GANGS

A HANDBOOK

FOR

COMMUNITY

AWARENESS

GANGS

A HANDBOOK

FOR

COMMUNITY

AWARENESS

Rick Landre,
Mike Miller, and
Dee Porter

☑® Facts On File, Inc.

Gangs: A Handbook for Community Awareness

Copyright © 1997 by Rick Landre, Mike Miller, and Dee Porter

Facts On File, Inc.
11 Penn Plaza
New York NY 10001

Library of Congress Cataloging-in-Publication Data

Landre, Rick.
    Gangs : a sourcebook for community awareness / Rick Landre, Dee Porter, and Mike Miller.
    p.   cm.
    Includes bibliographical references and index.
    ISBN 0-8160-3359-5 (hc)   ISBN 0-8160-3724-8 (pb) (alk. paper)
    1. Gangs—United States.   2. Crime prevention—United States.
I. Porter, Dee.   II. Miller, Mike, 1956– .   III. Title.
HV6439.U5L35   1997
364.1'06'60973—dc20
                                                                95-25314

Facts On File books are available at special discounts when purchased in bulk quantities for businesses, associations, institutions, or sales promotions. Please call our Special Sales Department in New York at (212) 967-8800 or (800) 322-8755.

You can find Facts On File on the World Wide Web at http://www.factsonfile.com

Cover design by Whizbang! Studios
Text design by Cathy Rincon

Printed in the United States of America

MP FOF 10 9 8 7 6 5 4 3 2

This book is printed on acid-free paper.

Contents

Acknowledgments

I would like to recognize and thank all my colleagues, countless friends, and family who provided constant encouragement and assistance in obtaining information and proofreading the unpublished text. They helped keep me going on the project over the last few years. I especially want to thank my children, Jase and Kaci, whose patience and understanding were unlimited while I worked on the material for the book. Finally, my most heartfelt thanks go to my wife, Linda, whose endless hours of typing my many drafts was invaluable to the completion of this book.

—Mike Miller

To Debra and Joy who motivated me to write, to Christina and Mathieu who tolerated me while I was writing, and to my partner, Lance, who made our work an experience to write about.

—Rick Landre

To the gang kids and their families who let me peek into their lifestyle and understand. To my fellow writers, colleagues, and friends who encouraged this project from beginning to end. To my husband Jim, daughter Barbara, parents Carl and Vivian, who provided the needed support and motivation both in working in the Gang Alternative Program and on this book.

—Dee Porter

And a special thanks to the editors at Facts On File: Nicole Bowen, Emily Ross, Laurie Likoff, Hilary Poole, and Jim Chambers. Throughout all the editing and changes in format they have been extremely helpful and approachable, making the transitions run smoothly.

—Dee, Rick, and Mike

About the Authors

Rick Landre, a detective in the Lodi Police Department gang unit, met Dee Porter, an author, when she was doing research on gangs for a mystery novel in 1990. The two worked together to produce a video documentary about gangs for the local cable access channel.

While doing the research, they discovered that there were criminology textbooks that talked about gangs and books on specific topics, such as girl gangs or the L.A. CRIPs and Bloods, but rarely did these books include any solutions to gang-related problems or refer to the vast network of resources now available on gangs. Also, while the books often contained much information, they were dry and unimaginative, making it difficult for the reader to maintain interest.

Landre and Porter decided to write a book for the general public that could be useful for educators, law enforcement, and community leaders as well. Meanwhile, Landre helped to form a community-based Gang Alternative Program, of which Porter became chairperson in 1992.

Although Landre and Porter felt ready to pursue the book in 1993, they decided they needed an individual knowledgeable about gangs in the school environment and in the youth incarceration system. They asked Mike Miller, then an educator with the California Youth Authority, to join their team.

Rick Landre, a graduate of Bradley University, Peoria, Illinois, moved to California and became a police officer at age 31. He worked as a detective in the Lodi Police Department in Lodi, California, for six years. During that time he served as a gang investigator, working primarily with Hispanic, white, and prison gang members. He produced a department training video on street gangs that aired on cable television. In 1990 he wrote a booklet on street gangs that was distributed by the San Joaquin County Board of Education to faculty and administrators. He was awarded the department's Police Officer of the Year award in 1991 and also received a Meritorious Service award in 1993 for his work with gangs in the community. As of January 1, 1996, he was transferred to the patrol division, where he works as an officer in the police equestrian unit. Landre continues to teach about gangs in the State Police Academy on the campus of San Joaquin Delta College. Rick and his wife Christina have a son, Mathieu, and live in Lodi, California.

Dee Porter has been involved in a variety of creative interests that include writing nonfiction, fiction, and screenplays. Porter has won awards for her fiction and has published many articles and columns. She also taught writing for five years.

In addition, she is an officer in the California Writers Club and founded the Lodi Writers Association. She has worked with youth for over 25 years and has chaired the Lodi Gang Alternative Project since 1992, directing the outreach program and working with youth personally. In January 1997, Porter became the manager of a teen center that she helped to create. She believes problems must be understood before they can be solved. Porter lectures on "A Community's Look at Gangs" through the university and community college system. She lives in central California with her husband of 30 years, Jim. They have an adult daughter, Barbara.

Mike Miller has been involved with education and youth most of his adult life. After graduating cum laude from the University of North Dakota, he served four years as an officer in the United States Army Military Police Corps. His experience with youth includes managing adult and juvenile group homes, working as a counselor at San Joaquin County Juvenile Hall, and teaching for five years at the California Youth Authority's O. H. Close School in Stockton, California, where he specialized in programs for boys between the ages of 12 and 18—criminal offenders committed mostly for gang-related offenses. He was twice selected as the school's Chapter 1 Teacher of the Year. He is presently teaching in an opportunity program for at-risk youth at Oak Ridge High School in El Dorado Hills, California. In his spare time, he volunteers as a coach for youth football, soccer, and baseball. He and his wife Linda have two children, Jase and Kaci.

Preface

California attorney general Dan Lungren spoke at an August 1994 California Gang Investigators seminar and shared some sobering statistics: juvenile arrests for murder are up 119 percent nationwide, and 130 percent in California, since 1986. The population of gang members in California alone is expected to reach 250,000 by the year 2000 unless aggressive steps are taken.

But the problem does not stop at the California border, or even at the borders of our metropolitan areas. Gangs that once roamed only urban streets have spread to smaller communities and rural areas. Because residents of these areas often don't know the warning signs, or how to deal with their growing problem, they ignore it until their community is overrun by violent gang members toting guns and dealing drugs. The problem of gangs is universal. Indeed, there are few places in the United States or in neighboring countries that will not be affected by gang problems before the end of the century.

Law enforcement agencies around the country agree that just arresting the youth involved in gang warfare is not the long-term answer. Communities must work together to combat gang problems with alternative programs that combine methods of prevention, intervention, and suppression. This book is designed to help ordinary citizens, as well as professionals whose work involves gangs, clarify what they may already know and build upon that knowledge so that they can develop or join a community-based anti-gang program in their locale. It will also direct readers to related resources and provide assistance in acquiring additional information.

The book is organized into six sections, each with a different focus. The first section gives a general background and comprehensive view of gangs; it addresses commonly-asked questions about street gangs that the authors hear in their professional and social contacts.

The second section discusses the various types of gangs, based upon ethnicity, sex, place of origin, and beliefs. It delves into the idiosyncrasies of each gang's graffiti, dress, monikers, and slang.

The third section focuses on the violence associated with the gang lifestyle. From the initiation to the burial, these chapters cover numerous signs of gang membership, including the use of weapons and drugs.

The fourth section addresses the impact gangs have on our everyday lives. Chapters are dedicated to the influence of gangs in schools, in the media, and in corporate boardrooms.

The fifth section identifies problem-solving methods available to the various sectors of a community. It cites community-based anti-gang programs around the country that have used the combined resources of local businesses, service organizations, law enforcement officers, educators, parents, and youth to successfully control gang violence.

The sixth and final section is a comprehensive resource guide and bibliography for readers desiring more information.

Whether you're a parent, an educator, a member of law enforcement, an elected official, or just a concerned citizen, you will find answers to your questions about gangs in these pages. The easy-to-understand format incorporates anecdotes, dramatizations of real-life gang activity, and specific gang information.

Special features include "Voices from the Front," actual accounts from gang members, ex-gang members, and citizens personally affected by gang violence; and "Rick's Reports," true-life anecdotes from gang unit officer Rick Landre. Rick also interviewed several people whose names appear throughout the book. These include B. K., Huero, Oso, Payasa, and Flaco, who were incarcerated in California prisons. B. K., an African-American female, and Payasa, a Hispanic female, were paroled in 1994 after serving time in the California women's facility. Huero, a white male, was incarcerated for his criminal actions while participating in a Hispanic street gang in Sacramento, California. Flaco was paroled to Los Angeles after serving his sentence in a northern California prison. He plans on turning his life around and playing professional baseball. Oso was convicted of murder in a gang-related shooting and hopes to be paroled in 1998. Excerpts from the interviews are listed throughout the book as quotes taken from the prisoners.

Gangs Defined

If a girl is a CRIP, and she meets
a boy she likes and he's a Blood
. . . well, she can do whatever
she wanna do but she can also
be assassinated. You cannot
betray your own kind. You
will die!

—B. K.

VOICE FROM THE FRONT

INCREASE THE PEACE

TO: Sandra Davis, founder of Mothers Against Gang Wars

My name is Stanley "Tookie" Williams. I am cocreator of the notorious Black street gang called the Crips. The Black-on-Black violence this gang has helped spawn is a legacy I truly regret. I apologize to the Black collective for this legacy.

While writing these words to all of you, the bitter act of being here on San Quentin's death row for over 14 years, and facing a possible state of execution, is a humiliation that I must strongly bear each day. However, it does not, nor shall it ever, weaken my determination to help better the position of the Black man, the Black woman and the Black child regardless of who and where they are on the face of this earth.

The major crisis that confronts us, the crisis that will be discussed here today, is a Black crisis. This Black crisis revolves around the stagnation of our growth—economically, socially, technologically and educationally. And only collective Black wisdom, Black strength, Black affection, Black economics and Black participation can effectively reverse this momentum towards Black destruction.

This is not an individual struggle. In fact, the cycle of Black-on-Black destruction will persist as long as we Blacks remain physically, mentally and ideologically divided. So, we must give up the selfish philosophy of individualism and make new choices from a collective viewpoint.

I'm honored to have had the chance to participate in today's Increase-the-Peace Jan. '95 and I extend praise to Mothers Against Gang Wars for having the courage to host this forum where the critical issues that challenge the Black community can be discussed, and where significant strategies that will solve the problems that afflict us can be developed.

Faith, power and love to all of you.

—Stanley "Tookie" Williams
San Quentin
June 1995

(Used with permission)

FROM: Richard "Peebody" Cooper
      West Side Denver Lane (gang)
      Founder of the United Blood Nation (UBN)
      Los Angeles, California
      Locked down 16 years for murder. Sentence 15 to life.

TO: Sandra Davis, founder of Mothers Against Gang Wars

Every organization has a purpose or a cause. Regardless of what your cause is or what you represent, it is universal that there be respect. On the streets it should not be about being real and being respected. But before we can demand respect from others we must first respect ourselves and our loved ones. When gang banging first got started, it was about being respected or disrespected. It had nothing to do with the color of one's skin nor clothes he wore. It is our responsibility as "big homies" to set examples and to educate the youngsters. Whether they are our children, young homies, siblings or relatives of our comrades, it's our duty as soldiers to properly educate and strengthen the minds of all who are close to us. All of you homeboys, homegirls who are able to vote, must do so. Your voices are just as important as anyone else's and must be heard.

    Remember there is strength in numbers. United we stand, but divided we fall. Increase the peace with "no color lines." One nation under a groove.

              —Peebody
              W/Side Denver Land 4 life

              (Used with permission)

Colors and Crime: Gang Characteristics

If someone wears blue into our neighborhood you try to kill them. You let them know you can't be disrespected like that.

—Oso

ETHNIC ORIGINS

Gangs have typically been categorized as white, black, Asian, and Hispanic, and are often rooted in the historical experience of discrimination and economic struggle. However, it should not be assumed that any particular ethnic background or ancestry leads to gang membership. Only a small percentage of any ethnic group chooses the life of gang membership.

White gangs exist mainly to promote and act on racist beliefs. They are concerned with committing hate crimes and trace their origins in this country to the Ku Klux Klan. The most violent of these white supremacy groups operating today is the Skinheads, who have formed alliances with the older hate groups.

Black gangs formed mainly for protection from other gangs. They have evolved into an enterprising street network focused on the sale of narcotics. Although the neighborhood is an important concept to black gangs, it is much more important to the Hispanic gangs.

Hispanic gangs are typically concerned with the self-respect and integrity of their neighborhood. In the past, as Hispanics settled in small communities in the Los Angeles area, they took a great pride in their barrio (neighborhood) and banded together to protect it from sometimes hostile outside forces. Today the barrio is still sacred, and problems may arise if people from outside the neighborhood interfere.

Asian gangs are perhaps more organized than either the Hispanic or black street gangs and have been associated with gambling, prostitution, and narcotics on a more sophisticated and profitable level than other types of gangs. Well known for home invasion robberies usually carried out against wealthy Asians, Asian gangs are more mobile than the other gangs. They crisscross the nation committing crimes purely for financial gain. One particular pair of Southeast Asians drove over 90,000

4

miles in less than one year, back and forth between Stockton, California, and Houston, Texas, committing robberies and searching for new victims.

Rainbow Gangs

Though the above characterizations are still valid for some ethnic gangs, this system of classification is becoming obsolete due to the rise of a phenomenon known as "rainbow gangs." Rainbow gang membership is as racially diverse as the surrounding community. Though the original gang may have been a traditional, single-race, street gang with affiliates of the opposite sex, it has evolved to include two or more races and possibly members of both sexes. The rainbow gang represents a more sophisticated street gang with a broader recruiting base and a wider network of information and ideas.

Formerly Hispanic gangs may now contain Anglos, blacks, or Asians. There have even been some Norteño cliques without a single Hispanic member. One such clique was comprised solely of Pakistani and Arab youth. There are numerous examples of Crip sets that contain only members of Cambodian descent. Integrated gangs often form in smaller towns, where fewer people wish to participate in criminal street gangs.

Some ethnically integrated gangs form because of language barriers. It is not uncommon to find juveniles who speak Spanish, Vietnamese, and Cambodian hanging out together. Recent non-English-speaking immigrants tend to live in the same neighborhoods and associate with each other; their camaraderie is formed of necessity and proximity.

Traditional Street Gang Classification

Asian	Black	Hispanic	White
Southeast Asian	Blood	Sureño	White hate groups
Laotian	CRIP	Norteño	Neo-Nazi
Cambodian	Jamaican/Rastafarian	Blue Circle	Skinheads
Vietnamese	People Nation*	Black Circle	SHARPs*
Hmong	Folk Nation*	Native American	Satanic
Minh		Latin Kings*	Stoners
Chinese			
Korean			
Filipino			
Japanese			
East Indian			

Biker	Prison	Organized Crime Families
Hell's Angels	Mexican Mafia	Mafia (La Cosa Nostra)
Banditos	Aryan Brotherhood	Triads/Tongs
Pagans	Black Guerrilla Family	Yakuza
Outlaws	La Nuestra Familia	Colombians
Sons of Silence	Texas Syndicate	

*Depending upon location, they may be single race other than black, or a rainbow gang.

Gang Alliances

Gang alliances such as Blood, CRIP, People Nation, Folk Nation, Sureño, Norteño, SWP, Blue Circle, and Black Circle are not to be considered as monolithic, organized groups. They serve more as a means for small street gangs to identify themselves as belonging to a greater association of gangs. Many gangs decide to associate themselves with one of these factions due to the need for alliances to protect them from rivals. If their rivals identify themselves as Norteños, they select a Sureño affiliation for themselves. Some gangs may have historical reasons for identifying with a certain alliance. Just because two gangs belong to the same alliance does not mean that they will not be rivals. Very often, CRIPs fight CRIPs and Bloods fight Bloods. There are even occasions when gangs that are members of rival alliances cooperate, especially when money is involved.

With the creation of rainbow gangs, we are no longer able to say that a gang belonging to an alliance will be composed of a specific ethnic group. White gangs are known to claim CRIP or Blood, or even Norteño or Sureño affiliation.

GRAFFITI

Hispanic gangs are known for displaying the most sophisticated and artful graffiti. Their writing is often in block letters or in something similar to Old English script. Black gangs prefer graffiti that is spray painted or written in either red or blue.

These graffiti found on a tee shirt show membership in the Sureño street gang. The word SUR appearing next to the figure's head along with "Sur X3" on the brim of the hat show that this is a Sureño drawing. Trece, written as "3 ce" above the bed of the truck, is another way of showing an association with Sureños.

The red bandanna, red web belt, and the red cap, worn together or separately, are indicators of gang membership. What is written on the cap is not as important as the color of the cap.

Perhaps the most primitive graffiti is that of the white gangs. Crude and often written in a hurried and sloppy manner, white gang graffiti is not as prevalent in most communities as the graffiti written by other gangs. Until recently, there has been little graffiti written by Asian gangs. They have been more secretive in nature and have just begun displaying their gang names and monikers to the public.

COLORED CLOTHING

As seen in the movie *Colors*, gang members at one time dressed from head to toe in red, blue, green, purple, or any other color that suited the gang. A member may have worn a red hat over a red bandanna, a red shirt, red pants, and red shoes with red shoelaces. It didn't take more than a casual glance to identify the person in red as a gang member. Gang members who were dealing drugs seldom wore colors for this reason. They were carrying drugs and knew better than to give police officers a reason to stop them. But soon the wearing of so much "color" became a hindrance to all gang members. Slowly eliminating the predominant color from their dress, gang members attempted to blend in with citizens.

Today there is still a common color associated with most gangs, but it may be harder to identify from one quick glance at a member. A red cross around the neck, a red baseball cap, or perhaps just red shoes are the only sign. Only when four or five members are together will one notice a predominant color.

Gangs are territorial in nature and usually take on the name of a specific geographic location, such as a street, park, neighborhood, or part of town. Examples of such names include the following:

South Side Lodi (SSL)
North Side Gangster CRIPs (NSGC)
East Side Gangsters (ESG)
Third Street Bloods (TSB)
18th Street
North Side Aryans
Hayes Park Sureños (HPS)
West Side Mob (WSM)

CRIMES

Most violence is carried out between gangs of the same ethnic or racial background. For example, Vietnamese gangs are known for preying on other Vietnamese gangs. They know that they can rob other Vietnamese, who will rarely notify the police.

Though most gang-related crimes are committed between members of opposing gangs, innocent citizens are often hit by stray bullets. They also may be the victims of such gang crimes as robbery, burglary, and auto theft. In most cases gang members will not fight or shoot at innocent citizens unless provoked or, to use their term, *disrespected*, often shortened to *diss*.

Gang members participate in all forms of criminal activity, either for personal economic gain, for revenge against another gang, or out of hate for the victim. Crimes committed include, among others, assault with a deadly weapon, arson, grand theft, sale/possession of narcotics, and murder.

The weapons in these crimes have become more sophisticated in recent years, evolving from hands, feet, and knives to automatic handguns, automatic rifles, sawed-off shotguns and, in some cases, pipe bombs, Molotov cocktails, and hand grenades.

We would go out on a weeknight, steal two cars. There would be about eight guys. We would drive to a nice neighborhood at about four in the morning. I would knock on the door, then harder and harder with a screwdriver. If nobody answered, a couple of guys would go around the back and check the windows. Pretty soon we would have the garage door up and the guys would be bringing out TVs and stuff. The whole thing would take about 15 minutes. One time my friend couldn't get into the door that went from the house into the garage so he shot a big ol' hole in the door with the police shotgun. I went back to the car. The backseat was already full of stuff. I got into the car and drove away. I almost hit lots of cars cause I can't drive good. . . . We sold the stuff to some CRIPs.

—Huero

Graffiti

Most gangs perform acts of vandalism, including writing graffiti, which is often the first sign of gang presence in a community. A gang uses graffiti to advertise its existence and its claim on a particular territory. Some gangs, such as taggers, exist solely for the purpose of writing graffiti. They vandalize property in an attempt to outdo other tagger crews.

Hispanic gangs are known for displaying the most sophisticated and artful graffiti. Their writing is often in block letters or in something similar to Old English script. Black gangs prefer graffiti that is spray painted or written in either red or blue.

Perhaps the most primitive graffiti is that of the white gangs. Crude and often written in a hurried and sloppy manner, white gang graffiti is not as prevalent in most communities as the graffiti written by other gangs. Until recently there has been little graffiti written by Asian gangs. They have been more secretive in nature, and have just begun displaying their gang names and monikers to the public.

Drive-bys

I live in Stockton, California. It's a quiet area but we all get together, drink 40s, sell a little dope, have a little money. Sometimes we go wide and go gang bangin', go wide and do drive-bys. We don't be under the influence when we do drive-bys. We be straight headed. That's just the way we feel.

—B. K.

The majority of gang-related homicides can be blamed on drive-by shootings, which is the type of crime committed most frequently by gangs. In some gangs the drive-by is a rite of initiation for new members. Full acceptance into the gang might depend upon the initiate shooting a rival gang member.

In general the drive-by offers the gang a chance to commit a crime and flee the area before the police can be summoned. Some gangs steal cars to use in drive-by shootings. Afterward the car is dumped, leaving few, if any, traces to the identity of the suspects. The sawed-off shotgun is the weapon of choice for most gang members because it offers better odds of hitting a mark. It is not important who is shot as long as someone is hit. In some cases male shooters will meet a carload of female gang members after the shooting and transfer the weapons to the females' car in an attempt to hide their involvement if stopped by a police officer.

Illegal Drugs

The use of illegal drugs among gang members ranges from casual use of marijuana to addiction to heroin. For those gangs involved in drug sales, some members use and sell drugs; others only sell them.

Drug sales among gang members are more common in larger cities than in rural areas. Large cities offer a broader customer base that makes selling drugs a more profitable business. Gangs in these cities have claimed certain areas as their territory. Within their territory, they have established sophisticated organizations for the manufacture and sale of illegal drugs. Gangs have also taken control of vacant properties, turning them into crack houses where fellow gang members can come to use drugs.

Most rural gangs use drugs rather than sell them. Their members are likely to have started using drugs prior to joining the gang, and the drug use includes, but is not limited to, marijuana, crack, anabolic steroids, cocaine, and sniffing paint or glue.

2

Homies, Wanna-bes, and OGs: Gang Structure

To me the worst kind of gang member is not the hard-core OG (original gang-ster). It's the one that's coming up trying to make a name for himself. They're the most dangerous.

—Huero

LEADERSHIP

The internal organizational structure in a gang provides a hierarchy of power, or at least a method of operating, that extends throughout all membership categories to exercise control over gang members and their activities. Gangs with a formalized organizational structure have titled leadership roles and clearly defined operating rules for members. Other gangs are more informal with constantly changing group leadership. In these gangs, the social communication skills of members dominate the decision-making process. Gang organization is classified into three types: traditional, committee, and social.

Traditional Organization

A traditionally organized street gang is controlled by an individual who may be known as president, number one, godfather, or head honcho, among other terms. This position of leadership is not always permanent. One member becomes the leader, usually through group consensus or by being the "baddest" one in the gang. Some gang leaders must fight to obtain and then maintain their position of authority. The leader has to make what he sees as the wisest and best decisions for the gang.

Votes to change leadership usually occur when there is a disagreement within the gang over a major decision. Under these conditions, leadership can change quickly. Such conflicts may still leave many gang members dissatisfied. An unhappy group will often break off and form its own gang as a way to resolve the disagreement.

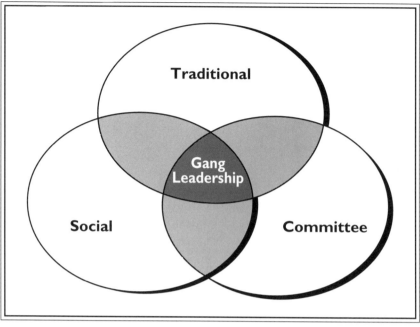

Gang Leadership

Committee Organization

The second type of structure is committee or council rule. This organization allows several members to be in control and to develop more of a consensus around the decision-making process. It also permits the gang to survive even if members of the leadership group are absent due to incarceration or death. This structure also trains members how to be responsible and allows them to gain experience in limited leadership roles. Members who want to participate in leadership but whose skills or expertise alone would not be adequate to leadership positions may find this system advantageous.

Street gangs that are large and have numerous sets or cliques tend to use this organizational structure. The representatives on the council or committee can provide a valuable service to the subgroups by using their own experiences and clout in order to help the smaller groups solve problems.

A rival gang that decides to attack one of the subgroups of the gang is actually going to war with a larger, more powerful organization. The larger group can also provide the subgroups with weapons, expertise, and soldiers. This less centralized leadership is an effective structure for controlling the members and activities of a disciplined, mature gang.

Social Organization

In the social organizational structure, identifying members in leadership positions tends to be the most difficult. As one gang member put it, "We don't have any leaders. The OGs sometimes call the shots. But, we just look out for each other and back up our homies when they need it." Since this gang structure operates at the whim of its members, leaders are constantly changing. The individual or individuals who can be the most persuasive at any given moment determine the gang's activities. By its nature, this organizational structure tends to be ineffective since a decision or project can be easily changed or dropped whenever someone comes up with something else for the gang to do. A single dominant member can use well-developed communication skills to persuade gang members and control their activities.

Such skills of communication and persuasion, however, may not be enough to keep the gang members focused when they encounter difficulties, and they may find it easier to move to another task. When a leader is removed from such a gang, there is usually little or no observable effect, since someone else easily becomes a leader, even if such new leadership is only temporary. Members in this gang structure feel equally powerful in their influence on the gang's decisions and activities. They also believe no one is forcing them to do anything.

MEMBERSHIP

Sets/Cliques

Gangs can be broken down into smaller factions consisting of specific sets or cliques. Black gangs refer to the smaller groups as *sets*, while Hispanic gangs call them *cliques*. These smaller groups usually incorporate a geographic term, such as Val Verde Park CRIPs or North Side Norteños, into their name.

These subgroups are also a way of identifying factions of different ages or gender within a larger gang structural unit. An individual may change his status throughout his career in the gang. Some members become more dedicated and loyal as social contacts outside the gang decrease, while others drop their close gang ties until their gang activity is infrequent. Members of this last group are never really out of the gang, but their level of involvement has subsided for various reasons.

Gangs are organized with leadership drawn from the most enthusiastic and active members. Around that leadership are members of varying degrees of loyalty. The gang's strength is determined not by numbers, which can range anywhere from a few to hundreds, but by the dedication of the individual members to the gang. The following categories describe the different levels of commitment found among members of most gangs.

Levels of Individual Gang Involvement

Level I—Fantasy (Imitators)   10 Percent of Gang Membership

- Knows about gang, primarily from newspapers, newscasts, and movies.
- Knows gang members but does not associate with them.
- May like, respect, or admire a gang, a gang member, or the gang lifestyle.
- Sees gang members as "living out a fantasy."

Level II—At Risk (Homies, Wanna-bes and Peripherals)   20 Percent of Gang Membership

- Negative view of past, present, and future; sees no viable alternatives.
- Casually and occasionally associates with gang members.
- Lives in or near gang areas (turfs) or has gang members in family.
- High rate of absences, truancy, antisocial behavior in school.
- May like or admire the gang lifestyle but not fully participate.
- Low level of self-esteem; high level of self-contempt.

Level III—Associates   40 Percent of Gang Membership

- Personally knows and admires gang members.
- Regularly associates with gang members.
- Considers gangs and related activity as normal, acceptable, or admirable.
- Finds many things in common with gang members.
- Is mentally prepared to join a gang.
- Sees gangs as source of power, money, and prestige.

Level IV—Regular Gang Member   20 Percent of Gang Membership

- Is officially a gang member.
- Associates exclusively with gang members to the exclusion of family and friends.
- Participates in gang crimes and other related activities.
- Has substantially rejected the authority or value system of family and society.
- Is not yet considered hard core by fellow gang members or others.
- Sees intimidation as a source of pride and power.

Level V—The Hard Core   10 Percent of Gang Membership

- Totally committed to the gang and gang lifestyle.
- Totally rejects anyone or any value system other than the gang. Is considered hard core by self, other gang members, and authorities.
- Will commit any act with the approval or a demand from the gangs.
- Does not accept any authority other than the gang.
- Has fully submerged personal goals for the collective goals of the gang.

From The National Youth Gang Suppression and Intervention Program. *Youth Gangs: Problem and Response*. University of Chicago, 1990.

The Hard Core

These are the few individuals (5–10 percent of gang members) who thrive on the gang lifestyle. Their daily activities revolve around the gang and the commission of crime. They are often the leaders of the gang, based on their street knowledge or past incarceration. The hard core and their leadership determine the gang's level of violence. They delegate criminal acts to other members and participate in criminal activity on a regular basis.

Regular Members

These are the soldiers who serve the gang as directed by the leadership. In the case of one street gang member arrested after a drive-by shooting, the directions did not have to be explicit. "Nobody told me to shoot that *vato*, I did it just because my homeboys would have done it and I didn't want to let them down." These members

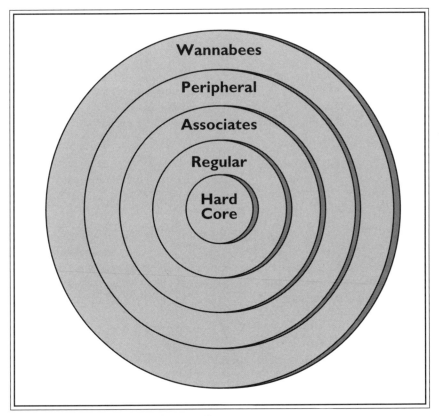

Gang Structure

have a sense of loyalty to the gang and are willing to work because they derive a sense of power, as well as financial gain, from their gang involvement. They also may perceive no real alternatives to the gang lifestyle.

The Associates

These are the members who associate with the gang for status. They regularly attend gang functions and dress in gang attire. Associates belong to the gang more for the emotional needs the gang fulfills than for the thrill of criminal activity.

The Peripherals

These members may associate with the gang on an occasional basis, yet their daily activities are not centered around gang involvement.

The Wanna-bes

Often referred to as the "gonna-bes," these individuals dress and mimic the gang in their neighborhood. Such activity has been documented among individuals as early as preschool. Wanna-bes find gangs intriguing and view the hard core as role models.

Imitators

These individuals dress, talk, and generally try to act like gang members, but they are not members. They are dangerous in that they may influence others and give an impression of the presence of gang activity. They can be even more dangerous to themselves due to the attention they may attract from actual rival gangs, thereby becoming targets of violence.

Homies (Homeboys/Homegirls)

The homey may or may not be a gang member but usually has some tie of friendship or allegiance to the gang. The term is used among gang members and those they include in their extended circle of friends.

ORGANIZATION

Street gangs can be categorized into three types: nomadic, territorial, and corporate. These classifications are based on the gangs' general intentions to provide unified protection to members or to make money. Although sociological studies have pointed out that a complex set of intentions probably drives the formation and activity of most gangs, these basic terms are meant to help people understand the general principles of organization in a gang. For a fuller treatment of the intentions of gangs, see Dr. Carl S. Taylor, *Dangerous Society*, Michigan State University Press, 1990.

Nomadic Gangs

The nomadic gang, as its name implies, is not found in any one specific area. It may claim some territory, but this claim is not really important to its existence. Instead of claiming turf, such gangs tend to roam cities looking for mischievous or criminal activity.

Many would refer to the nomadic gang as a band of juvenile delinquents. With an inconsistent membership, nomadic gangs have more members on the fringe than in the hard core. Juveniles in nomadic gangs tend to seek out the gang and its activities more as a diversion from what they consider the boring straight life. They can also easily hide their misdeeds under the cover of the gang and not fear being singled out. The nomadic gang lacks real commitment to anything, and its members are not very committed to the gang, though they may profess commitment. Dependent upon members who feel they don't fit in anywhere else and who need the gang for a social outlet as much as for protection, this type of street gang will usually fall apart whenever pressured by law enforcement. Some members may seek out another group to replace the disbanded organization.

Territorial Gangs

A territorial gang claims a geographical area as under its "protection." Their "hood," "turf," or "barrio" is sacred ground, and anyone coming into it must be respectful of them. Such a gang is usually in a constant state of war with other gangs who come into the territory and commit drive-by shootings in an attempt to show superiority.

The territorial gang also tries to lay exclusive claim to any criminal activity within its area, especially drug sales, which provide a very lucrative income. The territorial street gang sometimes comes into conflict with another gang over the distribution of drugs in its claimed territory. This can lead to an increased level of violence as one gang attempts to push another out of an area that is a good distribution point.

The territorial gang may also work as a franchise for another larger gang, selling drugs in their claimed territory. The territorial gang, by necessity, usually has a somewhat formalized structure with a steady membership that can be counted on to back up the gang and defend its territory. Members usually remain close to their territorial home where they feel safe and are "on duty" protecting the neighborhood from rival gang invasions. Even though they claim to be defenders of the neighborhood, they readily victimize its inhabitants through drug sales and gang violence. As members of this type of gang mature, they tend to become the older gangsters (OGs) to the younger gang members.

Corporate Gangs

The corporate gang's intention is to make money, and the gang will commit itself and its members to whatever is necessary to achieve this goal. The corporate gang needs a lot of members to operate successfully. Often beginning as a large territorial gang, the corporate gang may soon evolve and take on more and more territory, branching out across a city, into other cities, and sometimes out of the country—as in the case of the Crip and Blood gang sets spreading to Belize. They will make any deal that allows them to increase their revenue and will even work with supposed enemies. Their income is from robbery, extortion, and the sale of drugs.

Like Prohibition-era gangs, this type of gang uses violence to further its profit-making objective. Any other reason for violence is secondary. The gang becomes highly organized, with special groups set up to perform specific tasks. To the members, the gang is a business, and they conduct themselves accordingly. This structure is most common among Asian and black street gangs, but there are some Hispanic and white gangs adopting it as well.

Although street gang organization is presented here in specific categories based upon leadership, membership, and structure, it is best to remember that any street gang is a dynamic or constantly changing group. It can appear and disappear rapidly and change its members, leaders, and structure just as fast.

3

Jumped In: Gang Membership

*What you straight people don't get is that gang bangers don't have no choice
but bangin'. We can't get no jobs and bangin's all we can do.*

—Street gang member

RECRUITMENT

A 16-year-old boy, harassed for years to join his neighborhood gang and sell drugs
in New Haven, Connecticut, was shot while trying to protect his younger brother
from the gang. Despite offers of money and threats of physical violence, the victim,
a member of the high school basketball team, had always refused to join. He felt
the shooting was intended to demonstrate to others in the neighborhood that the
gang would not tolerate opposition. He said that once released from the hospital,
he would continue to refuse the gang's overtures because selling drugs wasn't right.

This incident demonstrates the lengths to which gangs go to meet their recruitment goals. As old members die, fade away, or go to prison, the gang struggles to
maintain its membership roles. Its method of recruitment will vary depending on
its needs at the time, its status in the streets of the community, and the type of
individual it wishes to attract. The street gangs look for new members all the time,
but the best times for recruiting are during summer vacations and at the start of the
school year. Individuals join street gangs for different reasons, and they are drawn
into the gangs through three styles of recruitment—fraternity, obligation, and
coercion.

Fraternity

Fraternity-style membership recruitment requires that a street gang appear very
desirable to potential recruits. Prized recruits, those thought to possess great
potential for becoming active members, are drawn into the gang through social
events. The benefits of gang life, such as drugs, alcohol, money, excitement, power,
influence, and access to members of the opposite sex, are displayed at these social
events. The recruits see the street gang as a path to the better things in life that they
may feel are unavailable through legitimate channels. The recruits are then enticed
to join so that they too can share in the benefits. Gangs using this recruiting style

may find that the recruits are more than willing to share in the benefits but are not totally prepared to do the "work" required to achieve them.

Therefore, this initiation style may require a relatively long period of socialization, whetting the recruit's appetite to increase his/her desire to work for the gang. The gang also has an opportunity to turn away recruits who have insufficient desire to work. A recruit who does not seem able to maintain or add to a gang's reputation will also be turned away as an undesirable addition.

Obligation

Street gangs that are territorial in nature will use an individual's sense of obligation as a method of recruitment. The gang's strong identification with a neighborhood can work to its benefit in attracting new members. The territorial gang will play up to the recruit's desire to be identified as a defender of the "hood" and, of course, family and friends who live there.

Failure to join the gang is considered a betrayal and thought to show a lack of respect. Individuals living in the neighborhood may have family members who have been in the gang and done their service for the neighborhood. These individuals grow up with the sense of responsibility and desire to join the local gang.

Gangs that recruit this way usually have age-delineated groupings, sets, or cliques that recruits are expected to join. The individual joins the appropriate group level and endures an initiation process to formalize his or her membership. Gangs using this style of recruitment usually accept all those who want to join and are able to endure the initiation process. They also are limited in their potential recruiting base since they draw new members only from the immediate neighborhood.

Racist street gangs also use obligation as a basis for recruiting new members. Playing on perceived fears of other racial groups, members promote those fears and attempt to develop a sense of racial responsibility among recruits. Once members create an enemy, they can convince their recruits that they are needed as soldiers to protect their lifestyle or culture.

Coercion

This type of recruitment relies on intimidation and fear. Individuals who do not actually want to join a gang may find themselves threatened with physical harm to themselves or family members if they fail to join.

Gangs using this method of recruitment must maintain a level of fear to ensure continued gang loyalty and cohesion. They must make a strong example of any member straying from the gang. This least desirable method of recruiting may be necessary if a gang has a high turnover rate due to incarceration or death of members.

BECOMING A MEMBER

In general gangs satisfy many of the social needs that young people have, including the need for companionship, activities, training, protection, status, and a sense of belonging.

Reasons for Joining a Gang

- Family tradition—second- or third-generation gang members in family.
- Fear of other gangs and a need for protection at school and in the neighborhood.
- Desire for the recognition and status that membership seems to offer.
- Lack of family concern and support at home.
- Low self-esteem in one's daily life or activities.
- Desire for action and adventure.
- Lack of alternative recreational or social outlets.
- Access to drugs, money, weapons, and members of the opposite sex.
- Distorted view of gang lifestyle as portrayed by the entertainment media.
- Poor potential for educational and/or job opportunities.
- Absence of positive role models in daily life.
- Rebellion against surroundings.

Requirements for Membership

- Recruits must usually be "jumped in." Typically, this involves a beating administered by other gang members or the commission of a crime.
- Most gangs have begun accepting members from all racial and ethnic backgrounds.
- Members come from *all* socioeconomic backgrounds.
- Often a tattoo is required to show loyalty after being jumped in.
- Females have begun taking a more active role in what, at one time, were male-dominated organizations.
- Gangs consist mostly of individuals between the ages of 12 and 24 years who associate on a continuous basis.

The value system of the street gang is different from that of the average person, and those being admitted to the gang usually must go through an initiation rite that proves their support of the gang's value system. Potential candidates for membership arrive at the point of initiation through a variety of routes. Some are born into joining the gang; they have never thought about having a choice of whether or not to join. A second type of potential member wants to join because of the perceived benefits of gang membership. The third type wants to join the gang for protection, either from the gang he or she joins, or to be protected from other gangs.

Defining and Tracking Gangs

A loose-knit organization of individuals usually between the ages of 14 and 24. The group has a name, is usually territorial, or claims a certain territory as under its exclusive influence, and is involved in criminal acts. Its members associate together, and commit crimes against other youth gangs or against the general population for property, money, or anything of value.

—A youth gang as defined by the California Attorney General's office

NATIONAL EFFORTS

Definitions

In this book the terms *gang, crew, mob, posse, set,* and *clique* are considered synonymous except when used in a special context. They have, in most cases, lost their original distinct meanings due to the impact of television, music, and film. Some, however, are still more popular than others in certain geographical regions and specific ethnic groups. The term *set* usually denotes a subgroup of a specific black street gang, or the gang itself. *Clique* has a similar meaning for a Hispanic gang. These two terms are most popular in the western United States.

Posse seems to have originated with Jamaican drug gangs, who have won notoriety for their violence as a result of extensive media coverage of their crimes. This media coverage has helped to popularize the term, which is frequently used by black street gangs in the Midwest and eastern United States. Those adopting the term into the name of their gang, as in the case of the South Side Posse, attempt to capitalize on that violent reputation and create a sense of fear in potential opponents.

The term *crew* is used primarily by ethnic street gangs in the eastern and Midwestern United States. The word has some interesting connotations since it usually implies a group of individuals organized to do a specific job. Many gangs that deal in drugs see their activities as business or work, so the term is popular with them. Tagger gangs—those who do graffiti—have also freely adopted the terms *posse* and *crew.*

Another term occasionally used in place of *gang* is *mob*. A gang's use of this term may demonstrate aspirations to organized crime or it may serve as another example of psychological warfare. Many young gang members are enamored with films about organized crime and its accompanying violence, and they believe that using these terms helps to promote an image of success and ruthlessness.

The difficulty in accurately naming gangs reflects the overall problem in defining them. There is no clear, nationally recognized definition of what constitutes street gang membership or a street gang crime. Meanwhile, most law enforcement agencies across the country use some combination of the following nine criteria in determining youth gang membership:

1. The individual freely admits membership.
2. The individual has gang tattoos.
3. The individual associates with gang members.
4. The individual wears gang colors or clothing imprinted with gang names.
5. The individual has been photographed with known gang members.
6. Others identify the individual as a gang member.
7. The individual writes or has written about his/her gang affiliation.
8. The individual has family members or relatives who are known gang members.
9. Official documentation from police, probation, court records, or school records indicate the individual is a gang member.

If three (3) or more of the above criteria apply to an individual, he/she is usually considered a *gang member*.

If two (2) of the above criteria apply, he/she is considered an *associate of gang members*.

If only one (1) of the criteria applies, he/she is considered a *suspect gang member*.

The National Youth Gang Suppression and Intervention Program, established in 1987, decided on the following definitions after conducting a national survey of organizations that deal with street gangs:

> A street gang is a group of people that form an allegiance based on various social needs and engage in acts injurious to public health and public morals. Members of street gangs engage in (or have engaged in) gang-focused criminal activity, either individually or collectively; they create an atmosphere of fear and intimidation within the community.
>
> A gang for criminal justice purposes is a somewhat organized group of some duration, sometimes characterized by turf concerns, symbols, special dress, and colors. It has a special interest in violence for status-providing purposes and is recognized as a gang both by its members and by others.
>
> The notion of a youth gang incorporates two concepts: often a more undefined "delinquent group" (e.g., a juvenile clique within a gang) and the better organized and sophisticated "criminal organization." The latter may be an independent group of the gang, usually older youth, primarily engaged in

criminal income-producing activity, such as drug trafficking.

A gang crime incident is an incident in which there is gang motivation, not mere participation by a gang member. If a gang member engages in non-gang-motivated criminal activity (e.g., crime for strictly personal gain), the act should not be considered a gang incident. However, since gang members are likely to be serious offenders as well, information systems should record all types of crime but at the same time distinguish gang from ongoing crime.

It is important to note the difference between juvenile pranks and street gang–related incidents. A prank is a single incident that by its nature is intended to demonstrate an individual's or group's ability to perform an act that will achieve temporary notoriety or embarrass the target while causing limited physical harm and/or financial cost to the target. The gang-related incident has violence and terror, along with territorial claims, as its motive. The incident will intensify and be repetitive. Both types of incidents may involve legal disposition, but the gang-related incident will have greater meaning to the community.

Tracking

One of the major problems in acquiring accurate reports of gang and juvenile crime has been the use of inconsistent definitions of gangs. In addition, many local law enforcement agencies fail to list juvenile crime or gang-related crime separately from other statistics.

FBI UNIFORM CRIME REPORT

As of 1996, the most influential statistical database on crime in the United States, the FBI's Uniform Crime Report (UCR), did not compile separate juvenile street gang–related crime statistics, mostly due to a lack of clear definitions. This program, begun in 1929, collects information in eight categories of crimes reported to law enforcement agencies: homicide, forcible rape, robbery, aggravated assault, burglary, larceny theft, motor vehicle theft, and arson. Since 1991, at the direction of the president and Congress, the bureau has also collected data on hate crimes. The report presently collects data from over 16,000 law enforcement jurisdictions, representing 242 million inhabitants—95 percent of the total United States population. The UCR data is compiled annually and issued in a detailed report known as *Crime in the United States.*

Following the annual release of *Crime in the United States*, a rash of media reports usually attempts to sensationalize trends shown by the new data. It is important to know that the report itself uses only population size of communities as a correlate of crime. It lists several factors that affect the volume and type of crime occurring among locales:

- Population density and degree of urbanization with size of locality and its surrounding area.
- Variations in composition of the population, particularly youth concentration.
- Stability of population with respect to residents' mobility, commuting patterns, and transient factors.
- Modes of transportation and highway system.
- Economic condition, including median income, poverty level, and job availability.
- Cultural factors and educational, recreational, and religious characteristics.
- Family condition with respect to divorce and family cohesiveness.
- Climate.
- Effective strength of law enforcement agencies.
- Administrative and investigative emphasis of law enforcement.
- Policies of other components of the criminal justice system (i.e. prosecutional, judicial, correctional, and probational).
- Citizen's attitudes toward crime.
- Crime reporting practices of the citizenry.

Any attempt to make comparisons of UCR information gathered from various communities is somewhat faulty in view of the variables listed above. For example, the "crime reporting practices of the citizenry" will vary widely between locales. Does the community have a good, trusting relationship with its law enforcement? Perpetrators of hate crimes usually pick on immigrants, who may be from countries where police are corrupt. Would the victims report criminal incidents to an agency they fear and distrust? Central California has this problem with its Southeast Asian community.

The report is also limited by the fact that some local law enforcement agencies do not always contribute data to the UCR, and sometimes the information they do contribute is neither complete nor accurate. Several states now have legislated mandatory participation in the data collection system and/or created their own in-state system to gather data for the UCR. Presently, the UCR is being overhauled and redesigned to show more accurate data in a more usable format. The new system of obtaining the data, the National Incident Based Reporting System (NIBRS), is still undergoing evaluation.

NATIONAL CRIME VICTIMIZATION SURVEY

The second most influential evaluation of criminal behavior in the Unites States is the National Crime Victimization Survey (NCVS), conducted by the Bureau of Justice Statistics. Since 1973 United States Census Bureau personnel have assisted the NCVS by gathering data on the impact of crimes on victims during census interviews of 49,000 households nationwide. The NCVS does not measure the impact of homicide and any commercial crime, nor does it consider victims under the age of twelve. The NCVS does conduct separate surveys on special topics such as school crime. The findings from the surveys are published annually, and special reports are prepared on specific topics. The NCVS survey includes data on the average United States household's expectation that one or more of its members will become the victim of a crime category being measured by the survey. Presently it is difficult, perhaps impossible, to derive information specifically about gang violence from either one of the two major crime surveys. One can obtain information regarding age, sex, type of crime, race, etc., but any attempt to correlate these categories to some type of indicator of gang activity is futile.

OTHER NATIONAL STUDIES

Several national studies have been conducted by university researchers for the Office of Juvenile Justice and Delinquency Prevention (OJJDP) and the National Institute of Justice to determine the extent of gang problems. The first study, conducted by Harvard researcher William B. Miller and published in 1975, found 6 out of 12 large cities studied had acknowledged gang crime problems. Those 6 cities had an estimated number of gangs ranging from 760 to 2,700, and total gang membership ranging from 28,500 to 81,500. Another study in 1982, conducted as an outgrowth of the 1975 survey, measured gang membership in 286 cities. It estimated total gang membership at 97,940, with a total of 2,285 gangs. A third major survey effort, conducted in 1988 by the University of Chicago, found that in 35 cities recognizing the existence of gangs, there were an estimated 1,439 gangs with a total of 120,636 members.

The most recent significant survey was conducted in 1992 by the University of West Virginia for the National Institute of Justice. The survey conducted interviews with law enforcement officials in 79 of the largest U.S. cities and 43 smaller communities. Response to the survey showed 72 out of the 79 large metropolitan cities reported gangs as a problem, as did 38 of the 43 smaller cities. Of the areas surveyed, 91 percent of the major metropolitan cities and 88 percent of smaller cities had acknowledged gang problems. The results of this study indicate a national problem of significant magnitude.

This survey also revealed the impact gangs are having on a national scale. The cities responding indicated a total of 249,324 gang members belonging to 4,881 gangs. These gang members accounted for 46,359 gang-related crimes or 1,072 gang-related homicides in a 12-month period. The majority of juvenile gang members were identified as blacks or Hispanics, with an increasing number of whites and Asians. Females accounted for only 3 or 4 percent of gang-related crime during the same period.

In view of these findings, it would be of considerable importance for the NIBRS to include some type of category specifically for gang activity. The 1992 survey recommended this as a method to obtain more accurate data so that officials could at last gauge the extent and effect of street gangs in the United States.

Private organizations, both nonprofit and for profit, also produce statistical studies that are used for a variety of purposes. Large professional polling organizations are often contracted by news agencies and political groups to obtain opinions on certain topics as a means of getting a pulse on public sentiment. These polls are based on random surveys to obtain unbiased results. Most often the surveys employ yes/no questions, but more lengthy questionnaires are useful to obtain more substantial responses. Pollsters do gather information from diverse groups, and may attempt to break down responses by sex, age, or any other relevant category that may affect results. Organizations in the business of conducting surveys must provide dependable and reliable results.

The accuracy of opinion polls varies, and is based on several factors. It is important for the reader to evaluate the information in statistics, studies, opinion polls, and/or surveys, with several questions:

- Who or what organization conducted the study?
- Why was the data collected?
- How was the data collected?
- When was the data collected?

After evaluating the answers to these questions, the reader should be able to draw conclusions about the study or survey's credibility and decide if it warrants further consideration.

Currently, the only tools we have to measure the growth and extent of juvenile street gang crime are surveys conducted as a part of individual government and private research projects. The information gathered to date is from a sampling of jurisdictions across the country. The data certainly indicate a growing national problem, but we will better understand the true scope of gang-related crime when a more complete information gathering and reporting system is in place. In order for this to occur, we must establish a clear, nationally accepted definition of a street gang and of gang membership.

Sampling of Gang Populations and Crime

Based on 1990 census figures unless otherwise noted.

City	Pop. (1990)	# Gangs	# Members	# Gang Crimes
Abilene, TX	106,654	10	200	75
Albuquerque, NM	384,736	111	6,000	unknown
Chicago, IL	2,783,726	125	29,000	5,351
Cincinnati, OH	364,040	35	495	48
Clinton, IA	29,201	5	unknown	unknown
Colorado Springs, CO	281,140	50	375	unknown
Dade Co., FL	1,937,094	52	3,500 ('89)	unknown
Denver, CO	467,610	145	5,100	3,387
Des Moines, IA	193,187	8	300–400	unknown
Evansville, IN	126,272	10	150–200	unknown
Fort Worth, TX	1,332,053	200	4,000	226
Glendale, AZ	148,134	30	1,100	94
Irving, TX	155,037	21	300	unknown
Jackson, MS	196,637	12	1,500	135

Lakewood, CO	126,481	174	600+	unknown
Las Vegas, NV	258,295	122	6,000	unknown
Little Rock, AR	175,795	8	200	unknown
Lodi, CA	51,874	10	300	100
Long Beach, CA	429,433	33	8,872	1,172
Los Angeles, CA	3,485,398	500+	49,800+	7,725
Louisville, KY	269,063	10	250	unknown
Rochester, NY	231,636	17	332+	unknown
Sioux Falls, SD	100,814	2	20	8
Stockton, CA	210,943	140	3,500	741
Wichita, KS	304,011	68	1,400	300

The above data was gathered from various sources of information from 1990–1994. Population figures are from 1990 census. Comparisons between cities are difficult to make due to a lack of a clear definition of gangs, gang membership, and what constitutes gang crime.

Rural and Urban: Seven Communities Fight Gangs

Police adopted a Community Oriented Policing Program (COPP) and developed a community watch program known as "Operation Bootstrap."

—Description of anti-gang efforts in Clinton, Iowa

The common perception that gangs plague only urban areas is inaccurate and comes from a lack of knowledge. Popular films and the news media share some of the blame for this lack of understanding about the extent of street gangs in smaller cities and rural communities across the United States. The news media tends to focus on stories about gang violence in major urban areas. When it does feature a story about gang activity in a smaller community, it usually frames it as something out of the ordinary. Films and television also depict the violence of gang lifestyles in large urban surroundings and ignore what is occurring in suburban and rural areas. This helps to create our misconceptions.

Gangs have spread to rural areas for numerous reasons, including, again, the collective media's portrayal of violence as acceptable and normal. This makes the growth of gangs and the "street mentality" more understandable to kids who have little direct exposure to such lifestyles.

A 12-year-old child in Nebraska watching a music video on television about the hard life of some gangster rapper from Los Angeles may begin to imitate what he or she sees as an exciting lifestyle. Such imitation is widespread. Normal teen rivalries that used to be settled by a fistfight in the school yard are now settled with guns thanks to the example set by music videos and films.

In the same way that television, film, and music lyrics have transported the gang lifestyle to even the most remote corners of our country via the airwaves, our extensive interstate highway system, built since the 1950s, has carried actual gang members to the hinterlands. Our society has become extremely mobile, and urban street gangs have found that these roadways provide access to new markets, where law enforcement agencies may not be prepared to handle their invasion.

Street gangs in urban areas have found that competition is fierce for new recruits, customers, and unwary victims. Law enforcement in urban areas is usually well aware of gang methods and routines; therefore, the gangs feel pressured to move to other areas where they can operate unmolested. In these new settings, the gangs operate freely for some time, while they become strongly entrenched and organized in their new surroundings. Informed communities can avoid this by being knowledgeable and proactive in their anti-gang efforts.

Provided here is a sampling of gang activity in seven cities of various sizes across the United States. This sampling demonstrates the growth and movement of street gangs, as well as the increasing violence. The cities were chosen as representations of average communities in their respective regions, and the intent is to show that street gangs are a concern of citizens everywhere. This sampling indicates that there are few places about which one can truly say, "There are no gangs in my town." Population figures are from the 1990 census.

Albuquerque, New Mexico

Founded in 1706, Albuquerque (pop. 550,000) is located in central New Mexico, approximately 255 miles north of the U.S./Mexico border. With a self-reported ratio of 1 street gang member per 65 residents, compared with Los Angeles's ratio of 1:100, community leaders are concerned. Estimates of active street gangs range from 115 to 300 or more, including gangs that are considered wanna-bes and/or gangs in a developmental stage. Police have determined that there are approximately 5,000 documented gang members, and the mayor created a Gang Task Force in 1994 to address the city's growing problems with street gangs and to coordinate efforts of government and private organizations in combating gangs.

Albuquerque experienced an extensive graffiti problem created by street gangs and graffiti gangs known as "taggers." The mayor recently declared a war on taggers, with increased efforts by city and private anti-graffiti crews working to combat the problem and providing stiffer sentences to youthful offenders. Drive-by shootings between gangs occur regularly, many never reported to the police. Drug flow into the city is aided by the intersection of Interstate Highways 40 and 25, giving drug traffickers easy access from the north-south and east-west axes. The city also has a large proportion of poor and low-income families, making poverty a major factor in the behavior of local youth.

Traditional territorial Hispanic gangs make up the major street gang population in Albuquerque. Many of these gangs have existed since the 1920s and 1930s but are now becoming more violent. They model themselves on the Los Angeles Hispanic gangs that they see portrayed in the media, even copying their gang names from them. The Juaritos, a group of local Hispanics with close ties to Mexico, are involved in drug smuggling and violence. The Mexican Mafia, a California-based gang created in the state's prisons, has been attempting to control the local drug trade. CRIP and Blood gangs from Los Angeles have been trying to spread and recruit in the Albuquerque area. Local white gangs, claiming allegiance to either the Bloods or CRIPs, also actively draw members from low income and middle-class areas of the city.

The community of Albuquerque has acted decisively to combat growing gang and youth violence. Youth Development, Inc., a private organization begun in the 1970s as a program to help troubled youth, has developed a three-phase strategy of intervention, prevention, and diversion to maximize their impact on gangs and youth in the community. Today the organization serves as an umbrella for more than 40 different programs in the community. By 1994, their main focus had shifted to the intervention model approach of combating gangs with a 10-week treatment and counseling program. Their over 20 years of experience with various types of gang programs has shown them that a strategy based upon individual and family counseling and education about gangs, directed at hard-core gang members and their families, tends to be more productive than a traditional recreation-based model. Youth Development, Inc. gets court-ordered placements and referrals from the police.

On the state level, the 1994 legislative session made long-overdue changes to the state's juvenile codes by rewriting the legal definitions of gangs and gang members and the sentencing guidelines to help judges and prosecutors combat gangs. The community has also instituted Teen Court, a peer-oriented, adult-supervised court that deals with misdemeanors. There has been a tremendous success rate of 2 percent recidivism for the court-ordered program.

Fort Worth, Texas

Fort Worth (pop. 447,619) is a working-class community compared to its neighbor to the east, the more cosmopolitan Dallas. Together the two cities are known as the metroplex. Street gangs are a major problem for the city of Fort Worth, as well as the metroplex. In 1994, police officially attributed the murders of at least 32 people in Fort Worth to gang-related violence. The Fort Worth community officially estimates that in 1995 the number of gang members was 2,400, but other estimates are as high as 4,000 in more than 200 designated gangs. Juvenile street gangs in Fort Worth are composed largely of black and Hispanic youth, with a small number of Asian and white gangs fighting for territory. Gang violence focuses around turf battles resulting in numerous drive-by shootings. There were 190 such shootings reported in 1993, and many more go unreported. In recent years the sale and distribution of drugs have also contributed to the rising violence among Fort Worth street gangs.

The community has received a lot of national attention for its anti-gang efforts in the last few years. It conducted a "zero tolerance" campaign during the summer of 1994, when police made use of extensive patrolling and sweeps through neighborhoods plagued by high concentrations of gang activity. Neighborhood watch groups were formed and given police radios to report crimes quickly. The most controversial program, with the backing of the mayor, police chief, and the city council, was proposed in May of 1993. It involved the proposed hiring of six current gang members as gang counselors at $10,000 each per year. Facing severe public objections, the plan was never carried out.

In November of 1994, Fort Worth began a program known as Comin' Up. It was founded with $580,000 from federal grants, donations, and a seized-asset fund. The program is run by the Boys and Girls Club of Fort Worth. It features seven neighborhood centers with recreation facilities and equipment. Each center has a local advisory board from that neighborhood and works closely to share information with other agencies and the police. Juveniles using the centers must pass through metal detectors and are forbidden to wear gang colors. Hard-core gang members and their families are selected for specialized counseling programs, and others are referred to the centers by courts and the police. Although still in its infancy, this program appears to be as successful as any other at changing gang members' lives, but only long-term evaluation will provide the answer.

Honolulu, Hawaii

Residents of this paradise state first became aware of growing street gang problems around 1986. Honolulu (pop. 365, 272) saw 13 gang-related deaths in the 1980s, a number considered significant. Hawaii is a unique state due to its island geography. The island of Oahu is the most commercial and urbanized, and Honolulu is the island's major city. Most gang activity is located here, but it has spread to other islands as well. Today, police acknowledge the existence of over 100 street gangs on the four major islands of the state. Oahu is the home to over half of the state's gangs. The majority of gangs are ethnically Filipino or Samoan; these two groups tend not to mix. However, there are racially mixed gangs as a result of racially integrated neighborhoods.

Hawaiian gangs are influenced by media depictions of gangs on the mainland, especially depictions of Los Angeles gangs. Many street gangs claim Crip or Blood affiliation, although their contact with these groups is reported to be more fantasy than fact. Wearing bandannas and/or hats of the appropriate color to show gang affiliation is common. Filipino gangs identify more with one of four basic gang organizations from the Philippines: Oxo, Sige Sige, Satanas, and Bahala Na Gang. Most gangs support themselves through robberies and auto theft. Drug dealing is not a central gang activity as much as a business enterprise by individual members who work alone for bigger profits.

Hawaiian street gangs are generally splintered and unorganized. One particularly dangerous gang was the Filipino immigrant gang known as the Hawaii Brothers. This gang developed its own written constitution, charged membership dues, and had positions in its organizational hierarchy for a business manager and a press officer to handle media relations. By 1990, this group's leadership was either imprisoned or deported due to fire arms violations, drug trafficking, and kidnapping offenses. Hawaiian law enforcement officials hope that this gang will not become active again and are closely monitoring the activity of gang members who remain free.

In 1990 the state legislature passed a special act because of growing gang violence in Hawaii and trends occurring on the mainland. The legislation, known as the Gang Response System Act 189, laid the groundwork to establish a strategy for combating youth gangs. It provided funding and authority to establish an information gathering and reporting system between state and local agencies. A second piece of 1990 legislation, Act 190, provided for the creation of the Office of Youth Services. OYS will coordinate the state's gang prevention efforts and focus funding into programs diverting youth from gangs. The recipients of most of this money have been the Boys and Girls Clubs, YMCA, and YWCA, as well as several other private organizations. The state decided to support currently existing organizations and their accompanying programs instead of creating new ones to fight gangs. Some limited funding did go to state police departments and the Department of Education for new program development.

One of the most notable programs created by Hawaii to combat gangs is Positive Alternative Gang Education (PAGE). Based upon the Paramount Plan from California (see Chapter 25—Gang Awareness Training), PAGE created an alliance between law enforcement and Hawaii's Department of Education. Students identified as truants by the schools must attend a special Saturday program with their parents. If they fail to appear, court action may be used as another intervention. Students are encouraged to stay in school. Gang activity and related criminal acts have been reduced by the program's efforts.

Las Vegas, Nevada

Las Vegas (population 258,295) is the fastest-growing urban area in the United States; with that rapid growth come the problems of a rapidly rising crime rate. The estimated number of street gangs ranges from 122 to 178, with probably 80 hard-core gangs in existence. Total membership is probably around 6,000, which includes associates or members whom the police consider to be on the fringe of gang activity. The level of violence is high, with more than 180 known drive-by shootings in 1993. The unusual working hours in Las Vegas, a city that never closes, mean that many juveniles are left home with a lot of unsupervised free time.

The draw of the streets and gang activity entices many juveniles as a recreational option. Claiming affiliation with CRIP and Blood gangs, Hispanic gangs are the most active in the community, but rainbow, or multiethnic, gangs are becoming more popular among juveniles in racially mixed areas. Graffiti is also a growing problem.

Police currently utilize several programs to combat these problems. Community Oriented Policing (COP) and Problem Oriented Policing (POP) allow the police to develop relationships with newly arriving residents and focus law enforcement resources in problem areas. Police support for Drug Abuse Resistance Education

(DARE), a well-known gang/drug prevention program, in the schools is also deemed an important part of the community anti-drug and anti-gang efforts. Recently the Las Vegas city council, in its efforts to reduce crime, changed the name of a portion of 28th Street to Avenida de las Americas because of the close association its previous name had with street gang activity. It is hoped that this will help to transform the area's reputation and decrease gang problems.

LaCrosse, Wisconsin

LaCrosse (pop. 51,132) is a small community located along the Wisconsin-Minnesota border on the eastern bank of the Mississippi River. Its gang problems are minor but growing due to the spread of gangs from Minneapolis–St. Paul to the north and Milwaukee and Chicago to the southeast.

The gangs seem to be looking for new drug markets and a population of potential new members. Besides recruiting local youth to sell drugs, the outside gangs also want locals to commit robberies and steal cars for them. The Vice Lords and Black Gangster Disciples, two major gang affiliations from Chicago and Milwaukee, are actively recruiting non-blacks in LaCrosse to join their ranks. Southeast Asian gangs from St. Paul are also known to be recruiting members from the large Hmong refugee community in La Crosse. Some local groups claiming affiliation with the Los Angeles–based CRIPs have also appeared, but police believe these to be mostly imitators.

Incidents relating to gang initiations, where minors assault and threaten each other with weapons, are appearing in juvenile court. Gang-related graffiti also appear more frequently in the schools and on downtown walls. However, a quick reaction to graffiti seems to have kept the problem under control.

Although the community has not yet mounted a forceful public reaction to the menace of street gangs, public officials are backing police efforts to control gang activity. Behind the scenes, school officials develop and implement dress codes to prevent problems over anticipated confrontations about gang affiliated clothing. Police are working with the district attorney and local judges to ensure that cases involving gang activity are given special attention. They are also using the DARE program in schools, as well as meetings with parents, to spread the word on gangs to juveniles and their parents.

Clinton, Iowa

In late August 1993, Clinton (population 29,201), a small rural community on the Iowa-Illinois border, was alerted to the gangs in their midst. Local police were aware of a gang presence but were not aware of its sophistication until they raided a street gang's storefront headquarters and found fifteen guns and a high-powered rifle with a scope located on the building's roof. Eleven members of a Chicago-based street gang, including one only 11 years old, were arrested in the raid.

The community has at least five street gangs known to police, three originating in Chicago, only 143 miles east of town. Law enforcement officials acknowledge the spread of street gangs from the nearby urban metropolises. This move into rural communities is attributed to better law enforcement in the urban areas, the competition for new drug markets, and the need to look for places where people are not familiar with gang behavior.

The Clinton community has responded to the growing street gang problem by effecting several changes in the way the city leaders approach gangs. Police adopted a Community Oriented Policing Program (COPP) and developed a community watch program known as Operation Bootstrap. The city council has created an adjunct teen council that serves as an advisory group to the regular council on youth issues in the community, and the juvenile court has even allowed some offenders who have already pleaded guilty to be tried in an adult-supervised court of their peers. The schools have adopted an anti-gang dress code intended to reduce potential conflict. This community is sending a message that gangs are not wanted, an excellent prevention strategy.

Colorado Springs, Colorado

Colorado Springs (pop. 281,140), an upscale community at the foot of Pike's Peak, struggles to control an existing gang problem. Police estimate that there are 50 hard-core gangs and approximately 375 documented hard-core gang members in the community. The large mobile military populations nearby and close proximity to a major road link, Interstate 25, make it easier for gangs to infiltrate this community. Groups readily travel from Denver, only 60 miles north, and from as far south as Albuquerque, New Mexico.

Due to the need to maintain security in the local military, Colorado Springs has received an unusual amount of support from federal agencies in its efforts to control gang activity. Several cases involving drugs and weapons procurement between gangs and military personnel have been jointly investigated. Its airport has been regularly utilized as a conduit for drug transportation into the area by gangs trying to avoid the major DEA efforts at Denver's Airport.

The city has a number of white gangs that are influenced by Skinhead doctrine and the Ku Klux Klan. Black gangs from Los Angeles and the Chicago area play a major role in the local drug trade of crack cocaine. In February 1994, one Los Angeles gang attempting to gain dominance over other crack-dealing gangs killed an ATF (Alcohol, Tobacco, and Firearms) agent in an escalation of inter-gang warfare. Local members of the Black Gangster Disciples participate in local politics and run for offices, following the model set forth by Disciples in Chicago. Hispanic gangs are a growing problem, too. They pit local groups against other Hispanic gangs from Albuquerque, New Mexico, or against juveniles accompanying migrant Mexican farm workers.

Colorado Springs' Gang Coalition meets monthly to share information among law enforcement organizations, schools, and community leaders. The police have also developed pamphlets to inform citizens about gangs in their community. In an effort to avoid using specialized gang units, the police force has developed a program called Gang Net to keep all patrol officers informed of gang activity and trends. The police also have a Power Shift with extra officers on patrol duty between 7 P.M. and 3 A.M., when most gang and violent crime occurs.

Rick's Report
RESPECT YOUR ELDERS

It was July, and my partner and I were working the noon to 10 P.M. shift in an unmarked unit. Cruising through the east side of town, we drove past a large yellow Buick occupied by four males. We recognized the two in the back seat as our local homegrown variety of gang bangers. The two in the front seat looked like something from the movie Colors. *They were each wearing red baseball caps over red bandannas that were tied around their heads, dark black sunglasses, and red shirts. A red bandanna hung from the rear view mirror.* Proud to be Norteños *was the message.*

We drove on and didn't think much of the situation. An hour or two later we happened to be near a supermarket and saw the same four guys as well as two more juveniles walking toward the food store. They entered the parking lot and stood near the same auto that we had seen them in earlier in the day. We parked across the street and watched them standing near the car.

Something didn't seem right, but we couldn't figure out what our instincts were telling us. After approximately ten minutes had passed, one of the gang members saw our car and alerted his friends to our presence. All six males immediately began to walk away from the car, leaving the vehicle's doors open. We drove into the lot and radioed dispatch to check the license plates in the computer. At the same time, dispatch was assigning a patrol unit to another grocery store to take a report of a strong-arm robbery that had occurred approximately 20 minutes earlier.

We knew dispatch would tell us that the car was stolen because the front license plate was blue and the rear plate was white. It was indeed stolen. We drove down the street and arrested the six Norteños. When we returned to the supermarket, I was met by a man who said he needed to speak with a police officer. He had been called by the supermarket manager who told him that his wife's purse had been found in the store parking lot. The gentlemen had come to pick up the purse because his wife was in the hospital. According to the elderly gentleman, his wife's purse had been stolen that morning in another town while she was at a shopping mall. Apparently a large yellow car had driven past his wife. A male leaned out from the car window grabbing her purse and knocking her to the ground. His wife was 73 years old and in the hospital with a bruised hip.

The officer that responded to the other food store said that he was looking for a large yellow car that attempted to steal a purse from a woman in the parking lot. He drove his victim to our location, where the husband identified our six gang members as the ones who tried to rob his wife.

One of the six juveniles was tried as an adult and sentenced to six years in state prison. In addition to the robbery charge, there was an enhancement for elder abuse, which added two years to his sentence. The remaining juveniles were back on the street within one week.

Ethnicity, Sex, and Beliefs: Gang Profiles

> You get respect when you join the gang. You get popular. You get noticed. You also make a lot of enemies.
>
> —Flaco

MASE SPEAKS

The following is an excerpt from the life story of a former Sureño gang member named MASE (Mighty Ass Sureño Empire).

This is the story of my life as a gang member. I am a nineteen-year-old husband and father, and I'm working on becoming an ex-Sureño, meaning southern affiliation.

It all started about seven years ago. I was twelve. I was born and raised in Lodi. I went to Heritage School from kindergarten to sixth grade. I was a normal fifth grader who liked playing football, soccer, and other things kids do at that age. I was just beginning fifth grade when I first heard about gangs.

After school, I would see a group of older guys hanging out. I talked to some of them, and they would tell me to bring the basketball so that they could play at the school around 5:00 P.M. I would go watch them once in a while, but then I started going every other day. The way that they treated each other and joked around made me want to be a part of that crowd. Back then there was no one to tell you to stay out of gangs. There were only two gangs: LK (Latin Kings) and SSL (South Side Lodi).

As time went by, I got to know them better and I was getting more interested in this lifestyle. Months went by, and I started seeing my classmates associating with this crowd. By now I was in the sixth grade, and gangs were influencing everyone. When I wasn't trying to hang out with the Latin Kings, I would go bike riding with two of my closest friends, Billy and Ruben.

They were also interested in gangs, and they would go with me to the skating rink on Friday night to hang out with the Latin Kings, who would be there with girls and wouldn't pay attention to us. They got a lot of respect from everybody, and they would stand by each other when there were problems. I think when you're twelve or thirteen you want to belong to a crowd and have people know who you are instead of being the kid with the black backpack or "hey kid."

After school the gang members would go to Billy's house to hang out. Since Billy was my friend, I would go too. They would talk about things that they did, things that they stole and fights they got into. Even though gangs interested me, I was still afraid to join and I would tell Billy and Ruben that they were dumb for being in a gang.

Since Billy and Ruben were gangsters now, they had to write their name and their gang on the walls. They couldn't put their real names so they got nicknames. Billy was Ice Cube and Ruben was Sir Compton. They weren't as well known as "LK," but people knew they were around. I still hung out with them, but I didn't participate in any gang activities. Later on Billy took the name "Yogi."

I was just entering seventh grade when I found out about a rival gang—one who claimed or affiliated with the Norteños. I don't know how long they were around just that they were older guys that called themselves "South Side Lodi Norteños" and carried a red bandanna. They would chase my friends and throw things at them for wearing blue.

As the days went by, the gang grew bigger. At lunch time, a group would stand around and talk about what went down last night or talk to girls that would hang out with them, or I would hear Arturo this and Arturo that. I didn't know him well but I seen him a couple of times when he would pick guys up after school. He was older than the rest of the gangsters, and he was the leader. He was called MASE.

As the days went by, I would now wear blue more often and write gang things all over my books, in my hat, and in bathrooms. Even though I wasn't jumped in (officially initiated), I would still write "PBS X3" (Playboy Sureño) everywhere and sign it "Spanky."

Now that I started hanging out with the gangsters, I started getting a feel for it and understanding it better. My mom knew I hung out with them but she didn't think nothing of it. But now I could see that my attitude was changing. It used to be that when I came home from school, I would clean the house before my mom and dad got home. But now I wouldn't come home until 7:00 or 8:00 P.M. My mom wouldn't know if I had been home or not because my brothers would clean the house. My mom would think I came home, cleaned, then left.

Every year before school began my mom would take me and my brothers to get new clothes. We would always get Levis and regular shirts. But since all my friends were wearing T-shirts and dickies (baggy pants), I wanted some too. When me and my mom went shopping, I picked out some white T-shirts. She didn't understand why all of a sudden I wanted plain white T-shirts, but she didn't say anything. Then I went to look at the dickies, but she told me that I was crazy that those were old man pants. So, the next day after school I went with one of the boys to K-mart and stole my first pair of dickies. Since my mom didn't want me to have those pants, I would change at school. Two weeks had passed until I finally got caught. I was in the office being suspended for fighting and my mom came to pick me up. There was no way for me to change.

She didn't say anything about the pants, just said, "Wait until your father comes home." When he got home I got hit for getting suspended, not for wearing the pants. Now I felt like a gangster, and PBS was all I could think about. Everywhere I went, I would carry my rag (long colored handkerchief). Whenever I went to the store with my mom, I would ditch her and walk with my blue rag hanging then when I would see her, I'd put it back into my pocket.

My brothers were on a baseball team, and I would go with my mom to see their games. The first game was at Salas Park. When we arrived there were three games in three different diamonds. Instead of sitting with my mom at my brothers' game, I sat to watch the girl's softball. About twenty minutes later, a group of about five guys sat a few bleachers away from me.

They were all dressed in blue and one of them had a blue rag. I looked to see if I knew any of them. But they didn't look familiar. I looked again at the one with the rag, and it was Arturo. He looked at me a few times, but I don't think he remembered me because we only met a few times. I turned to see if my mom was able to see me. Since I couldn't see her, then I guess she couldn't see me. I reached in my back pocket and pulled out my rag just enough to be seen then I walked by them so that they could see my pano (rag—showing affiliation).

I went to the snack bar and bought a soda. As I was going back to my seat, Arturo and another guy approached me. Arturo asked me, "What's up? You a Sureño?" I said, "*Simone.*" ("Cool" way of saying yes) then he said, "*Orale* (same as "*simone*"), *yo soy* (I am) MASE *de* (from) PBS" and shook my hand. I said, "*Simone*, I met you at Yogi's pad." I could tell that he didn't remember me, but he pretended that he did. He introduced me to the other guys that were with him. Then we all were talking. I couldn't believe I was talking to the *vato* (local famous gangster) I heard so much about. He was telling me about how him and a guy named Qito started up PBS.

They all told my mom hi and then we went to watch the girls play. About 20 minutes passed when they asked me to get jumped in. I didn't say nothing till one of the Sureñas came up to me and said, "So you in or what?" I thought about it for a while then I said, "How do I get in?" MASE told me that they surround me, and when the time keeper says go, they all rush me, punching and kicking. And that if I want to hit back, they could hit me in the face. But if I don't want to hit back, then they can only hit from the neck down.

I asked for how long; he said for 30 seconds. I said only on one condition: If you give me your name. He told me if I wanted his name, I would have to fight him afterwards one-on-one since he had it tattooed on his knuckles. I don't know why, but I said yes.

We all walked to the end of the park and hopped the fence where the railroad tracks are. I wanted to say never mind, but I knew there was no turning back now cause either way I was going to get in. Arturo took off his watch and gave it to one of the guys. As I looked all around me it looked like there was more guys than before. Arturo asked if I was ready, and I said I guess. Then someone said go, and they all came at me. I tried to keep my eyes on the biggest one but someone hit me from behind. Now I was on the floor being kicked in the head and everywhere else. I didn't want to get up but I knew if I didn't then I would have gotten really messed up. So I got up and pushed some guys down and just kept waiting for someone to say time. Finally everyone broke off, and it was just Arturo. He said, "Now it's me and you." So I rushed him. But I tripped on something. Then he jumped on me and started hitting me in the chest. The last hit he gave me was the worst. When I tried to push him off and hit him in the ribs, he hit me on the side of my head and almost knocked me out. Then he helped me up, and they all took turns shaking my hand and saying how PBS was *por vida* (for life).

Later I found out the reason his last hit hurt so much was cause he had a railroad spike in his hand when he hit me to make his fist harder and heavier. As we walked back to the bleachers where the games were, I felt like a new person. I went to the bathroom to clean up and to look in the mirror. My face was all right, but the rest of me felt like I was hit by a truck. One of the guys gave me a pen in the bathroom and told me to go ahead and write my new *placa* (nickname) on the wall. First I wrote PBS XIII, then MASE. But I wanted to spell it different so I put MACE. When Arturo seen it he told me to write it with a *S* because it means *Mighty Ass Sureño Empire*.

So, I wrote it with an *S*. Then they told me to kick it (hang around, party) with them tonight and go to Qito's cause all the gang was going to be there. So when the games were over, I told my mom I was going to stay the night at Qito's house. She said okay and then asked why I had a bump on my head. I told her we were wrestling.

So we all went to Qito's house and kicked back for a while. Then he walked to the skating rink and tried to get in. They didn't let us in, so we just hung around outside. When we were out there we seen three guys across the street. They were just little kids, but one of them had on red Nikes. Arturo told me to go tell him to take them off so I did. I told him it was all about the PBS gang and to take off them red shoes before I took them off of him. So he did. Then as I walked back to my homies with the red shoes I felt unstoppable.

Then I got my first experience with Norteños when one of my friends invited me to his house in Bear Creek to spend the night. So I had my mom drop me off at his house. When I finally found it, he was outside waiting for me. After dinner we went in his front yard and played football about 20 minutes. We took a break and he told me that his neighbor was Gabriel, whose brother was a Norteño.

As we were standing there a car pulled into Gabriel's driveway. It was Gabriel who got out first. He walked fast to where we were at and told me to get in the house cause his brother was coming. I told him not to trip (worry) cause I didn't think his brother even knew me. Then two guys, probably in their twenties, walked up and said, "You a *scrapa*?" (derogatory name for a Sureño, meaning sewer rat). I said "No. I'm a Sureño." They said, "You better leave cause we don't want *scrapas* in our town." Then my friend took me in his house, and we went to his room. I was scared but I didn't wanna show it. My friend told me that those were two of the Norteños, but not to trip. Just not to fuck with them.

From that day on is where things started getting crazy. The Norteños in Lockeford would chase me every time they saw me. In Lodi, Sureños were hanging out at Angel's house and partying at Heritage School. I was meeting new gangsters every day. Now that I knew what was up in Lockeford, I told all my friends about all the busters (rival gang members). Now it was where I'd see someone in blue and they would be gang members. In time we all got to know each other real good and party with each other.

My mom knew I hung around gangsters but she didn't know how deep I really was. It wasn't till Lodi High when she started worrying. I was now a freshman and my world was changing so fast. PBS wasn't hanging out with each other no more and slowly we broke up. Now it was just me, Yogi, Ruben, Angel and a couple of wanna-bes (young ones wanting to be gang members).

Arturo and the rest of them other guys were doing their own thing and didn't really gang bang (be an active gang member) any more. By now I knew a lot about gang banging and about my friends. I knew from day one that Arturo was a liar. He liked to lie to his homies and steal from them. So now the so-called leader was no more.

But me and the others still banged PBS to the heart (engaged in very active gang activity). In school we would all hang out, mess around with WSV (West Side Varrio) and LK (Latin Kings). We would all call each other names like West Side Vegetables and little kids (LK) and peanut butter sandwiches for PBS. But it was all just for fun. Norteños were also showing up now with SSL (South Side Lodi) as well as new gangs called VCL (Varrio Central Lodi) and WXB (Woodbridge Boys). We still outnumbered them in school, but we would still rumble with them. We still went to school but would have a ditching party almost every day. Me, Yogi, and Ruben were still best homies but Yogi was in and out of juvie (juvenile hall) all the time. Now I was partying all the time and people I didn't even know knew me. PBS had a lot of wanna-bes, but we thought we would let them kick it with us anyway. I thought we were doing all right without Arturo and so did everyone else. In school, girls would hang out with us and after we would walk them home, and my mom would pick me up at Ruben's later.

The girls were fun to be around because they were excited that they knew gangsters. One of the girls that wanted to hang out with us asked Yogi how she could get jumped in. Yogi told her that to get jumped in, she had to pick two guys from the gang to sleep with. The next day Yogi told me that she had picked me and Ruben. I told Ruben and he just laughed. All day the girl kept following me around asking me if I would, but I told her that Yogi was just messing around when he told her that. She just got embarrassed and left.

At Lodi High, there were as many Sureños as there were Norteños. We were growing bigger and bigger. In Lockeford, I had turned some of my friends into wanna-bes. They would wear blue, but when the Norteños came, they would hide.

Since there were a lot of Norteños in Lockeford, I would go to Lodi. By now, my whole family knew I was a gangster, except my stepdad. But they all thought it was just a game, and so did I. A few months later I started to take it seriously. We had gunfights and got shot at by busters.

We had our first big rumble (fight) at Blakleys Park. We tagged (graffitied) on walls everywhere. We were making a name for ourselves. I was scared in a way but in a way I didn't care. When I would ride the bus to Lockeford after school, the Norteños would chase me home. But I didn't care, I would still walk everywhere. I was tired of running. I told myself, I am a gangster. I have to be down (act like a proud gangster).

For a while I didn't see the busters in Lockeford, so I would walk to Lockeford School and play basketball. I learned my first real lesson in Lockeford. I was so used to walking everywhere, I didn't even think about the busters. That's when I got caught slippin (not aware of what's going on). I was on my way to Lockeford School to meet my friends for basketball when a yellow minivan pulled up next to me and two guys jumped out. I took off running in the other direction when two other guys trapped me. They picked me up and threw me in the van. They took turns hitting me. I was still trying to fight them off when we finally stopped. We were at Lockeford School, and I was thrown off, then beat up again on the floor. I was hit in the face with a golf club, and then I passed out. When I woke up, I was full of blood on my friend's couch. He had seen everything and called his big brother to pick us up. I washed up and got a ride home. When my mom seen me she started crying. Then we went in my room to talk

I told her not to worry, I would take care of them myself. It was my decision to join a gang. We talked about gangs and that I shouldn't have joined. But she said she understood cause she was a kid once.

The next day I went to school and all my friends already knew what happened. Then I found out that after they got me, they went to Lodi and did a drive-by at Angel's house. Then they took off and flipped their car somewhere out in the country. One got killed, and the others went to jail. I was glad they got theirs.

We all had our gangs that we belonged to, but were united since we had the same enemies. As time went on, we all had trust in each other and were always there for each other. Then when school started up again, some of the homies starting changing. They wouldn't come around as much or wouldn't kick back with us in school no more. We noticed that all the changes were from one of the Sureño gangs. We didn't think nothing of it till one day they all didn't come to school no more. We found out later that they joined the Norteños. I couldn't believe how they could just backstab like that.

As time went on, I got into more trouble in school and finally got expelled. All those suspensions and ditching (cutting school) parties finally caught up with me. My mom thought that was better since I could have home study and do my work at home without some of my friends to distract me. But I just got worse. Now I would go out and wouldn't come home for days. By now so much had happened and we were getting more organized, but I would still look at all my friends and wonder who would be the next traitor.

My mom finally decided she was tired of Lockeford so we moved out to the country. She thought that by living out there I wouldn't go to Lodi no more. But that didn't stop me. The first day at the new house I ran away and went with my homeboy (fellow gang member) Angel to Napa to stay with his girlfriend. I partied with Sureños up there that lived in the apartment building where Angel's girl lived. We stayed up there for about two weeks and the first week I got my first tattoo. A homegirl from Lodi that went there with us talked me into it. I first got *Sureño* on my ankle and then three dots across my knuckles. I was scared of having the tattoos because of what my mom or stepdad would say. When we went back to Lodi, my friend Angel's mom said my mom called looking for me. She knew where to call since that's where I always stayed. So I called my mom and my dad answered.

He asked where I was and told me to wait there till he picked me up or the cops were going to arrest me for forging his name on a check I stole from him and cashed. Before we went to Napa, I had forgotten about that check because I only made it for 60 dollars. But he found out and he was madder than hell. He said if I ever run away again, he'd send me to juvenile hall. Since I left home before even unpacking, all my stuff was in the garage. He made me sleep out there since he didn't trust me no more. Two days passed, and I left again. This time I stayed with a white guy we had barely jumped in whose mom was always gone. The days went by, and we still partied more and got into trouble. We had a house that a single mother lived in that we could party at all the time. She would let all of us kick it there all day and night. But after a while the neighbors would complain and she got evicted. So now we had to plan where to party at.

For years we would go to Angel's house and kick back, but too many problems and fighting in the streets got his mom scared. Now all of us were good homies, and we partied with girls that were our Sureñas at the nearby school. But pretty soon it got too hot because we would graffiti all over it and leave beer bottles.

One night we planned a party and headed out to our house in Lockeford. It was still empty since my parents didn't want to rent it out yet. I got in through a window then let everyone else in. I told the guys to keep it down and I went to tell the neighbors that I was there so they wouldn't call the cops. We partied all night. Morning came, and we were all asleep on my old bed. There was about five people that stayed. As I woke up, I saw a shadow pass by. It was my dad, so we all jumped out the window to the neighbor's yard. Me and a guy and girl went one way; the rest went another. They got away but were caught by the neighbor. When my dad walked out of the house, I went up to him so my friends could escape. He told me to wait where I was at and then a sheriff came. I was arrested and taken to jail. When my mom found out, she picked me up. At home my mom and dad were arguing so I told my dad I wanted to leave.

He said since I didn't want to live there to get my stuff ready. He dropped me off at Angel's and that was it. Now I was free. I stayed with Kracker for awhile then moved in with my grandma. I lived with Grandma but was hardly ever there. I still stayed at Kracker's and only went to Grandma's to change. She was always nice and never told me nothing about not coming home. After a while we got busted for some drive-bys and two of my friends went to jail. One was a guy, the other a girl who also had a baby. I watched as they took her baby away from her and all five of us in the car were on file and released. Now, I was on the gang list and messed up for good. As time went by, I ended up in the police station more often and always with my best crime partner Kracker. My grandma would always pick us up and drop us off at his house.

Through the years, I've seen people come and go. Things were changing by the minute. Now the cops knew us all. Gangs were getting more violent and more recognized. I've been through good times and bad with my homies. But everyone has someone they trust more than the others. My crime partner was someone who just wanted to be accepted. He didn't look much like a gangster, and the older homies had their doubts about him. But I gave him a chance and he turned out to be all right. He got my trust and respect more than some of my homies I knew five years before him.

Now as I think of everything, all the new gangs, all the new gangsters, I wonder how long will it last. I can see that I'm different from the rest of the guys that I grew up with because I've always put my homies before myself. I would do anything I could to help them out. Now I have settled down a bit. I have a wife and daughter that come first. It's hard to understand gangster life unless you lived it. I put in work and been through so much I can't even explain how I was before.

Everyone thinks they know gangs and gang life. But they only know what they see on TV. I think gangs will never end because I've gotten into fights with guys my mom went to school with. People blame gangs on all kinds of things, but I think you can't blame your parents all the time. It's just that now you feel you have to be in a gang just to be safe from other gangs. Most of the gangsters now just have a wrong picture in their head. They think it's all they have and they like to have others scared. But they have to think about the future. Once you're marked you're marked for life. Then it's hard to change. Not only do you have rivals after you, but the police too. I don't regret being in a gang. Just some of my decisions I've made through life.

I'm glad I can tell my brothers and daughter that gangs just ain't worth it. I still hang out once in a while with my homies, but I made that decision to choose them over my family as a kid.

But by my experience, if I help just one person avoid it, then it was worth it. To anyone thinking of joining a gang—think first! Remember it's not that fun having to take 20 guys with you and your *ruca* (girlfriend) when you go to the fair. Life's hard enough without the extra pressure and bullets flying at you.

—Con Respecto,
MASE

Prison Gangs

When a member is released from prison, he must stay in contact with at least one member of either the unit he is leaving or the unit where he became a member.

—Rule 14 of the 16 original rules that apply to all members of the Texas Syndicate

As street gangs have evolved over time, members have moved from juvenile penal institutions to adult prisons. Both levels of incarceration contain gang structures with membership based primarily on race and/or area of origin. Some of the adult prison gangs have evolved from juvenile gangs whose incarcerated members have formed comprehensive and violent organizations that require obedience of street members. Prison gangs follow formalized rules and procedures strictly. Originally the prison gangs were established for self-protection; later they became involved with the control of drugs and favors in and outside of the prisons. Other groups formed in retaliation and for defense against the more powerful groups.

The influence that adult prison gangs have outside the prison and over juvenile street gangs varies and often depends on an individual adult member's reputation among his former associates in the youth street gang. An adult parolee returning to his former neighborhood may find himself idolized by the younger gang members, but his influence in the absence of leadership skills is limited to a reputation.

An adult who successfully recruits younger street gang members may become the middleman for the prison gang, responsible for directing the street gang to do the bidding of the prison gang. Such an alliance may appear mutually beneficial to participants. The influence and reach of the prison gang is increased, and the street gang itself is elevated by close association with the prison gang. The downside for the street gang is becoming involved in crime more serious than members may desire. In addition, members or their families become targets for retaliation by associates of rival prison gangs.

The main difference between the street gang and the prison gang is in their motivations for violence. The street gang usually commits a violent act to terrorize its enemies; a resultant murder is generally of secondary importance. The prison gang uses murder as a specific act of revenge; the terror created by the killing is secondary.

Following is a description of the most active prison gangs within the United States. According to the U.S. Department of Justice, Federal Bureau of Prisons, the major prison gangs are distinguished by their level of organization, the fact that they were formed in prison, and their potential for disrupting institutional operations.

The Bureau of Prisons lists the major gangs in 1995 as the Aryan Brotherhood, the Black Guerrilla Family, La Nuestra Familia, the Mexican Mafia, and the Texas Syndicate. It is important to note that several of the major prison gangs have expanded and include members serving prison terms throughout the country. In addition to the major gangs, the bureau documents approximately fourteen smaller prison gangs including the Northern Structure, the Texas Mafia, the Bull Dogs, the Dirty White Boys, the Mexikanemi, and the Arizona Aryan Brotherhood. There are also numerous disruptive groups throughout the country that are not categorized as prison gangs.

ARYAN BROTHERHOOD (AB)

History

The Aryan Brotherhood is one of four major U.S. prison gangs with origins in the California prison system. The Aryan Brotherhood started in San Quentin Prison, located in Marin County north of San Francisco, in the early 1960s. Originally called the Diamond Tooth Gang, its members would embed pieces of glass or diamonds in their front teeth as a means of identifying themselves and fellow members. Shortly thereafter the gang changed its name to the Bluebird Gang; members tattooed bluebirds on their necks as a means of recognizing each other. During this time period, the gang became known as the Nazis as a result of their racist, neo-Nazi philosophy. Between 1967 and 1968, the gang changed its name

Aryan Brotherhood drawings will have letters AB displayed somewhere within the drawing. Also present is the shamrock and, in this drawing, the numbers 666.

Creed of the Aryan Brotherhood

A brother I am without a care . . .
I walk where the weak and the heartless don't dare . . .
If by chance I should stumble and lose control . . .
My brother will be there to help me reach my goal . . .
For a brother, death holds no fear . . .
For vengeance will be his the brother still there . . .
A brotherhood means just what it implies . . .
A brother is a brother until that brother dies . . .
And if he was loyal and never lost face . . .
In each brother's heart there will always be a place . . .
A brother I am and will always be . . .
Even after my life is taken from me . . .
When my time comes, I'll lay down . . .
Content that I always stood . . .
With my head held high, walking proud . . .
In The Brotherhood . . .

—Unknown Author

one more time to Aryan Brotherhood. The Aryan Brotherhood may also be referred to as Alice, Alice Baker, Tip, or Brand.

In 1971 the Aryan Brotherhood was approached by a group interested in forming an alliance to assassinate political figures; the group would be known as the Revolutionary Alliance for Freedom or RAFF. The Aryan Brotherhood rejected the proposed merger and continued to emphasize crimes related to prison disruption, drugs, and robberies.

Organization and Beliefs

The Aryan Brotherhood admits only white members who align themselves ideologically with white supremacists. The Aryan Brotherhood philosophy was originally a blend of white supremacy and shared German and Irish ancestry. In the 1980s and 1990s, the gang has gravitated more toward admiring Irish ancestry and Norse/Viking symbolism and history. At one point, the main concentration of Aryan Brotherhood members was at San Quentin and Folsom prisons. All members vote to initiate new members, and one negative vote is sufficient to reject a potential member. Final approval is given by the gang leader, the "General." The Aryan Brotherhood has a "blood-in, blood-out" policy, meaning a member must kill in order to be admitted into the gang and must die in order to leave. In July 1995 in Stockton, California, it was reported that Candy Johnson, the leader of Aryan Brotherhood chapter 666 Devil Worshippers, was sentenced to two consecutive life terms for her role in the stabbing death of Anthony Bratton as part of an initiation rite.

Association with Other Gangs

While the members of Aryan Brotherhood are white, they are known to associate with Mexicans and blacks. Such association is formed of necessity and generally involves the sale of narcotics. The alliance between the Aryan Brotherhood and the Mexican Mafia came about as a means of protection and control of the narcotics trade. In addition, the two have banded together to carry out "contract hits" on both La Nuestra Familia and the Black Guerrilla Family. The Aryan Brotherhood has also been known to associate with the Hell's Angels and the Manson Family. It is not uncommon to see this alliance outside of prison, with parolees involved in armed robberies and drug sales.

Profile

Aryan Brotherhood members can usually be identified by their tattoos, which consist of the letters "AB," a shamrock, and three sixes. The three sixes are also a characteristic of satanic groups, signifying the mark of Satan. A nonmember found wearing an Aryan Brotherhood tattoo is at risk of being murdered by the Aryan Brotherhood. In addition to the above listed tattoos, Aryan Brotherhood members also wear Nazi tattoos such as lightning bolts and swastikas.

BLACK GUERRILLA FAMILY (BGF)

History

The Black Guerrilla Family was formed in 1966 by former Black Panther George Jackson. An all-black gang, they were originally called the Black Vanguard or Black Family and had links to the Black Mafia. Some original members were associated with the Symbionese Liberation Army, the Black Liberation Army, and the Weatherman Underground organizations. They changed their name to the Black Guerrilla Family in 1971.

Organization and Beliefs

The Black Guerrilla Family maintains an extensive and precise code of ethics in which they make several reference to their symbol, the dragon. The Black Guerrilla Family was formed as a Marxist/Leninist revolutionary organization with goals of

BGF Oath

If I should ever break my stride
And falter at my comrades side

This oath will kill me.

If ever my word should prove untrue
Should I betray this chosen few

This oath will kill me.

Should I submit to greed or lust
Should I misuse the people's trust

This oath will kill me.

Should I be slow to take a stand
Should I show fear to any man

This oath will kill me.

Should I grow lax in discipline
In time of strife refuse my hand

This oath will kill me.

—Unknown Author

overthrowing the US Government and abolishing racism. They are one of the most politically oriented gangs in the United States.

A prospective member must be nominated by an existing member. Acceptance into the gang requires a life pledge of loyalty to the Black Guerrilla Family. As black revolutionaries, members consider themselves above racism. Their goal is to consolidate all black colonies in order to promote revolution. The origin of one Black Guerrilla Family oath is unknown; however, it clearly states "The guerrilla must apply all of his resources to protect and build on the lives of the comrades as well as advance the revolution. We must never forget that there is no cure for the evils of the Western world other than through *uncompromising destruction*."

In addition to their political agenda, the Black Guerrilla Family also facilitates drug sales. The Black Guerrilla Family draws most of its members from all-black street gangs, including both CRIPs and Bloods. They maintain close ties with street gangs to enhance the flow of narcotics and in some cases have been known to provide protection for drug dealers rather than deal drugs themselves.

Association with Other Gangs

The Black Guerrilla Family remains rivals with other prison gangs such as the Aryan Brotherhood, the Mexican Mafia, and the Vanguards. These rivalries exist within the correctional facilities, but have been known to carry over onto the streets.

Profile

Black Guerrilla Family members may have tattoos of a Chinese dragon, a rifle and sword crossed with the letters BGF, or just the letters BGF. Some tattoos consist of a dragon encircling a prison guard tower.

LA NUESTRA FAMILIA (NF)

History

La Nuestra Familia is a Hispanic gang formed within the California prison system during the mid-1960s. Sources vary as to which exact prison witnessed the gang's beginnings; the Federal Bureau of Prisons has written that the gang formed in Soledad Prison, while the California Department of Corrections maintains that it originated in Deuel Vocational Institution in 1966 and then moved to San Quentin in 1967.

La Nuestra Familia recruits predominantly from northern California. The fact that a large portion of the members come from rural areas explains why they may be referred to as "sod busters" or "farmers" by their enemies.

Organization and Beliefs

La Nuestra Familia originated in order to protect young, rural, Mexican-American inmates from the Mexican Mafia. It was set up along military lines, including such

Nuestra Familia

If I go forward, follow me
If I hesitate, push me
If they kill me, avenge me
If I am a traitor, kill me
Forward onto victory.

—Unknown NF inmate

This is a typical example of La Nuestra Familia drawings. The hat is modeled on those worn by rural farm workers. The dagger is a symbol of the gang's violent behavior.

ranks as generals, captains, lieutenants, sergeants, and soldiers. Because of its rigid organization and obvious chain of command, La Nuestra Familia was prosecuted in the early 1980s under the federal RICO Act (Racketeer Influenced and Corrupt Organizations). This prosecution temporarily stunted the gang's expansion.

Association with Other Gangs

La Nuestra Familia associates with the Black Guerrilla Family (BGF), the Northern Structure, and a splinter group of the Texas Syndicate. Some theorize that the Northern Structure, a Northern California–based group that is aligned with Norte/Norteños, is a spin-off group of La Nuestra Familia, but La Nuestra Familia members say that the Structure is a separate entity. La Nuestra Familia are bitter enemies of the Mexican Mafia, the Mexikanemi, and the Aryan Brotherhood.

Profile

La Nuestra Familia uses various types of tattoos including the words "Nuestra Familia" or "NF," a sombrero with a knife through it, and a five-pointed star. This is symbolic of the North Star because La Nuestra Familia is a northern California gang. They also favor the color red and may have a red rag (bandanna) in their possession.

Norteño

A bright red rag, the Norteño flag,
He wears on his head with pride.
Lentes disguise the hate in his eyes
and he's always ready to ride.

He's on the yard and strolling hard
He's always on his toes.
He packs a knife to guard his life
and takes it wherever he goes.

A few months back I saw him attack
this *vato* from way down south.
He took a stand, blade in hand
cut him from neck to mouth.

I could tell by the way he fell
that the *vato* was going to die.
Blood has spilled
and an inmate was killed
and no one still knows why.

For six months they've had us
on a lockdown status
pending the investigation.
Time gets hard without the yard
it's a fucked-up situation.

Fed in the cell miserable as hell
a runner can't be found.
1/2 an hour to take a shower
placas all around.

Over and finished
lockdowns diminished
the *vatos* still on the line.
Back on the wall, standing tall
his tumbler full of wine.

      —Author Unknown

NORTHERN STRUCTURE

History

The Northern Structure was created in 1983 in northern California's Folsom Prison. Some sources indicated that it was a spin-off of La Nuestra Familia designed to divert the attention of corrections staff. It was also a means for La Nuestra Familia to conduct their business covertly after the recent RICO prosecution.

Organization and Beliefs

Similar to other prison gangs and La Nuestra Familia, the goal of the Northern Structure is to control the trafficking of narcotics within the prison community as well as out on the streets.

Association with Other Gangs

Adversaries of the Northern Structure include the Aryan Brotherhood, the Mexican Mafia, a faction of the Texas Syndicate, Sureño street gangs, and a new and growing gang called the Fresno Bulldogs.

The Northern Structure's membership is primarily Hispanic, and the gang is affiliated with the Norteño street gangs.

Profile

The main color of the gang is red, and they use the symbol of the Aztec eagle, as does La Nuestra Familia. The Northern Structure and La Nuestra Familia also may use the Roman numeral XIV as a means of identification. The number 14 represents the fourteenth letter of the alphabet, which is *N* (Norte, Northern Structure, Nuestra Familia) and therefore appears frequently in their graffiti and tattoos. Other symbols include a solid blue five-pointed star and "XIVERS." The Northern Structure may also be referred to as the Nuestra Raza or New Structure.

MEXICAN MAFIA (EME)

History

The Mexican Mafia, or EME, was formed in the 1950s within the California Department of Corrections. The word *eme* is the Spanish pronunciation for the

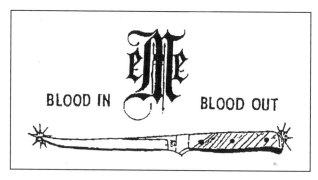

The Mexican Mafia's motto, "Blood In, Blood Out" is shown with a dagger

letter "M." The EME, which promotes ethnic solidarity, is a Hispanic gang that originally included members from east Los Angeles. The gang grew during the 1960s and expanded its control over gambling, extortion, and the drug trade within the prison system.

Organization and Beliefs

Known for viciousness, the EME murders as a form of inter-gang intimidation. It is also notorious as one of the most disruptive prison groups within the federal prison system. Its drug trafficking is carried out by a paramilitary organization that includes ranks from general to soldier. In September 1993 in Los Angeles, California, the Mexican Mafia put out the word to all Latino street gangs that drive-by shootings were to stop. Apparently, uncontrollable gang violence had affected the Mexican Mafia's ability to dominate the distribution and sale of narcotics on the streets. The prison gang promised retribution to anyone violating the edict. Strict guidelines dictated that rival gangs were still allowed to avenge each other, without harming innocent bystanders. Police noted a 15 percent decrease in Latino gang-related murders during the months after the edict was issued.

Association with Other Gangs

The EME enlists members from urban areas, while its major rival, La Nuestra Familia, recruits its members from rural America. In addition to La Nuestra Familia, the EME maintains adversarial relationships with the Northern Structure, Arizona's New Mexican Mafia, black street gangs, the Black Guerrilla Family, and Norteño street gangs.

Allies of the EME are the Aryan Brotherhood, Mexikanemi, and various Sureño street gangs. There have been cases where the EME has also been shown to have ties with the Italian criminal organization known as La Cosa Nostra. Primarily, the Aryan Brotherhood and EME are associates and occasionally will take "hit" contracts for one another, meaning that they will "murder for hire."

Profile

EME tattoos consist of the letters *M*, *EME* or *MM*. In addition, members may have a tattoo of a black hand called the *mano negro* in Spanish. Often, tattoos portray a large bird of prey with a serpent hanging from its mouth, as seen in the Mexican flag.

TEXAS SYNDICATE

History

Although the Texas Syndicate, or Syndicato Tejano, was formed at Folsom Prison in California during the early 1970s, the group's strongest membership lies within the state of Texas. It was organized for protection from the Aryan Brotherhood and the Mexican Mafia, who were attacking native Texas inmates, and for the control of drug trafficking within the prison. As of 1995, the gang primarily concentrated on drug trafficking and also engaged in "selling" protection in prison.

Organization and Beliefs

Membership consists primarily of Mexican-Americans incarcerated within the Texas Department of Corrections. The rule allowing only Latinos into the gang is no longer followed. Several inmates who reside in Texas but are actually Cuban

The dragon shaped in the form of the letter S wraps itself around the letter T representing the Texas Syndicate.

and Colombian have been documented as Texas Syndicate members. Membership began rising in 1994 with recruitment of Latin American members.

According to the Texas Syndicate, there are sixteen original rules that apply to every member in every state. The penalty for violating any of the rules is death. The rules are as follows;

- A member must respect other members and their families at all times.
- A member must never lie to another member.
- Once a prospect becomes a member, he is a member for life. There is no out.
- A member comes first and last before all nonmembers. This includes mother, father, wife, child, brother, sister, friend.
- Every member must share all things with other members, there are no exceptions.
- Only the first five rules will be shown to prospective members.
- A member will never talk to anyone but other members about the organization.
- The *TS* tattoo will be put on every new member as soon as possible.
- Every prospect to become a member must be voted upon by every member in every unit.
- If a member is designated to carry out a hit then he will have two weeks to do so or else he will be hit himself by another member.
- Only Mexicans will be allowed to become members.
- No one who has ever been a turnkey or building tender (correctional officer) will be allowed to become a member.
- When there is going to be hit on a unit, the chairman will make several slips of paper and on one of the slips will be the victim's name. Each member will draw a slip and whoever draws the slip with the victim's name on it will carry out the hit.
- When a member is released from prison, he must stay in contact with at least one member of either the unit he is leaving or of the unit where he became a member.
- The member who sponsors a prospective member will be forever responsible for the prospective member's actions if he should become a member.
- A member will carry himself with respect at all times and abide by all the rules forever.

Association with Other Gangs

The Texas Syndicate aligns itself with the Texas Mafia and the Dirty White Boys. Its enemies include the Aryan Brotherhood, La Nuestra Familia, EME, and Mexikanemi.

Profile

The primary group symbol of the Texas Syndicate is the letter *T* with the *S* running through the lower part, often disguised as the figure of a snake. Another symbol is a cross with a ribbon running through it in the shape of an *S*.

White Hate Gangs

We think the white people are the chosen people. It's going to get to the point where every race is going to be going against every other race and that'll be the '95 Race War.

—Archie Johnston
18-year-old Imperial Wizard
of the Independent Knights of the Ku Klux Klan
October 1993

In the early 1990s a new crime classification evolved in the law enforcement community and became known as "hate crimes." Police officers all across the country began training in the fine art of determining hate crimes and speaking to the victims of such crimes. Suddenly, a fist fight that would have been classified as a battery could now be classified as a hate crime, depending on what one person may have said before punching the other person in the nose. If the suspect made mention of race, religion, sex, sexual preference, or a host of other items, that suspect could face a more serious criminal charge.

White supremacist groups such as the Skinheads are responsible for committing many of the hate crimes that occur each year throughout the country. They have a long history in America that dates back to the Ku Klux Klan, which was founded after the Civil War. Though the KKK and other white supremacist groups have existed in America for a long time, it is the Skinheads that have won notoriety in recent years for their organizational skills and violent tactics.

SKINHEADS

History

The Skinhead movement originated in England in the 1960s among the children of blue-collar workers. Though they originally wore long hair and frequented Jamaican reggae clubs, the teens began to shave their heads in the sixties and seventies in an attempt to be unique and as a defense against having their hair pulled in street

This Skinhead drawing shows the close link between U.S. Skins and their counterparts in Britain, where the movement originated.

fights. They wore boots and suspenders (also called *braces*), and fought frequently, often attacking the police, soccer players, homosexuals, and hippies.

Their music is called *oi*, a term originally used to greet a friend, and is very important to the Skinheads. Characterized by a pounding rhythm, it is very simple and pure. The slam dancing phenomenon took root in this movement, and Skinheads were known for gathering on the dance floor of clubs and, as the name suggests, literally slamming into one another, often causing injury to the dancers.

This white supremacist drawing states the philosophy that racial purity is a component for Aryan security.

The letters SWP, meaning Supreme White Power, are carved into this club. Weapons such as this are used for attacking rival gang members.

In England in the 1970s, there was a split in the Skinhead movement. One faction was referred to as the "2 Tones," and they primarily focused their attention on Jamaican reggae music. The other faction became more politically oriented and concerned themselves with unemployment, immigration, and other social woes.

The Skinhead movement crossed the Atlantic and spread to the United States in the mid 1980s. In 1987 there were an estimated 300 Skinheads in the United States. According to a special report from the Anti-Defamation League (ADL), as of 1993 there were over 3,500 members in approximately 40 states across the nation. The ADL states in the report that Skinheads are the most violent of all white supremacy groups and that there is no single national Skinhead organization. Instead there are numerous groups operating independently within the country, including such groups as American Front, Northern Hammerskins, Aryan Resistance League, and the SS of America. In addition to these smaller territorial groups, Skinheads have formed alliances with the older, more established hate groups such as the Ku Klux Klan, White Aryan Resistance, and the Church of the Creator. The older groups often refer to the Skinheads as their "front-line warriors."

Organization and Beliefs

The Skinheads are divided into two separate organizations. The majority of Skinheads across the country are racist, neo-Nazi whites who feel threatened by Jews, nonwhites, and homosexuals. Another group, Skinheads Against Racial Prejudice or SHARP, are not racist and actually fight the racist Skinheads. Other names for this group include Racial Unity Skinheads, Anti-Racist Action, Two-Tone Skins, and Mad Skins. Since SHARP dress like racist Skinheads in Doc Marten boots, braces, and flight jackets, it can be hard to tell the two groups apart.

The main difference between Skinheads and SHARP is that nonwhites as well as whites can be SHARP members. In Portland, Oregon, in 1990, the SHARP movement received press coverage for its attempts to rid the City of Roses of all racist gangs. Many Portland citizens thought that the city could only benefit from having a group in town working to eliminate Crips and Bloods and Skinheads from the streets. However, the SHARP never explained that the "method of elimination" would include severe brutality and that their goal was to control the city and claim it as their own turf.

On-line communications

Skinheads often communicate via the Internet. It is not unusual to find chat rooms with juveniles discussing the Skinhead philosophy. The following profiles were taken from a chat room of a major on-line service in February of 1996. Each person using the service usually has a profile listing demographic and other information. The following profiles belong to customers that were chatting in a room entitled "Oi."

Screen name:	Bird
Member name:	Jennifer
Location:	San Antonio, TX
Birthdate:	11/17/77
Sex:	female
Marital Status:	single
Computers:	who cares
Hobbies:	TALKIN TRASH, DRINKING, AND WHATEVER COMES AFTER THAT
Occupation:	WORKING CLASS SKINBIRD
Quote:	KEEP YOUR BOOTS ON AND YOUR PRIDE HIGH

Screen name:	Stomper or Skinhead
Member name:	Todd
Location:	Tacoma, WA
Birthdate:	'76
Sex:	male
Marital Status:	single
Computers:	Mac
Hobbies:	Romping and stomping in my steel cap boots and listening to real SKA
Occupation:	Working Class Skinhead
Quote:	"Strappin on the braces, lacin up the boots, Skinheads, Skinheads on the loose."

What follows in an excerpt from the conversation that took place in that particular room. "Author" is the name I used when in the room that evening.

bird:	life sucks all the time
skinhed:	the only thing good about today was band rehearsal, and the fact that i'm getting a tat soon
bird:	well lets see . . . i got some new boots today!!!!!!!!!!!!!!!!!!!!!
skinhed:	mine are on the way
bird:	doug . . . what kind of boots are you gettin?
skinhed:	10 hole oxblood steeeelies, size 10

bird:	i got some undergrounds . . . . . 10 i's oxblood . . . steel and bump toes . . . . .
bird:	from crash and burn
skinhed:	nifty
skinhed:	how much
bird:	i got some new braces too . . . and a patch . . . $130
Author:	hey, whats the steel toes for?
skinhed:	i got my docs for $85 or something shipped :)
bird:	kickin shit
Luv oi:	kickin the shit out of people :)
Luv oi:	heheheh
Skinbird:	CRACKING SKULLS
bird:	right on skinbird
skinhed:	I could stomp some skulls right now . . . .
bird:	i wants to stomp some skulls tonite . . . . bonehead skulls!
Luv oi:	author . . . . i take it yer not a skinhead?
skinbird:	I WANNA GO CURB SOME NAZI'S
bird:	right on skinbird!!!!!!!
skinhed:	i am so pist i wanna roll over and die . . . . . curbin nazis would be cool too
Author:	hey skinhed, whats curbin nazis mean?
skinbird:	U LAY THE FUCKERS HEAD ON THE CURB AND STOMP ON IT
rudy:	woohhoooooo
bird:	On their heads!!!!!!!!!!!!!!!!!!!!!!
bird:	break some motha fuckin teeth
rudy:	you about to bust some heads?
bird:	birds rule the world!!!!!!!!!!!!!!!!!!!!!!!!!

In addition to the chat rooms, there are various newsgroups and Web sites that cater to and are set up primarily for racist groups. The on-line customer merely types the area of interest, and the computer searches for similar groups. Two skinhead groups were found in a matter of seconds, each containing notes posted from members worldwide, with information on new music and future rally dates. In December 1994, The Simon Weisenthal Center sent a letter to the Prodigy computer on-line service protesting the "continued use of Prodigy by bigots to promote their agendas of hate." The Weisenthal Center said that it has tracked over fifty hate groups using the service to disseminate their information.

Association with Other Gangs

Skinheads and the Ku Klux Klan are not the only white supremacist groups. In the absence of an organized movement, communities can expect to find juveniles aligning themselves with such groups such as Supreme White Power (SWP). This particular gang does not have a hierarchy, nor is it usually linked with similar groups in other states or counties. For the most part, SWP members are isolated within their respective cities and have little or no contact with other SWP factions. Similar to the Skinheads, SWP members will tattoo themselves with swastikas, lightning bolts, White Pride, and the letters "SWP." Unlike the Skinheads, SWP members do not dress in braces and Doc Martens.

A one-time leader of the Ku Klux Klan, Tom Metzger started a movement known as the White Aryan Resistance (WAR). WAR is headquartered in Fallbrook, California, and boasts a membership of approximately 3,000 people. Metzger and his son, John, have been responsible for enlisting the youth of America into the white supremacist party. John Metzger became president of a WAR affiliate in 1987. The movement is known as AYM, Aryan Youth Movement. At least half of this group's members are Skinheads from groups in San Francisco, Portland, New York, Detroit, Cincinnati, and Tulsa. One method of recruitment that was extremely successful for the Metzgers was the use of music. In an article in his WAR newspaper, Tom Metzger said, "Music is one of the greatest propaganda tools around. You can influence more people with a song than you can with a speech."

The rock band Screwdriver is perhaps the best known racist or "oi" music band to distribute records in England and the United States. Other groups include The

SKINS

The White Aryan Resistance has also used the skull and crossbones as a means of intimidation.

Excerpts from *Young Nazis*

Dress

"The dress of the skin is rough, smart, and clean. The boots skins wear are 'Dr. Marten' boots. Suspenders are worn by most skins but not all. Fred Perry–type polo shirts or T-shirts are standards worn by skins. Flight jackets and Levi Jackets are preferred. The skins' hair is either zero-zero cut up to a number three. All in the skinhead uniform is working class, ready to fight because our heads are shaved for battle!!!"

Skinhead Girls

"A Skinhead girl's dress is similar to that of a Skinhead guy, the Fred Perry, jeans, and Docs, etc. But even more feminine is the kilt skirt, preferably wool, and mini-skirts. These skirts are worn with fishnet stockings, and DM boots or DM shoes. A Skinhead girl usually sports a fringe haircut and hooped earrings."

Attitude

"The attitude of a skinhead is generally ready to fight and on guard all the time. Skins do not usually go around and start trouble. It's only when people start to make the jump on skins. When that happens, the skins end up winning! Skinheads are mad and tired of the system screwing them over. Skinheads are the All American white youth, they love mom and love their flag!!!"

Klansmen, Brutal Combat, Warrior Kids, Evil Skins, Elite Terror, and Brutal Attack. The most popular songs bear such titles as "White Rider," "White Warrior," "The New Storm Troopers," "Take the Sword," "Fists of Steel," "Heads Kicked In," and "Reich 'n' Roll."

Other groups sprout up around the country in big and small towns alike. For example, in Brockton, Massachusetts, in January 1995, a 20-year-old man was sentenced to forty-six months in prison after pleading guilty to painting swastikas on a synagogue and harassing blacks. The man admitted being the founder of the New Dawn Hammerskins, a neo-Nazi Skinhead group.

Profile

The typical Skinhead is between the ages of thirteen and twenty-five. Both males and females are involved in the Skinhead organization. Most Skinheads sport shaved heads; however, a shaved head does not necessarily mean that a teen is a Skinhead. Skinheads do not usually have any facial hair with the exception of sideburns. As in any gang, this is only a generality. Some Skinheads wear their hair long in order not to draw attention to themselves. Females do not usually shave their heads, but rather wear more of a punk-style haircut, sticking out in all directions or dyed in bold colors such as green, yellow, or purple.

The most popular jacket worn by Skinheads is the air force flight jacket. The jackets are usually embellished with patches to denote certain affiliations. Common patches include the Confederate flag, the United States flag, the Ku Klux Klan, Aryan Nations, swastikas, and other German war memorabilia.

Skinheads refer to suspenders as "braces" and wear them for special occasions or everyday wear. Some Skinheads choose not to wear any suspenders at all. The color of the braces has different meanings in different parts of the country. The color red signifies blood and a readiness to fight for their cause. White braces signify that they are proud of "white" and all it stands for. The braces may be worn attached to tan work pants or blue jeans. Some Skinheads prefer to wear camouflage pants and to take on more of a militaristic style. When the Skinhead is dressed up and on the street, he usually rolls his pants up to the top of his Doc Marten boots.

Doc Marten boots or "Docs" are the boot of choice for Skinheads. If Doc Marten boots are not available, the Skinhead will wear old work boots that lace up the front. The Doc Marten steel-toed boot is the boot of choice as it comes from England and the steel toe is a useful tool in street fights. The laces of the Doc Martens signify different attitudes. The red laces signify that the wearer is a neo-Nazi and ready to shed blood for the cause of the Skinhead movement. White laces denote white pride or white power, and green laces signify that the wearer is a gay basher. Yellow laces have no particular meaning.

Like other street gangs, Skinheads have a whole assortment of tattoos and emblems. Skinhead tattoos may include the words *white pride* or *white power*, the Nazi *SS* symbol (lightning bolts), a strand of barbed wire typically worn around the biceps, swastikas, Iron Crosses, and the words Nazi or Skins. Emblems might include swastika patches or the Nazi flag.

Black Gangs

I as a 415 Soldier, will come from the bleeding heart of this constitution, and flow as a true soldier across the sands I hereby fly the right solution, never before like no other black man, to achieve the goal of African opportunity, never before like no African others, and to embrace 415 African unity, to support the cause of my brothers and through the next four years to come, I shall honor and do my best by the banner until the job is done, I will never stop for rest, to be a winner is a faithful test, to be a loser is for the African Dead, that's why I march for the real conquest, with the faith of my 415 comrades, and should I ever fail my obligated deeds, under the banner that I fly may this prevail and punish me, for the reason that I did not try, forever forever to the 415.

—An oath taken by black gang members incarcerated by the California Youth Authority. The 415 refers to a former area code exclusive to the Oakland, California, area. Members of gangs from this area tend to band together when incarcerated for mutual protection from gangs originating in other areas or of a different ethnic background.

Black gangs in the United States, such as the Long Bridge Boys and the Fly Boys, date back to New York City in the late 1700s. The first recorded black street gangs appeared in Los Angeles in the 1920s. They roamed the streets, committing petty crimes such as robbery and assault. They had no real competition until the rise of neighborhood gangs in the late 1930s. Even then black street gangs posed little threat to communities and functioned primarily as social groups. Their most violent activities would be fights with other rival black gangs at school athletic events or dances. These gangs were not very territorial or turf-oriented, but they did look for ways to earn respect by being tough.

As the civil rights movement developed in the 1960s, many gangs lost their more aggressive or militant members to the organizations leading protests for political and social change. The lack of immediate reward for their efforts in fighting for civil rights caused many young blacks to join political groups such as the Black Panthers, and some street gangs became more politically oriented and aggressive due to lack of economic and social opportunity. By the early 1970s, black street gangs posed a threat to public order in many metropolitan communities.

Involvement in drug sales led some gangs to become more territorial and economically oriented. In response, many of these gangs formed informal alliances for mutual protection, and these alliances formed the basis for the umbrella groups most black gangs align themselves with today—the CRIPs and Bloods or People Nation and Folk Nation. Individual street gangs and sets usually fall under one of these umbrella groups.

A black street gang, known as a "set," can be as small as a dozen members or as large as several hundred. The size is dependent upon how long the gang has been in existence, its wealth, and its reputation. The smaller the set, the less organized it tends to be. When a set begins to get larger, it needs some type of leadership structure to hold it together. The more structural or organized set will probably have moneymaking as its objective and little if any room for error is tolerated from its members. Members can range in age from twelve to late twenties. Older gang members are either dead, in prison, or just "kick back" (retired) if they are lucky. Leadership in the smaller sets can be very fluid. Anyone who can control others through physical violence or persuasion is considered the leader or "shot caller." The larger sets require a more formal leadership structure with a variety of official positions depending upon the need of the organization. The leaders of these sets are usually more intelligent than the other members, but far more ruthless.

The image of the poorly organized black street gang should easily be dispelled by the example of the Detroit-based Young Boys Incorporated (YBI). This gang was the forerunner of the Los Angeles–based "super gangs" of the late 1980s. This street gang was highly organized and profitable. In 1982 YBI earned $7.5 million a week and over $400 million annually. It was broken up by federal agents that year, and twenty of its members were indicted for a multitude of crimes.

CRIPS AND BLOODS

History

The CRIPs originated around 1969–70 in the Watts, Willowbrook, and Compton sections of Los Angeles, California. The original members, students at Washington High School, rapidly expanded their operating area. The availability of automobiles increased this gang's extreme mobility, and they quickly established a violent reputation. Primary activities involved extorting or robbing students at local schools and assaulting anyone brave enough to oppose them. Members of Chicago's Blackstone Rangers who had moved to the area may have been involved in organizing the initial CRIPs street gang. The CRIPs began to recruit members throughout the Los Angeles area, establishing different sets that all "claimed" or were affiliated with the original CRIPs.

CRIP success led to the organization of rival gang sets, who would become known as Bloods. Founded in the early 1970s as a protection and defense against their more prolific and successful rivals, Bloods have been trying to catch up ever since. The Bloods originated in the Compton, California, suburb of Los Angeles. The first known Blood gang was formed by a group of young blacks on Piru Street in Compton, who called themselves the Piru Street Boys.

The Pirus had to be very tough, violent, and aggressive to survive the more powerful CRIPs. Perhaps as a result of the lower number of sets as compared to the CRIPs, Blood sets are usually more supportive of each other. It used to be said that Bloods didn't fight Bloods, but the reality of the streets has proven this to be false.

Organization and Beliefs

The introduction of drugs as a means of providing easy income has given new life to black street gangs. The CRIPs and Bloods previously committed robberies and car thefts to obtain money, but drug sales provide a much higher income for what they consider to be very little risk. The introduction of drugs to the street gangs also means that territory has become more and more important, not only to a gang's pride in controlling an area, but as a franchise site to sell drugs. Gang violence escalates as gangs have the financial means to purchase more deadly and sophisticated weaponry. Arms races between rival street gangs seeking the deadliest weapons have led to gangs becoming better armed than the Los Angeles Police Department.

The constant warfare, limited growth for sales, and better-trained law enforcement agencies in the Los Angeles area have forced many gang sets to seek new, more profitable, and safer markets. These gangs have discovered that the price of their crack cocaine is worth 300 to 400 times more outside of the Los Angeles area, so the gangs have set up franchise operations in other cities across the United States.

Sophisticated pipeline systems are established to transport the drugs to the new locations and to transfer money back to the base of operations in Los Angeles. Formerly minor street gangs have become major drug-running operations, or super gangs, on a national scale. Connections between them and international drug cartels have become obvious to federal authorities.

In 1985 and 1986 several metropolitan police departments in the United States began to notice that CRIP and Blood gangs were operating in their localities. Local street gangs at first complained to the police due to the loss of respect they received as the L.A. gangs moved into their territory and took over drug markets or developed them. Local gangs had the choice of either working for the L.A. gangs or being eliminated by them. Most often they joined and adopted the Blood or CRIP affiliation. By 1991 the Federal Bureau of Alcohol, Tobacco and Firearms had identified CRIP and or Blood sets operating in 32 states and 69 cities excluding California.

The drug trade has made several gang leaders very rich and powerful, creating what federal law enforcement agencies call "super gangs." Although some are only in their twenties, the leaders of these super gangs have been referred to as street gang "godfathers" by law enforcement agencies. Like other gang leaders, the godfathers have funneled money into legitimate businesses as a way to safeguard their fortunes and launder money from drug sales.

Another avenue to quick wealth for black street gangs has been bank and jewelry store robberies. This has worked successfully in California and surrounding states where the L.A.-based gangs use their mobility to hit targets and quickly disappear. The robberies are committed by groups of five or six well-trained individuals. They perform a thorough surveillance of potential targets in an area and select what they consider to be the most vulnerable and profitable. The group then raids the targeted bank or jewelry store and takes what it can in one minute. Two members stay casually in a parked vehicle outside the target to act as a lookout. Once the robbery is complete, the two groups meet up and leave the area in the observation vehicle. They can easily return to L.A. without drawing any suspicion and fence their stolen jewelry or divide the cash.

Association with Other Gangs

The CRIPs continued to grow in numbers throughout the 1970s and outnumbered gangs claiming allegiance to the Bloods by a ratio of three to one. Many long-established black street gangs in Los Angeles began to claim affiliation with the CRIPs or Bloods, and the division between the gang sets became formalized. Chapters integrated the name CRIP into their existing gang name and thereby became CRIP gangs. The large number of CRIP gang sets in Los Angeles led to intra-gang fighting, in addition to conflict with Blood sets. These various feuds became more violent and vengeful over the years as increasing numbers of gang members were caught up in the fighting. The animosities carried over into the Los Angeles County Juvenile Detention Camps and California Youth Authority institutions, where members of opposing factions were separated to prevent additional violence. These separations tended to reinforce the gangs' desire for confrontation and helped to support existing set allegiance and alliances rather than hinder them.

Despite this animosity, partnerships have formed throughout the U.S. with rival gangs working together, so as to spend more time making profitable drug sales than fighting each other. The sophistication and intelligence of gang members who are

Samplings of 1980s and 1990s Los Angeles Black Street Gangs

CRIP SETS   East Coast, Hoover, P.J. Watts, Eight Tray Gangsters, Playboy Gangsters, Front Street, 99 Mafia, Underground CRIPs, Rollin 60s, Watts Baby Loc

BLOOD SETS   Treetop Pirus, Bounty Hunters, Black P Stones, Kabbage Patch Pirus, Krenshaw Mafia, Sirkle Sity Pirus, Be-Bop Watts, Swans, Rolling Twenties, Skottsdale Pirus networking and branching out their drug sales across the country and internationally should not be underestimated.

Profile

There are several explanations for the origin of the term *CRIP*. One is that the term is a corruption of the word *Cribs*, a street gang that splintered off a 1960s group known as the Slauson Street gang. The story most often quoted about the origin of the name is that it was taken from the title of *Tales from the Crypt*, a comic book series popular during the period when the group first became noticed. Another version with a comic book origin is that gang members wanted to be known as powerful enough to kill even Superman. The name was then understood to be a corruption of the word *kryptonite*. Others believe the name came from a founding member of the gang who was crippled and used a cane, or that members carried canes as a weapon and means of identification. Members supposedly walked in a fashion that made them appear crippled, and the name CRIP was adopted.

Typical of gangs, the members adopt monikers (street names). Black gang members will use monikers that describe the gang member's perspective of himself, physical characteristics, and weapons. The words *bone*, *dog*, and *loc*, which is short for loco, are common suffixes. It should be noted that CRIPs will use the spelling *loc*, while Bloods prefer *lok*. This relates back to the belief that Bloods refuse to use the letter *C*. The following are examples of typical black monikers.

- **T-bone** *T* is the first letter of the member's first or last name.
- **P-dog** *P* is the first letter of the member's first or last name.
- **12 Gauge** Individual has or uses a 12-gauge shotgun to commit crimes.

Headgear usually consists of baseball caps of a particular color and college or professional sports team. Caps may be worn backward, sideways, or with the brim turned up. Price tags and manufacturers labels are also retained, attached to the headpiece. Civil War–style caps are popular with some People and Folk Nation sets. The People Nation wear the gray cap of the South and the Folk Nation prefer the blue cap of the Union.

Jackets were traditionally red or blue, but now can be of any color. The jacket may be green in some areas if the wearer is advertising that he is selling narcotics. Certain CRIP gangs will wear purple or green, as well as blue. There is usually some type of writing on the jackets, either a moniker or a set name. Black is usually considered generic, but still advertises gang membership.

Gang members who sell narcotics may be seen wearing necklaces with a dollar sign or a pierced earring with a dollar sign stud. Gold chains, rings, and watches are also worn conspicuously. Friendship bracelets with beads showing the preferred colors of the gang are now common.

Common Black Street Gang Terminology

ace kool	Best friend/backup
BG	Baby gangster
B/K	Blood killer
BOS	Beat on sight
beasting	Becoming physically violent
blob	Term used by CRIPs to put down a Blood
blood	Piru/non-CRIP
book	Run, get away
breakdown	Shotgun
buster	Phony, wanna-be gangsters
crab	Term used by Bloods to put down a CRIP
crew	Gang
cuzz	CRIP
dank	Marijuana
dead presidents	Money
deuce & a quarter	Buick 225 vehicle
donuts	Disrespect for Disciples
double deuce	.22-caliber gun
drop a dime	Snitch on someone
do-rag	bandanna wrapped around the head
dusted	Under the influence of PCP
essays	Mexicans
freak	Good looking girl
frog	Girl of low moral standards
gang banging	Involved in gang activity
get down	Fight
hittin up	Putting graffiti on something
homeboy	Someone from the same gang
hood	Neighborhood
hustler	Dope dealer
KC	Killer CRIP
kickin	Hangin out with the homeboys
man	Cop
OG	Original gangster
packing	To conceal a gun
player	Individual interested solely in girls
popo	Police
posse	Gang or group of friends (East Coast)
rag	Bandanna (blue or red depending upon affiliation)
rooster	Piru
sagging	Wearing your pants lower than your boxer shorts
sets	Individual CRIP or Blood gangs

slob	Term used by CRIPs to put down a Blood
TG	Tiny gangster
tray eight	.38-caliber gun
vicky lous	Disrespect for Vice Lords

British Knight gym shoes are often worn by CRIPs. The letters *BK* take on the meaning of Blood Killer rather than British Knight. Red or blue Nike gym shoes are also popular. Shoelaces of particular preferred gang colors may also be a common sign.

Dress has been an easy method to identify gang affiliation, so the more savvy gang members have given up the stereotyped dress for less obvious attire. This way they can continue their activities without immediately drawing attention to themselves. Some hidden style of dress or indication of gang membership may still be present, especially tattoos, which are usually homemade.

Popular among black gangs is an intricate system of hand signs, which are used by gang members to identify themselves, advertise their presence, or challenge others. Flashing one's hand sign can start a fight quickly for what may seem to be no reason at all to the uninformed. (See chapter 18, Other Gang Signs, for examples.)

Much clearer is the choice of blue as the color representing the gang. Blue was one of the school colors of Washington High School, and the founding members of the CRIPs attended this school. Blue has always been associated with CRIP gangs. Organized as a counter group to the CRIPs, the Compton Pirus (Bloods) adopted the color red from the local Compton High School colors. The Pirus referred to each other as "Blood" in conversation, and as a way to identify themselves and to challenge others as in, "What's up, Blood?"

CRIPs have traditionally referred to each other as *Cuzz*, a slang term for cousin. This identification may be used as a challenge or an insult to a Blood gang member, for example by asking, "What's up, cuzz?" Some of the more dedicated members will also refuse to spell correctly words with a "ck" combination since they believe the letters are an acronym for "CRIP Killer" and therefore a sign of disrespect. Conversely, they will gladly wear British Knights shoes, as they portray the initials *BK* on the shoes to stand for Blood Killer.

PEOPLE NATION AND FOLK NATION

History

Although ethnically diverse, the People and Folk gang alliances are discussed with black groups because they are similar to the black gangs in behavior and media coverage. These two gang alliances originated in Chicago street crime in 1979. Prior to this, the gangs had operated independently, forming temporary alliances to fight common rivals when the need arose. Larger, more influential street gangs had been around since the 1950s and 1960s in various forms. Incarcerated street gang members formed informal alliances for protection from rivals inside the state prison system and juvenile institutions. Since the gang members were forbidden by authorities to show gang affiliation during incarceration, they identified themselves as being either People or Folk. This identification was especially useful as these informal gang alliances were racially diverse and did not fall into the single race categories of earlier gangs.

By 1979 these loose alliances were formally acknowledged with a treaty signed by the Black Gangster Disciples and the Simon City Royals, (the two largest black and white Chicago area street gangs, respectively) and over twenty other area gangs. This alliance became known as the Folk Nation. As a protective counter to this move, the major rival of the Black Gangster Disciples, the Vice Lords, formally made a treaty with Chicago's largest Hispanic street gang, the Latin Kings, forming the People Nation, estimated to represent approximately 18 street gangs. The two affiliations established themselves as the opposing forces in battles to control the neighborhoods of Chicago. Although occasional rivalries inside each nation still occur, especially over drug territory, the antagonistic relationship between People and Folk draws the most attention.

Folk Nation Gangs	People Nation Gangs
Ambrose	Bishops
Ashland Vikings	Blackstone Rangers/El Rukn
Black Disciples	Cobra Stones
Black Gangster Disciples	Cullerton Boys
Black P Stones	4 Corner Hustlers
Braziers	Gaylords
Brother of the Struggle (BOS)	Insane Deuces
C-Notes	Insane Unknown
Campbell Boys	Jousters
Gangster Disciples	Kents
Harrison Gents	Kool Gang
Imperial Gangsters	Latin Counts
Latin Disciples	Latin Kings (many factions)
Latin Eagles	P. R. Stones
Latin Jivers	Party People
Latin Lovers	Racine Boys
Latin Saints	Ridgeway Lords
Latin Souls	Sin City Boys
Maniac Disciples	Spanish Lords
Orchestra Albany	Tokers
Popes	United Latin Organization
Satan Disciples	Vice Lords (many factions)
Simon City Royals	Villa Lobos
Spanish Cobras	Warlords

Organization and Beliefs

The rash of much-publicized gang truces and peace summits are directly related to the political ambitions of street gangs. Many of these peace negotiations appear to provide hope for an end to street gang warfare. The reality centers on the mutual benefit that street gangs and politicians gain through each other. The street gangs gain positive recognition and achieve political legitimacy when they participate in these events. They can then manipulate community leaders and further increase their own power and influence. Using the cover of their peaceful activities in promoting a truce, a gang can continue to operate with less pressure. Politicians, eager to look good, order police to ease up on the gangs in order to ensure continued cooperation. The "cooperating" gangs can then use the legitimacy and free publicity to build up membership and eliminate rivals during the truce.

Association with Other Gangs

Chicago's major street gangs have had some very unusual economic and political relationships since their founding in the late 1950s and early 1960s. After the civil rights riots of the mid- and late 1960s, several of the prominent gangs, such as the Vice Lords and Blackstone Rangers (also known as El Rukn), directly received large amounts of money from local, state, and federal government agencies as well as from private foundations. The gangs, becoming politically oriented and positioning themselves as potential community leaders, were supposed to use the money to finance job training, recreation, education, housing, and businesses to help the Chicago slums. The financially savvy gangs siphoned off money to purchase guns and drugs to strengthen their growing criminal empires.

Gangs and politicians used their newfound positive image for mutual benefit. As the facade of these images collapsed due to criminal arrests, the gangs returned full time to drug sales for the majority of their income. By the late 1970s, the Blackstone Rangers reinvented themselves as a quasi-religious organization. Calling themselves El Rukn, which is Arabic for "the cornerstone," the gang continued to grow to over 1,000 members. The most notorious episode for the El Rukns occurred in November 1986, when federal law enforcement agencies charged the group with conspiring with Libyan leader Muammer Qaddafi to commit terrorist acts in the United States in exchange for a payment of $2.5 million.

The latest run at political power by a Chicago street gang was during the 1995 city council primary elections. Wallace "Gator" Bradley, a Gangster Disciple, attempted to get elected to Chicago's Third Ward city council seat. Behind Bradley was the organization known as 21st Century VOTE, which is a new political action front of the Gangster Disciples. Although Bradley's campaign was unsuccessful, he was able to capture 31 percent of the vote in a four-way primary runoff election. The resurrection of the street gangs' political influence and the attempt to capture elected office may be related to a desire to gain access to government-funded programs.

According to federal charges for drug conspiracy filed against the Gangster Disciples in 1996, the Disciples have become a major criminal syndicate over a 25-year period, with operations in 35 states that claim 30,000 members.

Profile

People Nation street gangs use the left side of their body to represent their affiliation. This means that anything that they wear or do to identify themselves as being affiliated with People Nation is on their left side. Hats are worn with the brim to their left side, pants legs are rolled up only on the left side, jewelry is only worn on the left, and so forth. Affiliates of the Folk Nation represent themselves on their right.

People affiliates are also noted for using the following symbols: pitchforks pointed down, three- or five-pointed crowns, pyramids, crescent moons, and rabbit heads with straight ears. The Folk Nation symbols are upright pitchforks, rabbit heads with bent ears, and the six-pointed star of David. Latin Disciples sometimes use a backward swastika. These symbols in graffiti can give some idea as to which nation is responsible. Any symbol shown upside down is meant as a form of disrespect.

JAMAICAN POSSES

History

The Jamaican Posses are a major drug-peddling syndicate operating primarily in the United States, Canada, and England, with origins in the slums of Kingston, Jamaica. They were originally street gangs, or thugs, who controlled the rundown, poor areas of Kingston.

The posses' first significant appearance was noted in the 1976 Jamaican political elections, which pitted the leftist, self-described social democrat Michael Manley of the People's National Party (PNP) against the leader of the right-wing Jamaica Labour Party (JLP), Edward Seaga. Politicians used the Jamaican street gangs to control voters in their respective districts and funneled jobs, money, gifts, and food to voters through the gangs. The residents of the Jamaican slums became known as *sufferers* due to the hardships that they endured as part of their daily life.

Manley won the 1976 election, but both political parties and powerful international backers helped prepare for the next round of elections in 1980. Jamaican political elections had always been violent, but the 1980 election became infamous for the over 1,000 victims who died on both sides. The street gangs had been better armed and trained since the 1976 election, and the results were another high death toll. The PNP street gangs had been receiving automatic weapons and training from their Cuban backers, while the JLP gangs had obtained guns from the profits of their drug sales and via gifts of the U.S. Central Intelligence Agency. The street gangs on both sides were involved in the production, distribution, and sale of illegal drugs as a source of income.

Seaga and the JLP were successful in regaining control of the Jamaican government in the 1980 election, but had a new problem to deal with. The street gangs had become too flagrantly violent and were an embarrassment to the new government. Seaga and his government decided to turn on the gangs, utilizing police tactical units that violently hunted down street gang members, killing an average of 200 a year between 1981 and 1986. This resulted in an exodus of street gang members to other countries, especially the United States.

Organization and Beliefs

The Jamaicans found that they could easily support themselves in the United States by continuing to sell drugs, especially their home-grown potent variety of marijuana that they call *ganja*. The Jamaicans became imbedded in the United States drug scene, establishing themselves first in New York City and Miami. The posses, who originally had names that associated them with streets and/or districts in Kingston, Jamaica, were still opposing each other based upon their previous political orientation and now fought each other for control of specific areas for drug sales. Money made from the sale of drugs at first went back to Jamaica to support their communities and political affiliations, but these ties were gradually loosened. The first few Jamaicans found themselves quite good at making money by selling drugs in the United States, and put out a call for more help. This call for help resulted in the arrival of more than 20,000 Jamaican posse members into the United States, both legally and illegally, according to the United States Bureau of Alcohol, Tobacco and Firearms.

Jamaican Posse Vocabulary

bindle	Fake documents
blue posse	Police
ganja	Jamaican grown marijuana
sufferer	Jamaican slum dweller
yardies	Name for Jamaican Posse in England

Association with Other Gangs

The posses began to expand geometrically across the United States and Canada, developing ties to the Colombian drug cartels and selling cocaine, which they found even more profitable than ganja. The United States Drug Enforcement Administration reports that Jamaican ganja still accounts for 20 percent of all marijuana imported into the United States. The posses also began to expand their criminal activities to crimes in support of their primary business of drug trafficking.

Posses have developed a reputation for being extremely ruthless. Posse members who violate rules are subject to a practice known as jointing, whereby the individual is cut up at the joints and the pieces are returned to the family in Jamaica. The wrath of the posses is even evidenced in their style of executing rivals, which has been documented by Jamaican and U.S. law-enforcement agencies. Before shooting the fatal bullet to the head, posse members will shoot their rivals in various parts of the body to provide an example to others. The posses will even target a rival's family for execution in order to get their message across.

There are more than 40 separate Jamaican posses operating in the United States. Organizationally, the Jamaican posses have created a traditionally vertical criminal syndicate type of organization. The top leaders are known as dons. Dons are found back in the slums of Kingston, running the neighborhoods like medieval warlords. Supported by money from United States drug sales, they are able to provide for their neighborhood sufferers. Many of these dons were former posse leaders in the United States who have been deported back to Jamaica for a variety of reasons. They are still able to maintain control over their respective posses through subordinates known as generals. The generals run the posse operations back in the United States, Canada, or England and use subordinate captains and lieutenants to oversee their operations.

The leadership of U.S. operations is entirely Jamaican since they can be easily controlled with their immediate family still back in Jamaica as hostages. The soldiers who do the most work are Jamaican, but other black street gangs made up primarily of African Americans have become part of the organization at this level. The street gangs provide necessary additional manpower and are disposable when no longer needed. When law enforcement authorities begin to break up their drug operations, Jamaicans often flee, leaving the street gang members to fend for themselves.

The posses tend to retain control of all aspects of drug trafficking in order to improve internal security and maximize potential profits. According to the Drug Enforcement Administration (DEA), they import or directly purchase the raw material, such as cocaine, from the Colombian cartels or Chinese triads. The raw material is then brought to processing centers, also known as "controlling points." These centers are in charge of manufacturing and packaging.

The next level is staging sites or warehouses, which are responsible for maintaining a steady supply of drugs on the street and at crack houses. Crack houses are maintained in urban neighborhoods as distribution points and are carefully selected based upon security needs.

The posses may use a number of high-tech devices, such as radios and surveillance cameras, to provide an early warning about raids by law enforcement or rival gangs. The houses also have included several types of barricades and traps to stop or delay intruders. Some even have one or more escape routes built in to provide a quick exit for posse members. Crack house operations are frequently moved to stay ahead of law enforcement officials, and apartments and/or motel rooms are used to improve security and test the local market potential.

The posses' use of local street gangs to help sell their merchandise has even led to the migration of street gangs in the United States. Several gangs have willingly been recruited to set up sales networks in other cities.

The need to dispose of the massive profits from drug sales and to hide the money from authorities has caused the posses to invest in real estate and legitimate businesses. Some money is sent back to the dons in Jamaica, while most of it must be laundered through legitimate businesses in the United States.

Profile

Members of Jamaican posses are known to be extremely devious and to use disguises quite effectively. Many have at least five sets of false identification to help them travel in and out of the United States without detection. They have developed a very sophisticated inventory of false documents, which they freely transfer between one another to confuse law enforcement organizations. Sometimes posse members claim to be residents of the U.S. Virgin Islands to further confuse authorities.

Posse members are usually portrayed as wearing their hair in braids known as dreadlocks, but this can be deceptive as members will wear various hairstyles. Their style of dress also varies from camouflage clothing to business suits, depending upon the need. The posses are not only a threat in metropolitan areas, but have also been found in rural areas, where they can be just as deadly.

Asian Gangs

New York City Police report that 80 percent of Chinatown merchants pay monthly fees to street gangs.

Asian gangs have been operating in North America since the mid-19th century. Their roots can be traced back to the Asian homelands of their members. Similar to other ethnic gangs, Asian gangs often formed to provide protection for their community. The first Asian gangs in North America were Chinese gangs that became associated with the tong organizations. Their mission was to provide protection, support, and assistance to immigrating Chinese families that were attempting to establish businesses in California and the United States. They soon diversified to include extortion, gambling and prostitution, often preying on their own ethnic communities for financial gain.

ASIAN CRIME

Traditionally, Asian immigrants have lived in separate neighborhoods of major U.S. cities, remaining there usually through the third generation. This accounts for the present Chinatowns in most metropolitan areas and the developing clusters of new Southeast Asian immigrant communities. Asians' distrust of government and law enforcement is a natural extension of experiences many have had in their countries of origin, where both are seen as corrupt and untrustworthy. To them, reporting a crime is hardly worthwhile because it only brings shame on the family and further intrusion by strangers into their private life. Retaliation by the perpetrators of the original crime is also expected if one does report a crime.

Asian youth still believe in following some type of traditional authoritative hierarchical structure, if not in the family, then through another organization like a gang. They will also work hard and tirelessly for the gang, placing its needs above their own. In some Asian-American families, the traditional social structure does not function, as the parents become dependent upon the children to help them with language and daily living skills, causing the children to rapidly lose respect for their elders. These factors sometimes contribute to juvenile criminal activity in U.S. Asian communities. Following are the crimes most commonly committed by Asian gangs.

Gambling

Gambling is a favorite pastime for many Asians, a popular social or recreational activity. Since the laws of most U.S. states prohibit the operation of gambling establishments, illegal gambling rooms are operated by Asian gangs as a profitable business. This, in turn, leads to loan sharking, extortion, and money laundering from other illegal activities.

Prostitution

Prostitution among Asian Americans originally started to provide female companionship to male Chinese railroad workers and miners in the 1800s. Today, Asian women are brought to the United States under false pretenses, with student or tourist visas, and then forced to stay and work as prostitutes to pay for their travel. Some are placed in arranged marriages to American servicemen, or are set-up as mail order brides so that once they're in the United States they can work for the gangs as prostitutes. After a period of time, they are allowed to get a divorce. Many times the women are lied to about the type of work they will be doing, and for how long they will be required to do it. Once they are here, however, the gangs control their lives since their refusal to cooperate may mean death at the hands of the gang.

Drugs

Most drugs can be produced or bought cheaper in Asia than in the United States. Asian gangs with good connections can easily transport them into the United States and distribute them at a tremendous profit. In 1990 alone, 56 percent of the heroin seized in New York City, and 70 percent seized overall in the United States, originated in Asia.

Extortion

New York City police report that 80 percent of Chinatown merchants pay monthly fees to street gangs. Business owners despise this but are unable to protect themselves or their customers if they do not pay. The youngest members of gangs are usually sent to collect as they learn the business, and if turned in by the merchant, the gang members can easily retaliate as revenge. The gangs are also clever about how they collect the money, disguising it as donations to charity, sales of items at inflated prices, or investments. They will even accept payments such as free meals and/or clothes.

Home Invasions

This crime occurs when several gang members break into a home, usually Asian, while the residents are present. Since Asians tend to be distrustful of banks, they often keep large sums of money in their homes. Family members can be tortured until the hiding place for valuables is revealed. Sometimes a female family member will be raped to insure that the police are not notified. It is considered a great disgrace for a family member to be raped, so the crime will probably not be reported for fear of the rape becoming public knowledge. Home invasions occur all year long, but increase dramatically before the Chinese New Year, due to the likelihood of more loot being available in Asian homes during this time of gift-giving and celebration.

Smuggling

The importation of imitation products made in Asia, and sold to unwary buyers in the United States, brings in tremendous profits for Asian gangs. Illegal immigration from Asia, especially Hong Kong, also provides handsome profits. The gangs often charge as much as $30,000 per person and attempt to recruit the immigrant into the gang as well.

In reverse, the theft and smuggling of computer chips out of the United States to be resold at 80 percent of their value has been a very big revenue producer. In 1991 IBM alone is believed to have lost $45 million in chips due to theft from warehouses. Asian gangs have even committed armed robberies in daylight at plants throughout California's Silicon Valley to obtain these valuable chips, which are difficult to trace.

CHINESE GANGS

Tong History

Chinese immigration to the United States began in the mid-19th century when laborers were needed for railroad construction and mining. Confronted with racism and abuse, most Chinese settled in protective enclaves of major cities that were to become known as Chinatowns. To protect themselves and their interests, the Chinese formed mutual aid societies called *tongs*. These tongs were originally intended to be for assistance of Chinese immigrants, but some became front organizations for criminal activity such as gambling, prostitution, and the operating of illegal opium dens.

The tongs developed bitter rivalries as they competed with each other for control of the same markets for their illegal activities. Since these activities usually did not affect Westerners, little attention was given to the disputes or wars between the tongs. They were mostly apparent in communities that had a large Chinese

To Be a Flying Dragon

I, [name], born [date and place], now voluntarily and wholeheartedly enter into the Flying Dragons Tong. After being admitted into the tong, those who obey the mandate of heaven will live, while those who defy it will perish. As long as I live, I will be a member of the Flying Dragons Tong. Even if I die, I will still be a member. I will not feel remorse as long as I live. If I do, heaven and earth will destroy me.

After I join, I will obey all the rules and regulations of the tong. If I do not, I will die by gunshot.

My date of birth must be true; if not, I will be destroyed by electric shock.

The secret of the tong must be kept. If not, I will die by being stabbed a thousand times.

If the tong runs into difficulty or is in danger, anyone who knows about it and does not provide assistance will be destroyed by electric shock and/or burned by fire.

If anyone overreaches his authority and sends out an order to benefit himself or to try to gain more power, he will be punished publicly.

We are all each other's brothers; we must never spy on our brothers or sell them out. If there is hatred and hostility between us, public judgment should rule. Never dwell on it. After the public judgment between the hateful brothers has been rendered, put your feelings in the past.

If one of our brothers is captured or goes on a long journey, leaving his wife and children defenseless, we must try our best to help them. If anyone tries to take advantage of a member's wife, the punishment is death.

I must never be disrespectful to my parents or abuse my brother, sister, or sister-in-law. Anyone who commits such crimes shall be punished.

If anyone tries to betray the tong, the punishment is death. If one acts positive externally and negative internally, his death will come soon. The sword and knife will cut him to pieces, lightning will destroy his identity; thereafter, he will be in hell eternally with no hope for reincarnation. Since the sole judgment is by heaven and God, one who is loyal to the tong will be blessed by God.

The heaven and earth are my parents; the sun and moon shine upon us. we all should enjoy everything together, resolve all of our anxieties together. Even though we were not born on the same day, we will die together on the same day.

population such as San Francisco, New York City, Boston, and Chicago. One such war, which occurred in 1909–10 in New York City between the Hip Sing tong and the On Leongs, resulted in over 350 casualties, all Chinese.

To fight these wars, the tongs employed groups of young Chinese toughs organized into gangs known as highbinder societies. These societies were patronized by specific tongs and became known as their auxiliaries. Some of the highbinders were allowed, as a reward, to become members of the tongs for which they fought. The long-lasting tong war fought between the Sum Yop tong and the Sue Yop tong of San Francisco in 1897 resulted in an appeal by influential Western citizens to the emperor of China. The fighting was immediately stopped when the Chinese government imprisoned all Sue Yop family members still in China and threatened to behead them if any more Sum Yops were killed. By 1922 the six major tongs in San Francisco signed a treaty, and a relative peace was maintained for over fifty years.

By the late 1960s, groups of young Chinese boys who occasionally worked for the tongs began to form their own gangs and stake out territory in the Chinatown areas. These groups became more and more aggressive, and eventually the tongs could no longer control them. The young gangsters soon started taking over illegal gambling, drug dealing, prostitution, and extortion in their respective communities, and competing gangs began to violently confront each other.

The September 4, 1977 confrontation in San Francisco's Golden Dragon Restaurant between the Joe Boys and the Wah Ching resulted in five uninvolved restaurant patrons dead and eleven wounded. Two other major rival Chinese street gangs based in New York City, the Ghost Shadows and Flying Dragons, have had similar ongoing warfare since the 1970s. However, the New York–based tongs have maintained better control over their street gangs, adopting a similar relationship to the one developed with the highbinder societies before, giving protection and patronage to a specific gang.

Triad History

The origin of the Chinese criminal organizations known as triads is murky. Popular legend has it that they began when a Chinese emperor in the 17th century, fearful of the powerful Shaolin monks, had the monks killed and their monastery destroyed. Only five monks survived, but they separated and became founders of five secret societies that were dedicated to fighting against unjust rulers. They developed secret rituals, oaths, and signs of membership to protect their organizations from ever being infiltrated and betrayed. The term "triad" was coined by British authorities who first encountered these groups in their Hong Kong colony. The triangular symbol worn by members of these secret organizations represented the sacred relationship between heaven, earth, and man.

Over the centuries the original political goals of these societies became secondary or forgotten, and the triads became criminal in nature. Their close ties to the new republican government in China after the fall of the Manchu dynasty in 1911 became a convenient relationship for both sides. Corrupt nationalist government officials and independent warlords worked with the triads to build up their personal treasuries and armories. This relationship caused much infighting and civil disturbance in the new republic as rival groups fought each other for dominance. Even the invasion of China by Japan in 1931 did not cause the rival groups to work in harmony. Finally, when the Communists under Mao Tse-Tung drove the nationalists out of China in 1947, many of the triads, and their members who could, left the mainland for Hong Kong or Taiwan.

The Hong Kong triads are organized into four major groups—the Wo, 14k, Chin Chao, and Big Four—plus two smaller groups, the Ching Group and the Big Circle. The 14k has had direct ties to the Kuomintang political party of the Taiwanese Republic of China. The Wo group is considered by many to be the most powerful of the triads.

There are four dominant Taiwanese triad groups—United Bamboo, Four Seas, Tien Dao Mon, and Chao Tong. Since their home is secure and not going back to mainland control in the foreseeable future, they are less active overseas than the Hong Kong–based triads. However, the Four Seas group has been attempting to gain control of the Los Angeles area, and United Bamboo is active in both Los Angeles and Houston. The so-called invasion by these triad groups of the United States has many law enforcement agencies worried. The U.S. Department of Justice has declared the triads to be the second national priority in combating organized crime after La Cosa Nostra. Special funding has even been received from Congress to hire gang specialists from the Hong Kong police to work for U.S. agencies in fighting this new threat.

Today, the triads operate out of these U.S. locations and are attempting to extend their networks over the globe through Chinese and other Asian immigrant communities, especially in the United States, Canada, Australia, the Philippines, the Netherlands, Great Britain, and Belgium. This is most definitely true of the triads headquartered in Hong Kong.

These triads are making every effort possible to transfer their assets and operations out of the colony to overseas locations in order to survive the return of British Hong Kong to the mainland government in 1997. This has at times brought them into direct conflict with the established Chinese or Asian crime groups already at these locations.

Organization and Beliefs

The use of the street gangs by the tongs and triads follows a traditional model. The youngest members, 12 to 18 years old, are know as *ma jai*, or little horses. They are the soldiers who do much of the enforcement work. Usually put up at a communal apartment, they dedicate their whole life to the gang and give up their family, to whom they are considered an embarrassment. The gang provides these youths with everything, and in return they give their unquestioned loyalty. Recent immigrants are the preferred type of recruit due to their vulnerability.

The lieutenants form the next level. Known as *dai los*, meaning boss or big brother, they are in their twenties and have worked their way up by showing great loyalty and leadership. The rewards are a separate apartment and enough money to live comfortably. They keep the younger *ma jai* in line and ensure that they do not betray or disgrace the gang. The *dai lo* reports to members at a higher-level tong or triad, and hopes to work his way up to become a member of that organization. Another possibility is that he may eventually be set up by the gang as a legitimate businessman to serve as a front for illegal activities.

Association with Other Gangs

Triads usually serve mostly as an umbrella group under which several separate criminal syndicates operate. The triad provides some type of support and direction to the syndicates, with them turning over a percentage of their profits to the umbrella group in return. An example of this is the Wo triad of Hong Kong, which has several member syndicates. One of these, the Wo Hop To, is attempting to recruit and organize Asian criminal gangs along the United States west coast. Another triad syndicate is responsible for smuggling heroin into the United States through New York City. As rival triad syndicates vie for the same territory and/or criminal concessions, they begin to have open warfare until one group wins or a compromise is reached.

The recent arrival of triad organizations from Hong Kong and Taiwan into the United States has stirred some additional activity in the Chinese-American community. The triads have attempted to establish themselves as the dominant crime organization in these communities. Sometimes, by using existing gang structures or replacing them, the triads have moved in and taken control of the traditional tong-dominated Chinese-American gang activities such as drugs, smuggling, illegal immigration, prostitution, gambling, and extortion. This has caused a new wave of warfare among the street gangs as they attempt to stake out their territory and get approval from their new triad overlords.

Particularly interesting is the triads' use of non-Chinese street gangs to help establish their territory in the United States. The saying "Four Seas, One Brother" refers to the concept of cooperation among various ethnic groups being introduced in the United States by the triads. This means that it will probably be even harder for law enforcement agencies to infiltrate and track criminal activity by these gangs in the future.

Profile

Asian street gang members usually range in age from 14 to 25 years old. The younger gang members are often involved in the more violent activities, while the older members act as leaders and organizers. Older adults may also be involved in controlling a street gang's activity to benefit a more traditional adult organization's goals. This is true in the case of the Flying Dragons street gang in New York City, which follows the orders of the Hip Sing tong. Hip Sing uses the Flying Dragons as its soldiers to impose the tong's will on the community.

Initiation or "jumping in" for Asian street gangs will usually involve committing a crime to prove loyalty to the gang. The crime must be preapproved and witnessed by gang leaders in order to qualify as an initiation act. Vehicle theft has become a common form of initiation, although drive-bys and even murder are not unusual. Additionally, a lifetime oath of allegiance to the gang may be required. One can never leave except through death.

Asian gang members tend to be more secretive about their lifestyles than black or Hispanic gang members. This can be traced back to Asia, where the gangs kept a very low profile and were clandestine in their activities. This secretiveness also helped to promote a mysterious image.

SOUTHEAST ASIAN GANGS

History

Since 1971 over 3.5 million Asians have immigrated to the United States alone. Many came from war-torn Southeast Asia, bringing with them the psychological and social problems inherent in any culture destroyed by 50 years of war. These immigrants have established themselves in large and small metropolitan areas across North America, but younger members of the family often feel isolated and are without the usual extended family support upon which their cultures have traditionally relied. The result is fertile ground for the creation of gangs that can fill or supplant that void in their lives.

Organization and Beliefs

The majority of Southeast Asian gangs in this country are not as highly organized as the Chinese tongs or triads, which have been in existence longer; however, their crimes have become just as violent. Southeast Asian gangs are presently becoming organized under the overall control of Chinese triads as part of a plan to control all Asian American gangs.

Association with Other Gangs

A phenomenon known as *hasty gangs*, *casual gangs*, or *pickup gangs* occurs when a group forms a gang temporarily for a specific crime or spree of criminal activity. The hasty gang members usually have no previous ties, and they break up after completion of the crime or as a result of capture by the police. The members may then go on their own way to form other hasty gangs.

Profile

These gangs consist of youth from Vietnamese, Cambodian, and Laotian refugee communities. Typical members range in age from 12 to 25. Older Southeast Asian adults have formed some traditional criminal gangs that at times may control younger street gangs.

Asian gang members are well known for using identifying tattoos. Each group uses a different tattoo, but eagles, dragons, tigers, snakes, panthers, swords, daggers, and sailing ships are common emblems.

*T*s are found on Vietnamese gang members in groups of three, four, and five. Most often four and five *T*s are found tattooed on former inmates of prison or juvenile institutions.

The five *T*s are as follows:

Tinh = Love	T	T
Tien = Money/Wealth	T	or T T T T T
Tu = Prison/Detention	T	T
Toi = Sin/Crime		
Thu = Revenge (this usually is the fifth *T*)		

Another method of identification of Southeast Asian gang members are dots or burns in groups of three, four, or five. The burns made by either cigarettes or hot coins attest to the courage of the bearer. They are also representative of the previous *T*s.

Criminal activities of today's Southeast Asian gangs consist primarily of extortion, auto theft, auto burglary, residential robbery, also known as home invasions, and murder for hire. Most members do not carry identification and regularly use aliases. When apprehended, they also claim to be minors so as to confuse law enforcement intelligence networks.

These groups are very mobile and will often travel to other states to commit crimes. Some gangs known as *nomads, motel people,* or *cowboys* have no permanent home and travel between Asian-American communities, committing crimes and moving on before local law enforcement can catch up.

F I L I P I N O

History

Filipino street gangs in the United States are primarily active along the West Coast from Alaska to California, but they can also be found in Texas and Louisiana.

Today there are probably over three million Filipinos residing in the United States, with one-half of that number living in California. The people are a diverse cultural blend of Asian and European background. This cultural diversity has created a separation of the Filipino people based upon race, language, religion, and lifestyle. Today there exist eight major language groups with 87 different dialects. The national language is known as Tagalog, but English and Spanish are also quite common. Approximately 80 percent of the people are Catholic, the remaining being Muslim, Protestant, Shinto, or Buddhist. Since 1965 the immigration rate from the Philippines has been substantial as Filipinos try to escape from a very high unemployment rate.

The origins of today's Filipino-American street gangs date to the 1940s in the Philippine prison system. Similar to the origins of some gangs in America, there began two rival prison gangs known as Oxo and Sige Sige, the latter meaning "hurry up" or "let's go." Each gang began to have internal rivalries, and infighting soon occurred which gave rise to younger factions of the gangs in the 1950s.

The Oxo younger members called themselves *crossbones*, and the Sige-Sige younger members were known as *Sputniks*. The older members became known as *Sigmas*. The rivalries between the gangs gave rise to two more gangs, the Bahala Na Gang and Tres Cantos. These rival gangs became involved in gang wars around the streets of Manila and in government prisons. This fighting lasted from the early 1960s until September 1972, when martial law was proclaimed by the Marcos regime. The level of gang activity decreased dramatically due to the creation of a government crime task force with extensive power and authority. Many gang members were kidnapped and never seen again, apparently executed by the military or the police. Many Filipinos who feared the Marcos regime began to immigrate to the United States, and with them came gang members too.

In the United States, the Filipino gangs made their first notable appearance around 1972 in Washington and Alaska. Many Filipino immigrants had gone there seeking jobs in the canning industry, and the criminal gang members followed them. Due to cultural differences, the gangs were able to organize workers into rival groups, and occasionally assaults and even murders occurred. The gangs also had some union affiliations which made local law enforcement authorities suspicious about their possible ties with American organized crime.

In the Los Angeles area in the early 1970s, a former Sige Sige Sputnik member, Billy West, began a Filipino street gang known as the Santanas or STS, which means devils. Most Filipino street gangs in southern California trace their roots to the Santanas. Opponents of the Santanas formed a rival gang called the Temple Street Gang, and Filipinos from Guam formed the Barkadang Guam in the 1970s.

As the Marcos regime in the Philippines tightened its control, many more Filipinos immigrated to the United States. These new arrivals moved into established Filipino communities in the United States and discovered the existence of the new incarnations of the Filipino street gangs. Although these people were often educated professionals, their children soon became victims of the gangs and, in order to protect themselves, either joined or formed their own rival gangs. Divided by ethnic factions, these gang rivalries result from the cultural diversity of the

Philippines and are based on differences in language, religion, and area of Philippine origin.

Organization and Beliefs

Filipino gangs attract family members, which in the Philippines include extended family as distant as fourth cousins. This is partly due to the background of the people who lived a lifestyle known as Barangay, in which families lived on boats tied together and shared everything communally. This made the people very family oriented and self-sufficient. It is not unusual to find Filipino gangs in which most members are related to one another.

Association with Other Gangs

The majority of Filipino street gang members participate in the gang for social interaction as well as financial gain. Their crimes are committed against rival Filipino gangs, and they will travel considerable distances to attack any adversary. Some gangs claim allegiance to the original Philippine gangs, while others align themselves with Crip or Blood factions.

Profile

Many Filipino hard-core gang members have tattoos, which play an important part in identifying gang members. The use of burn marks to show gang membership is another common practice among Filipino gang members. Like other Asian ethnic groups, they use a hot coin or cigarette to burn marks on their body as proof of their personal strength and courage. With a Filipino gang member it is sometimes customary to use an odd number of burn marks to show that one is an active gang member and an even number to demonstrate that one is no longer active. In addition to tattoos, some gangs have been noted to wear all black or a "ninja" style of clothing.

The types of weapons used by Filipino street gangs are diverse, but they have been known for the use of the *Balison* or butterfly knife. This unique weapon is very impressive when used by a practiced handler. Filipinos equate owning a gun with manhood and consequently have a high regard for anyone carrying a gun. This goes back to their history of fighting rival ethnic groups and invaders in the Philippines.

This attachment to guns fuels a business in smuggling guns into and out of the United States. They are deeply involved in smuggling guns into the Philippines and other Asian countries, where a profit of five to ten times the original price can be made.

KOREAN

History

Although not a major source of juvenile gang behavior in the United States, Korean gangs possess some unique qualities as a crime organization. Korean immigration to the United States was insignificant until the Korean War in the 1950s established a link between the two nations. The American military presence in Korea made immigration from Korea easier to achieve and less of a culture shock. Koreans used to dealing with Americans came to the United States for education and established small businesses here, where they saw an opportunity for more economic freedom. The autocratic form of government in Korea also forced many democratically minded Koreans to leave, sometimes in order to save their lives and those of family members. Along with the wave of immigrants fleeing Korea's oppressive government came members of the Korean Central Intelligence Agency, or KCIA. Their job was to keep an eye on their countrymen and insure that they did not attempt to agitate against the Korean government.

Organization and Beliefs

Korean gangs are organized in a vertical class structure made up of three distinct levels. These levels tend to operate independently and are delineated by age. The top level is composed of adults aged 25 years and older. This group controls the lower two groups and provides the organizational management and direction.

The second level in the Korean criminal gang structure consists of young adults whose ages range from 18 to 24 years old. This level of middle management provides muscle for the organization. It is primarily used to carry out the orders of the older adult leaders in extorting money from businessmen and to provide leadership to the third level of the gang structure. This third level is composed of juveniles who range in age from 12 to 17 years old. Though limited in what activities they can perform, these gang members can be just as deadly or destructive as those at the upper levels. Their criminal activity is mostly limited to robberies, burglaries, and auto theft. They may also work as intelligence sources or lookouts for the activities of older group members.

Korean gangs are tight knit, well organized, and sophisticated in their operations. The gangs' motives are primarily profit oriented with any activities geared toward supporting the gangs' income balance. These gangs do not usually claim any territory except Korean businesses, and they often travel great distances between Korean immigrant communities. The Korean gangs usually have prepared well before committing any type of crime. The home or business targeted for a robbery will have been placed under observation for some time, and members committing the robbery will be well informed as to what to expect. The robbery plans often include a backup procedure in case things go wrong. It is often difficult for law enforcement to get cooperation from victims of Korean gangs because of their genuine fear of retaliation. Korean gangs also use sexual assault against a crime victim's family members as a means of insuring that they do not cooperate with police.

Association with Other Gangs

Many of the Korean CIA agents who immigrated after the Korean War developed strong ties with the Korean crime world and used this relationship to put pressure on immigrant Korean businessmen not to support Korean dissident groups. They also extorted protection money from the businesses. This relationship still exists today with some legitimate businesses still paying protection money and being used to hide the illegal activities of Korean crime syndicates, such as prostitution, drugs, gambling, and smuggling of gold and currency.

Profile

The use of an identifying burn mark is common among Korean gangs as with other Asian gangs. They tend to be more secretive, however, about identifying themselves, so they place their burns in places easily covered up.

Within the Korean gangs, respect for elders is very important. The younger members are known as younger brothers, and older members are older brothers. The older members depend upon this structure of traditional respect to maintain control of the gangs. Often, a gang member having problems with another gang member has to ask permission before taking action against his opponent. The older members maintain some control over individual rivalries and groups in this manner, but today the younger more westernized gang members have a tendency to act without seeking permission. This has caused a rise in confrontations between Korean gangs and an escalation in violence. A prediction has been made by some law enforcement officials that gang wars between the older and younger factions of Korean gangs is not too far off.

SAMOAN OR PACIFIC ISLANDER

History

Mostly active in communities of Hawaii, California, and Washington State, these Samoan gangs have been active since the late 1970s and early 1980s. Originally forming groups around a nucleus of fellow islanders for social activity and a sense of security, these gangs today are involved in mainstream criminal activities like all other street gangs.

Organization and Beliefs

The Pacific Islanders have a strong sense of family and extended family, which is paralleled in the gangs' membership. Often gangs are made up of brothers and cousins and anyone else considered close to the family. Although typically clannish with their own people, the Samoan gangs are quick to accept whites, blacks, Hispanics, and other Asians into their gangs, partially due to the limited number of Pacific Islanders from whom they can recruit new members.

Association with Other Gangs

Samoan gangs are not as territorial as Hispanic gangs that claim a specific neighborhood, but they do tend to claim some area such as a school, park, or common gathering place. Many Samoan gangs have used the names and colors of the Crips and Bloods to identify themselves as rival factions of other Samoan gangs, even within the same community or school.

Profile

The style of dress adopted by these gangs is most closely compared to Hispanic gang styles. Many members prefer plaid shirts buttoned up high, khaki pants, and tank tops or sleeveless muscle shirts. A colored bandanna or colored deck shoes often represent their gang affiliation. Many members also now wear athletic jackets and baseball caps with gang graffiti embroidered on them.

Samoan gangs use graffiti to announce their presence in the community, and it will appear at schools, malls, and anywhere that gang members congregate. Their graffiti tends to use gang initials as the main theme with other messages written around the initials, such as words promoting their gang's affiliation and disrespecting others. These might include *cuzz*, *BK*, or *slobs* for Blood sets and *Blood*, *Piru*, and *CK* for CRIP affiliated sets. Like Hispanic gangs, the Samoans give nicknames or monikers to gang members that they keep for as long as they are with the gang.

The common criminal activities of the Samoan street gangs involve drive-by shootings, burglary, strong-arm robbery, auto theft, and drug trafficking. Members have readily admitted gang membership to law enforcement officials when questioned, since they still tend to see their gang's primary function as a social organization. Some gangs have even gone so far as to claim that they are dance groups by using a slang term such as *popping*, meaning street dancing or break dancing, as cover for their illegal activities.

Asian Street Gangs

Vietnamese	Asians with Attitudes, Black Dragons, Natoma Boys, Viet Ching, Banana Girls, Cheap Boys, Cobra Boys, Da Boys, Frogmen (adult gang), Kah Kwai Chang, Jr., Wally Girls, Innocent But Killers, Lonely Boys, Mohawk Boys, Oriental Boys, Ruthless Nips, V-Boys
Laotian	Lao Boys, Koray Boys
Cambodian	Tiny Rascal Gangsters, Asian Brotherhood, Exotic Foreign Creation, Cambodian CRIPs
Chinese	Big Circle Gang, Wah-Ching, Flying Dragons, Yu Li Chinatown Rulers (CTR), Joe Boys, Wo Hop To (Triad Group), Ghost Shadows, Hop Sing Boys, Cheung Chee Yee
Filipino	Sige Sige, Bahala Na Santanas, Pinoy, Rastas, Balboa Boys, Carson Pinoy Compadres, Pinoy Real, Supremo Gangsters, Supremo Pinoy Chicks, 8-Ball Posse
Japanese	Yakuza (organized crime)
Taiwanese	United Bamboo (organized crime)
Korean	Korean Crazies, Totally Down Koreans, Mickey Club, Asian Bad Boys, White Tigers, Korean Killers, American Burgers, Southbay Killers
Chinese-Vietnamese	(Vietchin) Viet Ching, Viet Boyz, Viet CRIPs (VC), Oriental Silent Boys (OSB), Ninja Clan Assassins (NCA), Born to Kill (BTK)
Samoan	Sons of Samoa (SOS), True Island Boys (TIB), Samoan Posse (RSP)

Hispanic Gangs

Mexican youths that claim to be Norteños will say that they are not Mexican, but Chicano. They will also say that even though both gangs are Hispanic, Sureños have no place in America because "they can't even speak English."

History

Hispanic gangs in the United States date back to approximately 1910, when there was a large influx of immigrants coming into southern California from Mexico. As the immigrants settled in southern California, it was common for them to locate in areas where people from their home town and states had already established home sites. Hence, Mexicans from Sinaloa would tend to live in neighborhoods where other Sinaloans had already moved, and the same held true for all the other states including Michoacan, Sonora, Baja California, Jalisco, and Durango, to name a few. Rivalries soon developed among immigrants from various regions, which led to the first gangs being organized.

The Latin Kings, a largely Hispanic group, originated apparently in Chicago during the 1940s. It was a small coalition of Hispanic-based street gangs incorporating Mexican, Dominican, Puerto Rican, and Italian and Portuguese gangs. It has spread throughout the United States since the 1940s and now is found all over, but predominantly in the Midwest and East coast down to Florida. This gang has developed a strong leadership structure and networked the individual gangs more than most law enforcement officials at first suspected.

The present leader of the Latin Kings in New York, Antonio Fernandez, known as King Tone, is attempting to gain official recognition for the Latin Kings to become a more legitimate political and social service organization similar to what has been occurring in Chicago with its black gangs.

Gang rivalries continued through the decades and perhaps were publicized most during what were called the "Zoot Suit Wars" of the 1940s. The name was given because of the type of clothing that the Hispanic gang members wore. Fights often occurred among Zoot Suiters and military personnel stationed in southern California.

The 1960s saw a dramatic increase in the amount of gang activity in southern California. This was in part due to the extended freeway system offering more mobility to gang members. Gangs could travel long distances in short time periods

Hispanic Gang Glossary

barrio, varrio	Neighborhood
blanca	White (female)
blanco	White (male)
caca	"Shit," drugs
Califas	California
carcancha	Junky car
carnala	Sister
carnal	Brother
carrucha	Car
catorce	Fourteen (XIV)
chale	No
chavala	Girl, little girl
checked in	Initiated into the gang
chiva	Heroin
chola	Female gang member
cholo	Male gang member
chota	Police
clika, clica	Gang
con safos (C/S)	Anything written over our graffiti goes back to you twice as bad
controlamos	We control
dedo	To finger someone
drop a dime	To snitch on someone
El Condado	County jail
EME	Mexican Mafia
ENE	La Nuestra Familia
ese	Homeboy
farmero	Member of La Nuestra Familia
frajos	Cigarettes
filero	Knife
ganga	Gang
gavachos	Anglos
homeboy, homey	One of the boys from the gang
huero	Anglo, Light colored
joto	Homosexual
jumped in	Initiation into the gang
jumped out	Process used to disassociate one's self from the gang
la migra	Immigration
La Raza	The Race (Chicanos)
leva	Silent treatment
LK	Latin Kings
MM	Mexican Mafia

mad dog	To stare at another, to challenge or intimidate
mad doggers	Dark sunglasses worn by gang members
maricon	Homosexual
mayate	African-American
MCP	Mexicans Causing Panic
movidas	Rules and regulations
N	Norte (XIV)
NF	La Nuestra Familia
negro	Black
Norte	Northern California (XIV)
Norteña	Female associated with Nuestra Familia
Norteño	Male associated with Nuestra Familia
pachuco	Contemporary Zoot Suiter
pinches	Bastards
pinta	Prison
placa	Name, sign, badge
por vida	For life
puto	Male prostitute
puto mark	Crossing out another gang's placa (graffiti)
rata	Rat, snitch
rifa	To rule
rifamos	We rule
saggin	To wear pants very low on the hips
simone	Yes
Sur	Southern California (XIII)
Sureña	Female associated with the Mexican Mafia (XIII)
Sureño	Male associated with the Mexican Mafia (XIII)
trece	Thirteen (XIII)
UNLV	Us Norteños Love Violence
vato	Man or boy
vato loco	Crazy man, gang member
veterano	Older gang member, veteran
vida loca	Crazy Life (usually seen as a tattoo, three dots)
13	Sur, Southern California, Mexican Mafia
14	Norte, Northern California, Nuestra Familia

to carry out acts of violence against rivals in other cities. At the same time, there was a noted increase in gangs throughout the northern valleys of California, which had formerly seen little gang violence. As parents moved their families in an attempt to better their lifestyles, new gangs developed.

Hispanic gangs are turf oriented and will fight to the death for the pride of their territory. Along with turf pride goes gang pride. To the Hispanic gang member, the gang is more important than any one of its individual members. Members are willing to give up their life for their gang. Due to the fact that Hispanic gangs have been in existence for many decades, it is not uncommon to find second- and third-generation gang members. The gang has become a family way of life. Fathers and mothers may take great pride in seeing their sons initiated into the gang just as their fathers took pride in seeing them initiated.

For many years the Mexican Mafia was the only prison-based Hispanic gang. Incarcerated Hispanics had to put aside their street rivalries and join the Mexican Mafia while in prison. In addition, the Mafia exercised significant control over street activity from within the prison walls. Leaders would send messages to their men on the outside to carry out hits or set up narcotics transactions.

According to the California Department of Prisons, a dispute took place in 1966 amongst Hispanic prisoners at the Deuel Vocational Institution outside Tracy, California. As a result of this dispute, a group of Hispanic prisoners separated from the Mexican Mafia and formed La Nuestra Familia. In English this means, "our family." La Nuestra Familia took a foothold in San Quentin prison and soon become the primary enemy of the Mexican Mafia.

The majority of prisoners aligning with La Nuestra Familia were rural farm laborer Hispanics, primarily from Northern California (at that time everything north of Bakersfield). In an attempt to differ from the Mexican Mafia, La Nuestra Familia began wearing red handkerchiefs rather than the standard blue bandannas worn by the Sureños or Mexican Mafia.

Today many of these distinctions still exist. La Nuestra Familia, or Norteños, still wear the color red. The Mexican Mafia, or Sureños, still wear the color blue. Problems arise when a southern Hispanic gang member moves to northern California or a northern Hispanic moves to the Los Angeles area. Such movement is common for families of Mexican migrant workers who work their way up the state of California, seeking employment in agriculture. As these southern families move north, their children may be confronted by Norteños and be accused of being Sureño gang members

Organization and Beliefs

Membership in the Mexican Mafia and La Nuestra Familia is restricted to adults incarcerated in the state or federal prison systems. However, street gang members do claim to be Norteños or Sureños.

What once started as a neighborhood gang based on pride and respect for family has turned into an avenue for crime. During the 1950s and 1960s, young men banded together to protect the neighborhood where their families had lived for years and sometimes generations. This is not the case today. Juveniles now get involved in gangs to accrue the benefits of power and money. It is not uncommon to find young men that have claimed to be Norteños or Sureños and at some point switched sides and joined the rival gang. Today, membership is based more on who your friends associate with than where your ancestors originated.

Mexican youths that claim to be Norteños will say that they are not Mexican, but Chicano. They will also say that even though both gangs are Hispanic, Sureños have no place in America because "they can't even speak English."

Hispanic gangs are not comprised solely of Hispanics. It is acceptable for non-Hispanics to also be jumped in to the Hispanic gangs. However, non-Hispanic gang members that are sent to prison are not always allowed to associate with the Hispanic prison gangs. For example, in 1992 a white boy joined a gang and had the numbers "1" and "4" tattooed onto his earlobes. He also had the Roman numeral "XIV" and the word "Norte" tattooed on his arms and chest. In 1994 the boy was arrested and sent to the Youth Authority in Northern California. The Hispanics did not accept him because he was not Hispanic, and the white population did not accept him because he has betrayed the white race by associating with the Hispanics. Hence he was left in a hostile environment with no protection and considered an outsider by both groups.

> The women participated in gangs. We would rob 7-Eleven stores, gas stations and do drive-bys. I did time for attempted murder when I was a juvenile.
>
> —Payasa

Females are also involved in the gang. Girls as young as 10 have been associated with gangs. They often dress similarly to their male counterparts. According to Los Angeles Sheriffs' Office statistics, the early 1990s showed an increase in drive-by shootings committed by teenage girls. In the 1970s and 1980s the primary role of the female was to carry the guns or drugs in their purses. After a drive-by shooting, the shooters would unload their guns into the car of a female associate. If stopped by the police while leaving the area, they would not have any guns in their possession. In the 1990s these young women are becoming more independent and sophisticated, forming gangs separate from the males.

Hispanic gang members can be separated into three distinct categories—pee wees, hard core, and *veteranos*. Pee wees are between the ages of 9 and 13. They will become the new generation of the gang. The hard core encompasses members aged 14 to 22. These are the truly committed members who actively carry out the gang's activities. The *veteranos* are aged 22 and up. They are considered leaders and may not actively participate in crime. *Veteranos* are highly respected for their past criminal accomplishments, as well as the fact that they have lived past the age of 22. They are known for hiding weapons and fugitives. Many *veteranos* have spent a portion of their lives in prison.

Association with Other Gangs

The population of a community will determine the number of gangs. Hispanic gangs tend to be territorial and will claim a particular geographic location as their territory. This could be a street, park, part of town, or an area code. Some examples include the 23rd Street Gangsters, Val Verde Park Norteños, "North Side Sureños,"

Norteño Gang Poem

1, 2, 3, 4, 5 this is norte do or die—
6, 7, 8, 9. 10 all the scrapas giving in—
in 1914 the N was formed 75 years and still going strong—
Red Rags Red Steel minds of still hearts of stone its just the norte moving on
    up the hills around the land—
be a man Kill a scrapa with your bare hands—
like the man huero past the test 14 years without a rest
Shank 1 Shank so just like him dare to lose but sure to win.
like Mr Rascal he is right cutting throats day and night—
like Mr Skwigy he is down beating scrapas to the ground—
so if you say that you are proud stand up and say puro norte loud
True love and deep respect is what the norte will always get—
minds of steel hearts of stone the mighty norte is moving along—
cant stop wont stop we will struggle to the top
so if you say your a man stand up and fight for norte land
Keep the scrapas on the run when you catch them slice there toung—
back a scrapa to the wall to his knees he shall fall
and when he starts to beg and cry tell him it was the norte that took his life
fill no pitty fill no shame because if it was you they'll do the same

—unknown author

(Grammar and spelling errors are as in the original.)

Poem Glossary
Norteño/Norte/N—Northern California Hispanic gang affiliation.
Scrapa—Term of disrespect for Sureños or Southern California Hispanic gang affiliation.
Shank—Homemade prison knife.
Mr Rascal/Mr Skwigy—Gang members, possibly dead.
Red Rags—Red is the color of the Norteño gangs
14—Represents the 14th letter in the alphabet N for Norteño. Gang Poem

and 209 Mafia. Each particular clique or subset may include anywhere from 3 to 100 or more members in larger cities. The 18th Street gang in Los Angeles has thousands of members from all over the city. The cliques will usually coexist peacefully alongside each other as long as they are both Norteño or both Sureño gangs. Rivalries amongst fellow Norteño or Sureño gangs are not very common.

Profile

Both groups use Roman numerals in their graffiti to designate their affiliation with the *norte* or *sur* (north or south.) The Norteños use the Roman numeral 14, XIV, and the Sureños use the numeral 13, XIII.

The 14th letter of the alphabet, the letter *N*, represents Nuestra Familia, Norte, and Norteños. Hence you will find either XIV, 14, or X4 in Norteño graffiti. The 13th letter of the alphabet is "M," which represents the Mexican Mafia. In Sureño graffiti this is expressed as either XIII, 13, or X3. The letter "N" is pronounced in Spanish as "ene." The letter "M" is pronounced "eme." These words, representing the letters, may also be found in Hispanic gang graffiti. The majority of Hispanic graffiti will include either the 14 or 13 to indicate who was responsible for the vandalism or is claiming that particular area as their turf.

Clothing plays an important role within the gang subculture and makes gang members readily identifiable. Clothing changes with the times and what was once indicative of a gang member may not hold true two years later. Gangs are portrayed and discussed on the television and in the newspapers. And when non–gang members dress like gang members, the manner of dress soon becomes fashionable. For example, in 1990 if a child wore a black Los Angeles Raiders jacket, he was considered to be in a gang by most uninformed citizens. But when teenagers began wearing the jackets, gang members chose a new way to dress.

For years, the typical dress of the Hispanic gang member has been the khaki pants accompanied by a white T-shirt or plaid Pendleton-style shirt. Bandannas, either red or blue, were very popular worn folded and tied around the head or simply draped from the rear pants pocket. In either case, the "moco rag" is there to inform others of gang membership. The point behind the clothing is to advertise gang membership. This may be because of gang pride; it also may serve to intimidate people. At one time, gang members would be dressed from head to toe in the color of their gang. This could be red, blue, purple, green, or any other color.

It did not take long for the gang members to realize that dressing in this fashion draws attention from the police. The extensive wearing of "colors" diminished over the years and by 1995 members might wear only one article of gang-colored

This personalized license plate shows the boldness of gang members. The plate has a meaning of Norteño y que. A loose translation is, "Norteño, what of it!"

clothing. Gangsters may wear gym shoes with the laces changed to red or blue, depending on their gang affiliation. The web belt sold in various colors is also popular. In the past, the belt had a silver buckle and would be cut at home to fit the waist size of the wearer. Today the belts are worn long so that the color red or blue hangs out below the jacket, shirt, or Pendleton. This is a subtle way of letting people know that you claim to be a gang member. In addition, the silver buckles are now sold with the an initial on the buckle. Most popular are the letters *N* and *S*. Recently gang members have been buying these buckles with numbers on them. The numbers are linked together to form a three-digit area code. A gang member might be found wearing a red belt with a "415" buckle on it, indicating that he is a Norteño from the San Francisco area.

A simple cross hanging around the neck has also become popular in the mid–1990s. The crosses will be made of braided string or thread and will be in red or blue. Again, this is a subtle way to let everyone know which gang you claim. Hats are an important part of the clothing. Hair nets are still worn, but the baseball cap has become more stylish. The caps are either red or blue and usually bear the logo of a sports team. The red and black cap from the University of Nevada at Las Vegas is popular with the Norteños. The cap has the large red letters, UNLV, across the front. According to gang members who wear the hats, this stands for "Us Norteños Love Violence." Sureños prefer the Dallas Cowboys shirts and caps because of the color blue.

Unique to Hispanic gang members is the habit of wearing cutoff pants and high knee socks. During the warmer months, you can find gangsters wearing their pants cut off right below the knee. These "long" shorts are worn in conjunction with

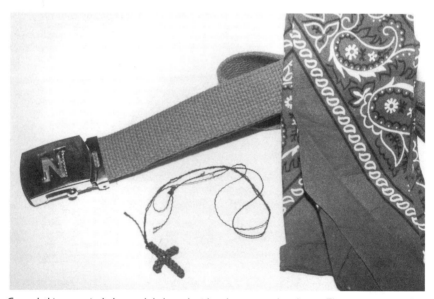

Gang clothing may include a web belt, embroidered cross or a bandanna. The items are usually the same color and worn together or separately. The belt buckle has the letter n on the face indicating the wearer is a Norteño.

Sureños Don't Play

We are born and raised in the Southern Land to kill with our bare hands. They send us up to Busterville and we arrive with the intention to kill. We walk around being proud of what we are. When we hit trade we look hard waiting to catch a buster off his guard. They try to hide but there are Sureños coming from every side.

They are not so deep so they get on their knees asking please don't hurt me. A homeboy laughs as the chap starts crying because he knows soon he will be dying. There ain't no mercy in a Sureños heart because killing our enemies is a beautiful art. The guards say Sureños have a strange mentality and that's from being raised gangbanging. If you are a Sureño you know what I mean, if you are a buster you better start running.

We are straight gangsters; not punks like chaps you see. Sagging their pants like wanna-bes. They are a disgrace to our Sur Raza. So when you see a buster, spit in his face. Sureños are men who mean what they say and when it comes to gang banging, we are down all the way. Don't ever forget what the wila says, Sureños control and don't fucken play. *Puro sur trece!!!*

—unknown author

white, knee-high athletic socks. This is an example of prison tradition being passed down to the street level. The theory behind the long shorts and high socks is that you never want to let the skin on your legs be visible. In prison, it's considered to be feminine to let your legs be seen by other men. This tradition is still practiced on the streets today.

Dress will vary from city to city and state to state. If parents have a concern about letting their children dress in a particular fashion, they should contact their local law enforcement agency.

Hispanic gang members use nicknames or monikers rather than go by their given names. Usually these monikers depict some physical trait. The monikers are usually in Spanish, but English names can also be found. Typical monikers include Flaco, Oso, Sleepy, Spider, Psycho, Gordo, Mr. Smokey, Wino, Lil Man, and Thopo. If an older member of the gang already uses a particular moniker such as "Lil Man," and a younger member also wants to use the name, he will usually go by the moniker "Lil Man 1." Monikers typically accompany the gang name in graffiti. Often there will be a list of all or most of the members of a clique written on a wall next to the gang name. This is referred to as a roster, and is useful to police officers when investigating criminal gang activity. Gang members know each other by their monikers and not their true names. Gangsters may associate with each other for years and never know their so-called friend's true name. Police officers not only need to know monikers, but must also be able to link a moniker to a gang member's true name. In large cities where there are several cliques, there may be as many Flacos as there are cliques. When a crime is committed and the suspect is merely Flaco, police officers must be able to identify which Flaco is the suspect.

Girls in the Gang

*The only guys worth going out with were gang bangers. They had cash, rides,
and dope, and I wanted it too.*

—Sad Eyes, a 15-year-old black female gang member

History

Traditionally, females were incorporated into more dominant male gangs or made
associate members. It was not uncommon for these young women to have personal
relationships with male members. The females supported gang activity by driving
the cars in drive-by shootings, hiding drug money and weapons for their boyfriends,
and performing other related tasks. Presumably, this association with gang members gave the young women status and power in relation to others who were afraid
of violent reprisal from gang members.

In addition to status, females are drawn toward gangs because they may receive
gifts derived from the proceeds of criminal activities. They also might enjoy access
to drugs. Finally, male gang members may provide attention and affection that are
otherwise lacking in their lives.

However, young women often pay a significant price when they join or
associate with a male gang. Females often serve as walking advertisements for the
male gang by wearing its colors in the streets and at school. The more attractive
and desirable a gang's female associates, the better image and reputation the gang
possesses for recruiting purposes. They are often considered the property of the
gang.

Many young women, hooked by the gang's access to money, drugs, alcohol,
and sex, soon find themselves totally involved; their lives are controlled by male
gang members. Others are labeled *hoes*, slang for whores, by male gang members
and find they cannot shed this reputation. In addition, many of these young women
become pregnant, losing their freedom to leave the gang lifestyle due to financial
dependence.

All of these factors have led to a growing number of females forming their own
gangs. They still tend to associate with specific male gangs, but they have distanced
themselves by committing their own crimes, usually drug sales and robberies,
which gain them financial independence. Female gangs have adopted the street
names, tattoos, drug sales, dress, territorial nature, and degree of violence of the

male gangs. Even the initiation rites of "jumping in" new members with physical beatings and/or criminal activity have been adopted as means of judging a potential member's desire to join the gang. Once they are full gang members, females get involved in different levels of crime, from violent felonies to misdemeanors, such as shoplifting, joyriding, and minor narcotics infractions.

Organization and Beliefs

Statistics indicate that girls are becoming involved in gang activity at a young age, usually between 11 to 18 years old. These young women represent between 10 to 15 percent of the total gang population in an area.

Some say that one reason female gangs are forming is to avoid being "sexed in" to a male gang. They're tired of being beat up, used, and abused. Gangs give them a sense of power in their lives, when everything else seems out of control. Female gang names have taken on a definite feminine format and are becoming more distinct, losing their previous titles of affiliation to male gangs. This divorce from the male gangs may be complete, but so is their violent imitation of them.

Association with Other Gangs

Hispanic female gangs are separate and often have their own cliques or sets within the group. While they may be from a larger group, such as the Sureños or Norteños, their set name may be Tiny Locas, Jokers, or La Pee Wees. The male gang members of that group may form attachments with them, or not, but they are expected to back up the girls should they need it and vice versa. These female gangs are becoming more involved in violent activities, such as drive-bys, and in luring rival gangs to their territory so their homeboys can shoot them. They also have a growing role in both the dealing or trafficking of narcotics and are abusers of marijuana, heroin, cocaine, and alcohol.

Black female gang members are usually mixed in with the male gang members, working side by side, especially when conducting narcotics sales. The females are rarely searched by male police officers, which makes their role very important. The black gangs that grow up in the same neighborhood feel as though they are "one big family." While the female gang members consider themselves equal to the males in respect to their loyalty to each other, they tend to be more discreet.

While they should be considered as dangerous as the males, the females are less boisterous, and their actions toward law enforcement are generally not as abrasive. Their clothing is also less likely to be as bold as the male gang member's. Their main role is to provide alibis; carry weapons and narcotics; and often "take care of business" when their mate is in jail.

Asian street gangs are involved in crimes such as commercial robberies and are the major perpetrators of gang-related extortion and home invasion robberies. The male gang members will use the females as getaway drivers, lookouts, and lures to draw rival gang members. The young women are also commonly used as a ruse to gain entry into locations they intend to rob. Recently, Asian females have begun to form their own separate gangs.

White supremacist female gang members participate in their gang's criminal activity, which often includes property crimes, drug trafficking, and hate crime. Unlike black or Hispanic gangs, white gangs do not consider their females as official members but as tag-alongs or girlfriends. However, the role of the woman is changing, especially in the Ku Klux Klan and the neo-Nazi movement. Here, women are becoming officers in some groups, retaining a certain sense of equality in the ranks. White outlaw motorcycle gangs consider their women to be property, and these women often wear patches on their clothing to identify them as such. These women tend to be older and to stay in the gangs out of fear for their own survival.

Profile

Most female gang members can be easily recognized. Their clothing is usually dark, in varying colors of black, blue, and brown. Hispanic female gang members sometimes wear the basic uniform or clothing that the men wear (Pendleton shirts and khaki or Levi pants). Hispanic gang females prefer pants and seldom wear dresses. They also wear bandannas around their heads, affix them to their attire, or use them as belts. They wear their own style of jewelry with the exception of a *chola band*, which is a thick black rubber band that is tied around the middle finger of their left hand and pulled across the top of the hand and around the wrist. This band signifies that they are married to the barrio or neighborhood where their street gang is located. They may even have the chola band tattooed to the top part of their hand.

Their hair is usually long and full, and they sometimes die it blonde or red. Facial makeup is usually thick and light in complexion. The makeup on their eyes and eyebrows is especially thick and dark.

Most hardcore female members will have tattoos, the most common being their gang affiliation, moniker, and boyfriend's name. Tattoos of crucifixes and rosaries on the chest or back mean that they will die for their neighborhoods. Three dots, shaped in a pyramid, which means *mi vida loca* (my crazy life), can often be found on the hand in the webbing between their fingers. They may have teardrops tattooed beneath the lower eyelid to signify they are crying for their barrio or a loved one in prison.

The black females have individual styles that differ from each other. While they may wear ordinary clothes, the clothing may be in one specific color, usually red or blue, to signify which group they claim. They also wear matching hair accessories, belts, socks and shoes.

Girl Street Gang Names

Sisters 4 Life
Pretty in Yellow
Best Side Posse
Sacramento Bad Girls
Wally Girls
Lady Rascal Gangsters
National Color Girls
Koreatown Crazy Chicas
West Coast Ladies
Southside Scissors
Masters of Destruction (coed gang)
Dirty Punks
Pomona Girls

Asian female gang members tend to dress in short black leather skirts, black tops, black stockings, and spiked high heels. Their hair and makeup are similar to the Hispanic girls'. Identification with the gang is discreet. They might wear certain colors of shoes, fingernail polish, and jewelry, that everyone else will recognize as their gang's color. Their tattoos are more conspicuous, since they are burned or cut into the skin in conspicuous places. They will be in the form of the gang logo, a nickname, or a boyfriend's name.

Society as a whole has been reluctant to accept that girls can be in gangs, much less commit the violent crimes dictated by gang membership. Law enforcement often disregards the girls as active participants because there are so many males caught up in the violent scene. Experts, however, feel that female gangs will continue to increase in number, independence, and violence.

Rick's Report
THE CASE OF THE CLOSET NAZIS

Most of the gang-related fighting in Lodi, California, occurs between Norteños and Sureños. Occasionally our white supremacist faction emerges from out of the closet and causes trouble, but it is usually short-lived and they retreat behind their dark cloak of anonymity. In the summer of 1994, the white priders decided to wage a war against the Sureño gangsters. This conflict could have been predicted due to the recent talk coming from Governor Wilson's office regarding illegal immigration from Mexico into California. Governor Wilson was demanding that President Clinton pay the state for enforcing illegal immigration laws and deporting illegal immigrants.

Girls in the Gang

The white priders adopted a form of guerrilla tactics, striking when they found one or two Sureños alone. Typically the whites would pile out of their pickup trucks wielding bats or tire jacks and proceed to assault their Sureño victims. Few of the Sureños spoke English, and those that did really didn't want to get the police involved. Consequently, only one or two arrests were made in what must have been a series of fifteen to twenty confrontations.

The group of white priders was clever in disguising their political and cultural beliefs both at school and on the street. Unlike the Hispanic gangs, they did not "fly colors" or wear a particular type of clothing. They were good students that came from good families and usually played varsity sports of some kind or another. They thought the way to handle the problem of federal budget deficits, unemployment, welfare reform, and illegal immigration was to beat the Hispanics all the way back to the Mexican border. Diplomacy was not a part of their vocabulary or their behavior.

I can't explain why, but our racist white pride contingent could always be found hanging out at the local Mexican fast food restaurant. It never made sense to anyone in the police gang unit why the white supremacists chose a Mexican restaurant as their gathering place, but they did. The Sureños knew that they could be found at this location on almost any evening. One night the Sureños decided that they had had enough of being beaten, and formulated their own plan of attack against the white priders.

As two truckloads of white priders drove along past the restaurant, they heard someone whistle. The sound came from the restaurant parking lot. They looked at the parking lot and saw three or four Sureños all dressed in blue Pendletons and their blue bandannas. As the white priders looked toward the small group of Mexican boys, the Sureños began "throwing" gang hand signs and yelling insults. This must have infuriated the guys in the pickup trucks, to see these "undesirables" insulting them from their white pride hangout. They immediately made a U-turn, cutting across oncoming traffic, and headed for the restaurant that was full with the evening dinner crowd. The odds were in the white priders' favor, and they were going to teach the Sureños a lesson that they would not soon forget.

As they leapt from their trucks towards the Sureños, they heard a loud whistle and were shocked by what they saw next. Out from behind the adjacent building came approximately 20 to 30 Sureños carrying boards, bats, clubs, sticks, and anything else that they could find. They proceeded to destroy the fancy new pickup trucks and chase the white priders from the parking lot. They chased them into the restaurant, through the dining area, over the counter, and into the kitchen before beating them with their weapons.

The people in the restaurant feared for their lives and the lives of their children. They were horrified to find themselves in the midst of a gang fight. When the patrol units arrived a couple of minutes later, all that could be found were the broken windows of the trucks and the broken bones of the white priders. With their pride crushed, the white priders returned to the closet and there were no more incidents of Sureños being attacked by white supremacists for two years. Fortunately, no one was severely injured, and none of the restaurant patrons were harmed.

from Initiation
to Burial:
A Culture of Violence

My daughter went out to the
trash can early Sunday morning.
This was in February of 1987.
My daughter came in and said
she thought there was a dead
man in the alley. I went to check
and sure enough, there he was. I
hear shots at night, look at the
clock, roll over, and go to sleep.
It just happens so often. Sometimes several times in one night.

—Resident of Playboy Gangster
CRIP terrtory

THE DRIVE-BY SHOOTING

The following incident is the fact-based account of an actual drive-by shooting in central California one summer during the 1990s. The information comes from interviews with the subjects.

Raul ("Gato") and Paco ("Smoky") sat in the darkest corner of the Charter Way Taco Bell, wolfing down burritos and Coca-Cola. Every so often, they lowered their glasses under the table and poured in liquid from the contents of a small brown-bagged bottle.

Dressed in the red colors of the Norteños gang, they were feeling good and raring to go gang banging. They wore the tennis shoes, the low-slung baggy pants, and Pendleton shirts buttoned to their necks, even on this hot night in Stockton, California. Their ponytailed hair was topped with graffiti-marked baseball caps worn over their eyes.

Raul, the short, stocky teen, finished his meal and lit a "weed." Breathing deeply, he passed the joint to his friend.

"So, Paco, what's you want to do tonight? Need money? Wanna jack a house?"

Paco, four inches taller and a year younger than his sixteen-year-old friend, blew out the sweet-smelling smoke.

"Naw, I got money. I scored some crack yesterday. In fact, now I wanna get me an Uzi."

"I know just the guy for you." He slid a .25-caliber semiautomatic out of his pocket and showed it to his friend. "Brand new. Twenty-five bucks. He can get anything you want."

"All right! Set up a meeting for me."

Raul suddenly went tense and grabbed the gun back, hiding it under the table. He murmured lowly, "Hey, man, get ready to ditch under the table. That's the third time that friggin Toyota has cruised by."

"Shit. And I don't have a piece on me."

Both boys got ready to dive under the table when a voice hailed them from the car. "Hey, Paco. What's happening?"

Paco peered into the car as the darkened window was rolled down and a grinning face appeared.

"That you, Joker?"

"Yeh. You guys wanna go cruising in Lodi? Teach some *scrapas* respect?"

Raul and Paco wandered over to the car, checking out the other riders. Besides Angel, his cousin, and a skinny white kid, there were two girls, one Hispanic, the other black.

Raul nodded to the other kids in recognition and asked, "These Lodi Scrapas, they do somethin' to you?"

"Yeah, a drive-by. Commin?"

"Sure, why not. Ain't got nothin else to do. We'll follow you over." They hurried to Raul's old low-rider Chevy Impala.

As they passed through the countryside on West Lane to Lodi, a small town eleven miles north, Raul asked Paco about this guy, Angel.

"I don't remember seeing him before. You sure he's Norte?"

"Yeh, I was at his jump-in."

Raul laughed, "I thought I recognized the bruises on his face. Must have been recent."

They followed the white Toyota through the quiet streets and parked two blocks away from the site. Angel stuck his head in the window.

"You guys bring weapons?" He had a metal bar in his hand and a knife. Paco showed his blade and Raul his gun. "Good. Let's go stomp some ass."

As they neared the house, a group of milling teens, mostly dressed in blue, belonging to the Sureño set, spotted them and started to move as a unit toward the small group. Realizing their surprise attack was foiled, Angel said, "Hey, Raul. Shoot the gun. Break em' up a bit and then we can go in."

Raul didn't like this. He seemed to be the only one with a gun. Man, there were a lot of guys coming at him. Maybe this wasn't such a good idea.

Angel and the others egged him on. "Come on. Shoot. You chickenshit? Shoot, shoot, shoot," the group taunted.

Raul was scared, but he wasn't chickenshit. Squeezing his eyes shut, he aimed at the crowd and pulled the trigger. A few screams and curses came from the mob headed in his direction. He opened his eyes and saw that the gang was still coming at him. He fired and fired until the magazine was done, and then he reached into his pocket for a new one, using that too. Now he was shooting wildly, hitting anything he could: cars, windows, telephone poles. There were screams and confusion. Then the sound of police sirens filled the air.

As the last clip emptied, he turned and ran back to his car, shoving the gun between the seats. The sirens came closer. He yelled, "Paco, come on." The door opened quickly and they were off, with a police car pursuing them. No matter how fast he punched the old Impala, he couldn't outrun the police car. Minutes later, Raul and Paco were leaning against the car being searched for weapons and "Mirandaized." An hour later, they were being interviewed about their actions that night. During the evening, they learned that one of the shots fired wildly had hit a man standing out in the street talking with his girlfriend—two blocks away; another hit a child who was sitting in his living room watching television.

Years later, after being incarcerated in a California Youth Authority facility for conspiracy and attempted murder, Raul would regret what had happened that night. And his conscience would bother him, especially about the innocent child who is now paralyzed from his bullet. How had he gotten started in gang banging? Could anyone or anything have stopped him?

Weapons

*At first I only carried a knife. Things started getting crazy and then I carried
a gun. Either a .38 or a 9mm or a sawed-off.*

—Oso

The rule on the street is, "The greater your firepower, the more respect you earn."
No longer satisfied with knives and clubs, gangs now use automatic submachine
guns and bombs. The ease of obtaining these weapons is a direct result of excessive
profits from drug sales, combined with a large volume of stolen weapons available
for sale on the streets.

The 1992 riots in South Central L.A. following the Rodney King trial verdict
reportedly placed over 20,000 additional guns on the streets. Once the looting
began, various gangs organized attacks on gun stores and pawnshops. The majority
of the weapons stolen during this period remain unrecovered.

According to the California Department of Justice, the firearms were stolen
from some 19 different locations. During the first night of disorder, a pawnshop
lost 970 guns and a gun shop lost 1,150 guns, most of which were either automatic
or semiautomatic. It was reported that a gang actually posted armed gang members
outside of one gun shop to prevent "general looters" from taking the guns.

Since the riots, hundreds more guns have been stolen in a series of "smash and
grab" burglaries throughout the Los Angeles area. "Guns—everybody has guns,"
Huero said when asked about the availability of weapons. "I once crawled in a
doggie door into a house and stole a guy's hunting rifle. I went to some apartments
and told the guy I would trade him for any other gun. I got a .38 special and six
bullets. The bullets had yellow tops . . . you know they got two different kinds of
colors on the bullets. That was my gun I did my crimes with. Ten minutes after I
got my gun, I shot at someone. I didn't hit him though."

Arms Race on the Streets

Street gangs unable to buy or steal their guns have the option of renting. Once the
crime is completed, the weapons are returned. Whatever the costs, gang members
find it increasingly important to possess sophisticated weapons arsenals. Recently,

Automatic and semiautomatic rifles are prized weapons of street gangs. This rifle has a bandanna with the gang's color tied to the gun.

laser sights and silencers have become popular. Gang members fashion "pop bottle silencers" from 2 liter plastic soda bottles. They attach the plastic bottle to the muzzle of the gun and pack it to muffle the sound of the gun shot. The improvised silencers prove effective, even though their size is often large and bulky, and they are not easily concealed. Law enforcement has demanded more modern weaponry to counter the street gang arsenals. Police are now regularly armed with automatic magazine-fed pistols carrying ten or more rounds.

On February 3, 1994, *USA Today* reported that "Drive-by shootings have become a major public health problem." The article listed the following statistics derived from 1991 Los Angeles police reports. The statistics are for Los Angeles in the year 1991.

- Los Angeles averages 48 drive-by shootings per month.
- 677 juveniles were shot at—in 583 incidents.
- 429 were wounded and 36 died.
- 71 percent of the juveniles shot were in street gangs.
- All the homicide victims were African American or Hispanic.
- 97 percent of the homicide victims were boys.
- Homicides represented 9 percent of all deaths among children.
- Overall, 2,222 people in L.A. were shot at in 1,548 gang-related drive-by shootings.

Children Killed by Gun Violence

On May 9, 1994, *USA Today* published a list of the deadliest counties in the USA for children. The statistics show counties (and four cities) that had children killed by guns during an assault or police shooting. Below is a partial list from that publication.

State/County	Rate*	State/County	Rate
Alabama		Indiana	
Jefferson	4.3	Allen	1.0
Mobile	3.4	Lake	3.4
Montgomery	3.8	Marion	1.0
Arizona		Iowa	
Maricopa	2.2	Polk	1.2
Arkansas		Kansas	
St. Francis	14.0	Sedwick	2.0
California		Wyandotte	2.5
Alameda	2.0	Kentucky	
Contra Costa	2.2	Fayette	1.3
Los Angeles	4.8	Jefferson	.9
San Bernardino	1.8	Louisiana	
San Joaquin	2.1	East Baton Rouge	3.7
Colorado		Jefferson	2.9
Denver	3.4	New Orleans	11.3
El Paso	1.0	Maryland	
Connecticut		Anne Arundel	.9
Fairfield	2.1	Prince George's	3.2
New Haven	1.4	Baltimore City	5.6
District of Columbia		Massachusetts	
Washington	15.8	Hamden	1.1
Florida		Suffolk	4.1
Alachua	1.7	Michigan	
Calhoun	27.2	Genesee	2.6
Dade	2.0	Saginaw	2.8
Duval	3.4	Wayne	5.3
St. Lucie	2.7	Minnesota	
Georgia		Hennepin	.4
Bibb	3.3	Mississippi	
Chatham	2.3	Hinds	5.1
Fulton	5.9	Washington	4.4
Illinois		Missouri	
Cook	3.9	Jackson	3.9
Kane	1.9	St. Louis City	10.8
Kankakee	4.2		

State/County	Rate	State/County	Rate
Nebraska		Rhode Island	
Douglas	1.2	Providence	.8
Nevada		Rhode Island	
Clark	2.6	Providence	.8
Storey	118.8	South Carolina	
New Jersey		Charleston	2.0
Essex	2.3	Pickens	3.2
New Mexico		York	2.3
Bernalillo	1.5	Tennessee	
New York		Rutherford	2.5
Bronx	6.6	Shelby	3.8
Dutchess	1.9	Texas	
Kings (Brooklyn)	5.0	Bexar	2.6
New York (Manhattan)	2.6	Dallas	4.7
Queens	1.9	Ector	2.5
North Carolina		Galveston	4.1
Cumberland	3.6	Harris	3.5
Durham	2.7	Hopkins	10.4
Forsyth	2.6	Tarrant	2.9
Orange	3.2	Utah	
Pitt	9.3	Salt Lake	.4
Cuyahoga	.21	Virginia	
Ohio		Halifax	10.3
Lucas	1.5	Norfolk City	6.1
Mahoning	2.3	Richmond City	5.9
Oklahoma		Washington	
Oklahoma	2.0	Yakima	1.6
Oregon		Wisconsin	
Multnomah	1.2	Milwaukee	3.4
Pennsylvania			
Philadelphia	3.6		

*Children killed by gunfire (per 100,000 people)

Pipe bombs also contribute to the latest escalation of the arms race on the street. A piece of metal pipe filled with explosive material and capped at both ends, the bomb explodes into tiny pieces of jagged metal when detonated. One advantage of this terrifying weapon is that its user does not have to be present when the bomb goes off—that is if it doesn't go off in the gang member's hands, which happens frequently.

In 1994 at least 15 cities reported arson-type gang homicides. In Atlanta, two informants were murdered after a gang member threw a Molotov cocktail into the apartment of an 18-year-old mother who was quarreling with the gang member's friend. In St. Paul, Minnesota, a boy witnessed a gang murder, and members of the gang firebombed his house. The boy wasn't home, but his five siblings were killed. In Los Angeles, 10 people were killed when gang members threw a firebomb into an apartment building. This type of firebombing is only one example of gang assaults. Arson has long been a gang tool, and is used as a means of extortion and retaliation. Arson squad reports in 1995 state that the majority of all arson crimes are gang-related.

Other types of weapons used by street gangs have become more technical and diverse. Knives of various types are common, and recently martial arts weapons such as throwing stars and nunchuks have been added. Handguns, too, are common; gang members also use electric guns (tasers) as terror weapons against robbery victims. The new electric toy squirt guns are also potentially lethal when loaded with caustic liquids intended to blind victims. In order to insure that their products no longer appear too realistic, most toy gun manufacturers paint their products bright colors. This is due to several incidents in which juveniles were mistaken by law enforcement officials as carrying weapons, which were in fact realistic-looking toys.

Acid-filled vials thrown at potential victims have been documented as another street gang weapon. Learning to build such items from published books, gangs have found a way to terrorize their enemies and the general population without immediately exposing themselves to their victims, opposing gangs, or law enforcement officials.

In addition to the above-mentioned weapons, hand grenades have become a valued tool in gang warfare. Southern California has seen an increase in grenade use in the past few years. In March 1992, a street gang member threw an M-67 grenade into a residence. The grenade did not go off because the gang member had failed to remove the safety clip. Police officials indicated that if the grenade had detonated, the residents and their neighbors could have been seriously injured or killed. In another incident, an undercover police officer purchased a live M-67 grenade from a black street gang member for $150.

Gang members buy practice grenades from army surplus stores. The gangs have devised a way to pack the grenades with black gunpowder and shrapnel and then plug the bottom of the grenade, thus making illegal and destructive weapons.

During the past decade, residential burglaries and illegal street vendors have been the most popular source of weapons for gang members. Recent investigations show that U.S. military bases are the source of some gang weapons. Investigations all over the country have revealed that both military personnel and civilian employees working on bases have stolen guns and replacement parts to be sold to gang members. Authorities have apprehended white supremacists, survivalists, organized crime groups, and street gangs that were stockpiling weapons stolen from military bases.

> Every time I leave the house I had a gun—a .38 or a 9mm. You can get a gun on any corner. No more than $25 for an auto. Hell, your friends may even just give you one.
>
> —B. K.

Teen Deaths

According to the National Center for Health Statistics, in 1990 teen deaths by gunfire hit an all-time high since the government began keeping records 30 years ago. Only vehicle deaths surpassed the 4,173 juveniles, ages 15 to 19, who died from gunshots. For African-American children ages 10 to 14, guns are the leading cause of death. Experts estimate that there are perhaps seven times as many children injured by guns than are actually killed. These shootings usually occur in inner-city neighborhoods among the Latino and African-American populations, but gang-related deaths among Asians have also escalated rapidly in recent years. The majority of these shootings can be related to the drug trade and gang activity.

Juveniles and Weapons

Despite the greater occurrence of gang violence in inner city neighborhoods, the problem of juveniles using weapons is not confined to gang members living in major metropolitan areas. A 1990 national survey by the U.S. Department of Health and Human Services revealed that "nearly 20 percent of all students in grades 9–12 reported they had carried a weapon at least once during the 30 days preceding the survey (not necessarily to school)." Guns and other weapons are reaching the hands of juveniles throughout the nation. The following examples occurred between 1990 and 1995.

Albany, NY— One in five New York state students admitted to bringing a knife, gun, or other weapon to school.

Ottumwa, IA—The School Board voted to expel three male students from Evans Middle School for bringing a gun to school and a basketball game.

Ashland, WI—Police seized three .22-caliber pistols from bags and lockers at Ashland Middle School, and five seventh-grade boys face charges.

Lafayette, IN—A 14-year-old middle school student who brought a loaded firearm to school will remain under house arrest until his sentencing.

Monogahela, PA—A 14-year-old boy was arrested for bringing his father's gun on a school bus. He fired the gun three times and struck another student in the arm.

Baton Rouge, LA—a 16-year-old boy was arrested after officials found a sawed-off shotgun and four shells stashed in his gym locker.

De Kalb, MO—A 12-year-old boy shot and killed a classmate in history class before killing himself with his father's .45 caliber hand gun.

Portland, CT—Using a 9-mm semiautomatic firearm, a 13-year-old boy killed a janitor and wounded the principal and secretary before taking a fellow classmate hostage.

Palo Alto, CA—A student was shot in the leg as an act of retaliation for participating in a rock fight in the schoolyard earlier in the day.

On July 18, 1994, Senators Diane Feinstein (Democrat, California) and Byron Dorgan (Democrat, North Dakota) introduced legislation that would require mandatory expulsions for students caught with guns on campus. According to the new amendment, any elementary or secondary school receiving federal funding that does not comply with the mandatory expulsion rule would be at risk of losing their funding. The Los Angeles Unified School District responded to the announcement of the amendment by stating that the U.S. government would be creating a "time bomb." All students that are expelled under the new ruling would end up on the street causing more problems for the community.

On January 30, 1994, three teenagers met with the nation's governors to discuss the violent atmosphere surrounding our country's schools. Their daily concerns centered more on school safety than homework. One of the students said, "A kid establishes himself by having the biggest gun and being willing to use it on anyone for any reason." Another student told the governors, "All my life has been spent around gangs. I dropped out of school because a friend of mine got shot and I didn't feel safe at school anymore." An 18-year-old student said, "We are now numb to what should shock us!"

The problem of youths carrying weapons has meant increasing levels of school violence. Students in some schools drop to the floor during drills to practice what to do if they hear gunfire. Several types of countermeasures have been undertaken by school officials to reduce the presence of weapons in schools.

Dealing with Weapons in Schools

SEARCH/DETENTION

Some schools now perform physical searches of the school and of students entering the premises. Metal detectors are placed at entry points, and students must pass through them. Students are also scanned by hand-held detectors. Additional physical searches may be required. Regular searches of student lockers are also conducted to keep the campus as weapon-free as possible. The school must be secure from unauthorized entry and/or the transfer of outside items to those already inside. Unannounced spot searches of lockers and bags are also used as an additional preventive measure.

EDUCATION

Students are taught that they are not snitches but responsible citizens when they report information on gang activity, possibly saving lives. Additionally, a conflict resolution program can teach students how to resolve problems through positive means without the use of violence. Several curriculums are already in place across the country for this purpose. This allows for a multiple assault on the problem. Students assume responsibility for their own safety and the safety of others. Students are encouraged to report the presence and location of weapons directly to staff or through an anonymous hot line system, such as Campus Crime Stoppers. It is of great importance to know that most juveniles carry weapons out of fear and for their own personal protection.

PREVENTION

These preventive measures make it difficult for weapons to be stored or transported in schools. The use of metal detectors reduces the chance of weapons getting into the school. Additionally, students are not allowed in their lockers during the day, only at the beginning and end of school. Some schools have even eliminated lockers as a safety measure. Students may be required to carry belongings in clear see-through or fishnet bags as a means of controlling the problem.

Juveniles who are found with weapons in school face at least a minimal suspension, if not expulsion. Additionally, they can be criminally charged along with any adult who allowed them access to a deadly weapon. Unfortunately, suspension or expulsion places the offender out on the streets. The problem is removed from school but pushed into the community. A more sensible approach in conjunction with the courts and legislation needs to be established to deal with the problem quickly and effectively.

Weapons Terminology

Uzi	Israeli 9-mm automatic machine pistol.
AK	AK-47 automatic Kalashnikov, communist-bloc mass-production, 7.62-caliber assault rifle.
Mac 10/11	Two different 9-mm machine pistols of small size, but with a great volume of fire.
bust a cap	Shooting at someone.
.38/tray eight	.38-caliber pistol. Traditional revolver size of police forces and U.S. military. Known for its stopping power.
.22/deuce	Small pistol caliber.

.44	Caliber of pistol made famous in *Dirty Harry* films.
9 mm	Standard European pistol caliber becoming more of a standard with police and U.S. military.
packing	Carrying a weapon.
Saturday night special	Cheap mass-produced pistol, easily available and legal.
M-16/AR-15/ CAR-15	Various versions of the standard U.S. military rifle in use since the 1960s.
revolver	Pistol type that holds ammunition in a cylinder between the pistol's barrel and hammer.
magazine	Spring-loaded box in a pistol's handle, holding ammunition.
automatic	A gun or mode of fire that produces multiple shots by squeezing a trigger and holding it.
semiautomatic	A gun which fires a single bullet with each squeeze of its trigger.
assault rifle	Sturdy military weapon that can fire in both an automatic and semiautomatic mode, usually of a large caliber.
shotgun	Single- or double-barreled gun whose size is measured by gauge. They can have their barrels shortened to enhance concealment, but this reduces effective range and accuracy. Effectiveness is also determined by the type of shell used.
dumdum/ cop killer	Type of bullet designed or altered to be as lethal as possible.

Drugs

Everybody in our gang used drugs. My friends were into a lot of drugs.
One time they took me and my cousins to a morgue, a mortuary, cause they
wanted to get some embalming fluid to stick cigarettes into and sell 'em.
It messes you up like sherm (phencyclidine) or something. . . . In our gang
everything revolved around drugs, robbing houses, and fighting other gangs.

—Huero

THE PBG GANG: A CASE STUDY

The Playboy Gangster CRIPs (PBG) gang lives for the most part in a small area of West Los Angeles. Founded around 1979, it is a relatively young gang in Los Angeles, where many gangs have been around for generations. The PBG started out as a typical juvenile gang that committed simple thefts and acts of vandalism, occasionally selling marijuana and other drugs as a lucrative sideline.

Sometime around 1982 the original members of the gang were getting out of jail or prison and expanded their activities into major drug sales. The younger members stood in awe of the flashy new cars and jewelry that older members secured from their narcotics trafficking. These younger members wanted a piece of the action, and the older members didn't hesitate to employ their services. The gang began to grow in numbers and influence.

By 1985 the surrounding community knew that there was a major problem on their streets. Burglaries, graffiti, and vandalism escalated. The police were notified and extra patrols were dispatched in the neighborhood. Even though gang members were being arrested, they were back on the street within days, if not hours, of their arrest.

Cocaine had just become popular and was being routinely sold in large quantities. When crack cocaine entered the market, the PBG were ready to distribute the product from within the boundaries of their neighborhood. Customers came to the neighborhood and often robbed the residents to pay for the crack. Violence was commonplace, and gun shots echoed throughout the once peaceful neighborhood. A tremendous number of juveniles, ages 12 to 17, manned the street corners, selling drugs.

What follows is a series of declarations taken from people involved with the Playboy Gangster CRIPs in Los Angeles. Their statements were made in 1987 and published in the Twenty-Seventh Annual Training Conference Manual for the California Narcotics Officer's Association in September of 1991.

When you arrested me, I flushed a thousand dollars of rock down the toilet. When I was released from juvenile hall, the dealer who gave me the drugs said that I had 24 hours to get his money back or he would harm me or my family. That is why I did the burglary. I can't tell you his name, I know what would happen to me if I did.

—A PBG gang member

I love my son and I keep trying to keep him away from the PBGs but in my heart I know that it is impossible. It's not just the kids, it's the adults. They keep the kids selling that dope and those evil ways just corrupt the kids. It is simple—the gang has more power over my son than I do. What worries me more is that I have younger ones and once one child is in the gang they soon get all your kids in it. We used to worry about pimps taking our daughters and corrupting them and now those same people are in control of the gang and it is our sons that are being pimped to sell drugs.

—Mother of a PBG gang member

You can send me to camp but you can't stop me from being a gang member. When I get out of camp and go back to the neighborhood, they will all be there waiting for me. They won't let me not be a PBG. The only way I could get out of the gang is to move a long way away from here.

—A PBG member

It all started for me at a very young age. I was eight or nine years old. I just kept on going in and out of juvenile hall, finally I ended up in juvenile camp. I was twelve then. I can't blame anyone, it was all my fault. I was just following the older guys. From there I graduated. I got out of camp, lasted a few months and went back to camp again. I didn't do so well. I ended up in the Youth Authority. I got respect when I got out of camp. More respect after the Youth Authority. And now after the penitentiary, I guess more. When I got out of the Youth Authority I started gang banging even more and did more serious crimes. Now I'm a heroin addict. I do most of my crimes to get money for a fix.

—A PBG member

CRACK AND GANGS

The phenomenal growth of street gangs and their level of violence parallels the introduction of crack cocaine into the United States in 1981. Prior to this date, street gangs had a small part of the drug trade, but they were well positioned to expand rapidly and take advantage of this new, relatively inexpensive drug. Traditional street drugs were expensive and required a well-organized operation to maintain for buyers a steady supply, which street gangs at that time did not possess.

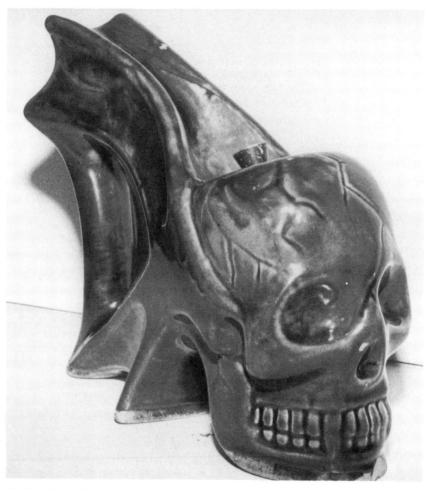

This "bong" used for smoking marijuana is an example of the drug parphernalia that is found in the possession of gang members.

But crack was different. After arriving on the streets of Los Angeles in 1981, the drug rapidly spread across the country due to its relative low cost, ease of production, and quick high for the user, who smoked it in a pipe. By 1995 a quarter of a gram of crack sold for approximately $20, and the user quickly developed an insatiable desire for more.

The product was very marketable, and young street gang members were soon earning large profits. As one former juvenile drug dealer put it, "I sell rock to anyone dumb enough to buy it. I don't care what happens to them. That's their problem." The vast amounts of profit from the crack sales financed the firepower that caused the drug and gang wars to escalate to a degree where law enforcement was at times outgunned.

Several "godfathers" who emerged from the L.A. street gangs organized national networks for crack distribution. They sent groups to major cities across the U.S. and started to recruit local gangs to sell their product. Some of these networks are still operating, and some have broken off to form their own organizations. As these changes occur, the fight to control markets and profits continues across the United States and Canada.

As a result, there seems to be an expanding, more sophisticated distribution network forming within the country. It makes sense to sell drugs in a location other than where they are being produced. The Chinese triads have been associated with the smuggling of heroin into the San Francisco Bay area, and outlaw biker gangs have been investigated for their role in the illegal distribution of narcotics, particularly the national distribution of methamphetamine. The motorcycle gangs have elaborate distribution methods that allow them to manufacture the drugs in remote areas, often in the western states, and transport them across country for resale in other states.

Typically, a gang rents an apartment or house in the area where it intends to sell or distribute its drug. Sometimes abandoned structures are convenient, especially

Stash cans are cans with false bottoms used for hiding narcotics. The cans are capable of concealing a large amount of narcotics.

in the inner-city neighborhoods. Customers are targeted, sometimes given free samples, and directed to the "crack house" to purchase and smoke additional product. Salesmen are also sent out to locate old customers and direct them to the location of the new distribution center. The operation continues until a police raid or until the gang moves on to another location to avoid detection and capture.

In addition to crack, LSD has returned to the contemporary drug scene. Very popular in the late 1960s, LSD causes an increase in pulse and blood pressure and is noted for its ability to create psychedelic effects. Stationary objects begin to move, and colors blend. The "trip" causes the senses to overlap, creating confusion in the user's sense of touch, taste, sight, and hearing.

Popular once again, the drug is showing up on seemingly harmless sheets of stamped images called blotters. Children can innocently lick these stamps and become unwitting consumers on the drug market. Knowledgeable drug users can easily conceal these blotter sheets from uninformed school officials and parents who may be unaware of a free flowing drug trade existing in their neighborhoods. This drug is cheap and easy to produce and, as previously stated, easy to conceal.

The upsurge in teenage smoking has been accompanied by a rise in the use of cigarettes soaked in or laced with another drug or chemical, such as phencyclidine, commonly referred to as PCP or sherm. The apparently common minor infraction of teenage smoking becomes another convenient method for concealing drug use. These drug users risk severe brain damage, respiratory impairment, and death. A closely related practice is the use of common chemical products purchased legally and then "sniffed" or inhaled to produce a "high." "I only sniffed spray paint one time," said a young user of inhalants, "but now I just laugh about stuff a lot. I think it really messed me up."

Behavior Signs that May Indicate Alcohol/Drug Abuse

A drop in work performance (quantity and quality)
Increased accidents and injuries
Poor attendance (sick days in conjunction with weekends)
Often late to work or school
Loss of energy
Often unaccounted for
Defiance of rules and regulations
Stealing money or property
Drug paraphernalia found in bedroom or vehicle
Defensive about behavior
Paranoia
Excessive emotional highs and lows
Withdraws from work or school-related functions
Change in physical hygiene and dress
Financial problems
Selling possessions
Legal problems

Marijuana and other commonly known street drugs have been joined by a new wave of "designer drugs." These are created in small chemical laboratories like those set up to produce crack. The producer sets up and creates his drug of choice, such as "crank" or "crack," and moves on before he is discovered and shut down by law enforcement. Drugs are distributed through drug traffickers and street gangs who sell and use the drugs. Much of the trade in designer drugs is carried out in dance clubs, where the drugs are used to enhance the sensation of sounds, lights, and dancing.

Oso, a gang member interviewed for the book, said, "We sold heroin, crank, marijuana. We sold lots of drugs to older people downtown. We made a lot of money then we go buy lots of red clothes, beer, and guns." It appears as if the majority of drug trafficking within the gang community is done for personal profit rather than the benefit of the gang.

Drug Terminology

amped out	Fatigue after being under the influence of methamphetamine
angel dust	PCP in crystal form
base head	Person hooked on cocaine
beam me up	Looking for drugs
bird	Refers to a kilo of cocaine
blow	Cocaine
bogey	$100 piece of crack
brown paint	Heroin
C	Cocaine
coke spoon	Specially made tiny spoons for inhaling cocaine
cokie, crackhead	Cocaine user
crank	Methamphetamine
crash	To sleep or come down from being under the influence of a stimulant
crumbs	Small pieces of crack cocaine
crystal	Methamphetamine
d	Drugs
dime	Ten; ten dollars
do up	Inject
dropper	Syringe
dusted	Under the influence of crack/PCP
eight ball	$1/8$ ounce of cocaine
8-track	$2^{1}/2$ ounces of cocaine
fix	To inject a drug
flash	Euphoria following the taking of a drug
flip crip	A drug house that sells small amounts of drugs
freak	Heavy drug user; scared
fried	Nonfunctional mind due to drugs

girl	Cocaine
graveyard	A drug house that has been closed by police
head	A drug user
high roller	A drug dealer
hubba	Crack cocaine
ice	Crystal methamphetamine
kick you down	Establish you in the drug trade
kit	Injection paraphernalia
lab	Place where narcotics are manufactured
LB	Pound
love	Crack cocaine
outfit	Injection paraphernalia
OZ	Ounce
point	A needle
primo	Marijuana laced with cocaine
rig	Injection paraphernalia
rock	A piece of crack cocaine
rollin good	Selling drugs
safe house	A place where large amounts of drugs and money are stored
script	Drug prescription
stingin keys	Selling drugs
snort	Sniff a drug through the nose
snow	Cocaine
seed	Methamphetamine
spun	To overdose on methamphetamine
speedball	A mixture of heroin and a stimulant
stacking	The simultaneous use of different anabolic steroids
tie off	Placing a tourniquet on a limb in preparation of injecting a drug
uncut	Pure form of a drug
wired	To be under the influence of a drug
works	Paraphernalia used to prepare and inject narcotics

Initiation

I got jumped in when I was twelve years old. That same day I got my tattoos.
I got jumped out when I was seventeen years old. I got twelve brothers and
sisters and we're all in gangs. I got a couple of brothers in Tehachapi (prison)
that are doing life for burglaries and bank robberies. My dad, mom, uncle,
sisters, brothers, and cousins are all in gangs. You grow up and you want to
follow in their steps. To get into the gang you had to get beat up by seven or
eight people for at least sixty seconds. The same thing to get out.

—Payasa

In the summer of 1993 a rumor of a nationwide gang initiation caused some panic
and concern until officially denied by various local police departments and news
organizations. The rumor stated that potential recruits were to drive cars without
the headlights on during hours of darkness. The requirement for initiation was to
kill the first occupants of a car to flash its headlights at the recruit's car. This story
was run on the local newscasts in major cities throughout the nation. Though the
rumor was a hoax, enough citizens took it seriously to require official denial.

The public's fear of being victimized as part of some type of gang initiation rite
is real. Drive-by shootings, conducted as part of gang initiations or retaliations,
threaten the lives and safety of the general public, who are innocent bystanders or
sometimes the intended target. All organizations have established some type of
ritual by which hopeful members must prove themselves worthy of acceptance.
The military services have their own basic training and boot camp rituals to test a
recruit's bravery and ascertain how he or she is likely to do in battle. College
fraternities have hazing rituals, during which a pledge has to undergo degradation
and humiliation to show his desire to belong to the select organization. Even
physicians continue to cling to the idea of an initiation rite, by which interns must
work long grueling hours to show their dedication to the medical profession. It is
not surprising, then, that street gangs have several types of initiation rituals.

Testing

Initiations that require some suffering, either physical or mental, serve several
purposes to the organization and to the individual. First, going through some type
of initiation makes it easier for other gang members to identify new members. In

the world of the street gang, this excludes the peripherals, wanna-bes, and just plain homies (friends or associates). Law enforcement doesn't necessarily observe this rule and considers an individual who regularly associates with gang members and participates in their activities to be a member. Through established initiation rituals, an individual formally acknowledges joining a street gang, leaving no doubt as to his or her loyalty.

Coming through the initiation, an individual accepts the street gang as much as they accept him or her. The rules of the gang become his or her rules, and the act of joining validates the gang's identity and group esteem. What good is it to be a member of an exclusive group if nobody else wants to join? The recruitment and initiation of new members also ensures that the gang will survive and hopefully gain new strength as it grows.

Gangs do not accept members who cannot contribute to the gang's status on the streets. An initiation that measures a recruit's physical and psychological limitations enables the gang to be sure of what it can count on from its new member. For the new member, it also clarifies the gang's expectations for performance.

Bonding

Another component of an initiation activity is the bonding created between the individual and the gang. The camaraderie between gang members and the new member is first defined by the shared experience of initiation. Whether this initiation involves a physical beating or commission of a crime, the common link is forged.

A gang member in West Palm Beach, Florida, describes his gang's initiation and resignation rites as follows: "Approach an officer with a revolver in a plain brown paper bag. If the pledged member walks away without being questioned by the officer, he's in. If the officer questions the contents of the bag, the pledged member must shoot. The only way out of the gang is by death."

The type of initiation a street gang uses depends on several factors, such as age and/or sophistication of the gang members and primary motivations of the gang. Local practices are influenced by traditions and media exposure. Many gangs will copy the initiation practices of other local gangs in a form of "keeping up with the Joneses."

If one gang's initiation practice appears to be harder than others, then they may be seen as the tougher gang on the streets. No gang wants to have weaker standards than others that they may have to confront. The age and sophistication of a gang's members can also help determine a method of initiation. The type of criminal activity the gang engages in can motivate a specific initiation, such as successfully burglarizing a home or stealing a car.

Gang sets or cliques composed of younger members may require a prospective candidate only to endure a physical beating or commit a minor crime in order to prove his or her worth. Since the younger gang members have usually known each other while growing up together and are already sure of each other's background and abilities, this seems to suffice. The older, more sophisticated gang members have more involved initiation rites to bond new members to the group.

The physical beatings that a candidate must undergo are only part of the initiation process. The commission of a crime, possibly violent, ensures that the candidate is not a police informant attempting to infiltrate the group. Participating in the crime also creates a commitment between the new member and the gang since they are now mutually involved in illegal activities. The new member is initiated into the expectations of supporting the gang and its members, even to the extent of breaking the law. The more violent the crime, the stronger that bond will be between the gang and its new member.

Street gangs use a variety of initiation processes individually or in combination which meet each gang's membership needs. Initiations can be categorized in four ways:

1. Joined in or walked in
2. Worked in
3. Jumped in
4. Sexed in

Joined In or Walked In

In this simplest style of initiation, a candidate becomes a member without the threat of violence. This may require a brief pledge or probationary period during which the candidate hangs out with the gang and participates in its activities. The gang members can then evaluate the potential member for compatibility and desirability as a gang member and accept or reject him or her in due course. Membership becomes official if the members vote on accepting the candidate, announce that the candidate is considered a member, or just let the candidate continue to hang out with the gang. This initiation style tends to be used by unsophisticated and loosely organized nomad-type gangs. As this gang type develops, more stringent initiation procedures will follow.

Worked In

This initiation process occurs among street gangs that are more sophisticated and mature. The gang desires a long-term commitment from prospective members and will use this method to achieve that goal. Being "worked in" refers to the commission of some criminal act to test the candidate's desire to join the gang. This criminal act might be as minor as spraying graffiti in a rival gang's territory or committing some other act of vandalism in the community. However, it could also be a violent crime, such as committing a drive-by shooting, participating in a gang rape, conducting a car-jacking, or holding up a convenience store. These acts,

It's Later Than You Think

Susanna Jones pulled her car up to a small convenience store/gas station in South Stockton, California, and stopped at the closest pump. Seeing the sign Pay in Advance on the pumps, she grabbed her purse and quickly hurried into the store to pay the cashier. A couple of minutes later she was back out at the car, pumping her gas. Suddenly, the gas flow stopped.

What in the world? She wondered. Surely, her tank hadn't filled that quickly. She looked at the gallon indicator and noticed that it had just put two and a half gallons in the tank. Susanna looked at her watch. Damn! She was going to be late for a dinner appointment! Frustrated, she marched into the store and demanded to see the clerk.

The manager took her aside and said, "Calm down, lady. We just saved your life."

Susanna put her hand to her mouth in astonishment and listened as the manager continued.

"While you were in here paying for the gas, I happened to look out the window and see a kid get in the back seat of your car. He's hiding on the floor right now. Don't worry, we've called the police."

Susanna turned to look out at her car, quietly sitting in the shade of the covered island. She wondered how this could have happened so quickly. She'd only been in the store for a few minutes. She usually locked her car doors, but today she'd been in a hurry.

When the police cars came with sirens blaring, a head popped up in the back seat, and the passenger door quickly opened. A short teenager climbed out and at first hid behind Susanna's car. As the patrol cars squeaked to a stop, he tried making a run for it, but the police caught him easily.

After questioning the young man, the officer in charge told Susanna that the sixteen-year-old had confessed that this was his gang initiation: to rape and kill a woman before midnight. He'd been waiting for hours for the right setup. He was real disappointed. He'd do anything to get in that gang!

besides testing a candidate's loyalty, also help to enhance the gang's violent reputation and provide income. Working in can also include selling drugs to help provide income for the gang. This can be a dangerous job because the seller becomes a target for addicts, the police, and other gangs.

Jumped In

This popular method is often used as a primary initiation ritual. The "jumping in" is in essence a physical beating by several gang members for a specific or undetermined duration. The intent is to test a candidate's ability to endure physical punishment and defend him or herself, as well as the reputation of the gang. Some gangs allow a specific amount of time for the beating; others let it go until someone or the group determines that the individual has received enough punishment and has shown some "heart," meaning bravery. Flaco, a gang member interviewed for the book, said, "I got jumped in four times. I wanted to make a name for myself. I wanted it to be a thing. I wanted to get jumped into 18th Street eighteen times. Cause I knew only a few people who had done it. I never made it that far. Most of the time they would give you eighteen seconds. That may not seem like a long time but they're slow. "One . . . talking to somebody else, two . . . go and get me a beer." Like that, so you got your butt kicked. Eight guys would just beat on you."

An individual who has recently undergone, or participated in a jumping in, may show telltale bruises or lacerations on the face and body. The ritual may be performed more than once, at a member's request, as a way to prove the new member's "heart" or how "down" (committed) they are to the gang. "I got jumped in a couple of times," said Huero, a gang member interviewed for the book. "Probably because I was the smallest one. One day we were all at the house. There was an older guy that had a house with his old lady. It was her mom's house but her mom was in prison. He kept it going by robbing people. It was a junky little house but the inside had nice stuff and even a couch. We used to get drunk there a lot. It was a Friday and everyone cut school to go to the house. I came outside and someone hit me in the face. They knocked me down and kept on hitting me. Another bigger guy grabbed me by my legs and held me upside down. Everyone was hitting me. They dropped me and started hitting another guy. I jumped up and ran over and started hitting him too. We went into the house and started smoking some more dope and drank some more beer. That's when they came up with my nickname [Huero]." Supposedly this demonstrates to the gang the individual's toughness, while enhancing his/her personal reputation within the gang.

Sexed In

Despite media publicity, this is not a popular initiation rite. Also known as "giving train," it is used by female gangs or for females desiring to join coed gangs. The practice probably originated among male-dominated coed gangs that required new female members to have sex or commit some sexual act with a specified number of members of the gang. A set number or roll of the dice could determine the number of sex acts or numbers of sex partners that the initiate would have to submit to in order to complete the initiation. This practice was, and is still, used sometimes in place of being jumped in, but gang initiates choosing this method are usually looked down on by other gang members and are considered second-class members.

Female gangs may require members to have sex with specific members of associated male gangs or specific local males. Although this method may prove a desire to join the gang, it doesn't demonstrate an ability to endure physical pain, and due to the epidemic spread of HIV, this method of initiation is no longer considered safe.

Male gang members may also use sex as an initiation ritual. The requirement may be to rape an unknown female in order to qualify for admission to the gang.

Resignation

The saying among gang members is "Blood in, blood out," meaning getting out of a gang can be as hard as, if not harder than, getting in. Quitting is known by gang bangers as "dropping the rag," or being "jumped out," or "violated." Traditionally, sociologists have observed street gangs maturing as members take several paths away from the gang. The preferred career path of gang members is to maintain their contact and loyalty to the gang while becoming somewhat legitimate, with a job and a family. This is extremely difficult if members become involved in criminal activity with the gang and start a cycle of incarceration and parole.

The infamous Chicago Forty-Two gang of the 1920s was the subject of research by University of Chicago sociologists in 1931. They found that the vast majority of the original gang members had been killed, crippled, or incarcerated, fates generally attributed to their original gang involvement. This prognosis may be even more of a reality today, as a report by the California Department of Health Services concluded. Based upon 1992 crime statistics for that state, homicide has overtaken accidents as the leading killer of youth between the ages of 15 and 19.

Many gang members feel trapped and without options for leaving the gang. They are truly afraid of what might happen to them or their families if they leave. Attempting to fade away from the gang scene doesn't always work. The gang can easily sense if a member is trying to avoid association and may issue a "beat on sight" (BOS) order for members who are shying away.

However, depending on the gang, an individual who acquires a full-time evening job or attends school to better himself may have found an acceptable way to "kick back" and avoid the criminal activity of the gang. Outreach centers with workable programs for helping interested gang members get back into school or obtain GED certificates or job training are often successful, providing that they don't insist on the member quitting the gang before joining the program. Thinking in terms of changing the direction of the gang rather than disbanding it seems to bring more members into these programs and result in a higher success rate.

Many families attempt to move away from areas where their children may be involved in gangs, or even send their children to places they think may be safe. Often, individuals bring their gang problems with them, starting new gangs as a way of protecting themselves in new environments or joining gangs already established in the area.

"I got initiated into my clique after hanging out with them for a couple of weeks," said one Hispanic gang member. "We were all just kicking it and drinking 40s when one of the guys asked me if I were down for the gang. I said yeah I was and then he said, 'Show me what you got.' I wasn't going to back down in front of him and everybody else so we started to fight and two other guys joined him. I don't know how long it lasted but it seemed like ten minutes. They kept knocking me down but I just got back up and fought back. When they got done, they said I was in and then we went back to drinking. Later, I told my mother that I got into a fight, because she saw my face was messed up, so she didn't keep asking me questions." It is very important that parents are aware of the danger signs and prepared to help youngsters obtain the needed respect and self-esteem from another source.

In some areas, the threat of violent street gang retaliation against former gang members and their families is very real. In Wichita, Kansas, an organization called Project Freedom was created to assist former gang members and their families in moving safely away from the gang's revenge. Police were also active in making this program a success.

The traditional social safety net of military service is no longer a viable option for troubled youth. They usually have below average educational abilities or felony criminal records, either of which are undesirable in military recruits. As of 1996 the California National Guard's requirements are possession of a GED certificate; a felony-clear record (before and after 18 years of age); 31 percent on the Armed Services Vocational Aptitude Battery test; no gang or racist tattoos; and aged between 17 and 35 years. Other branches of the armed services have even more stringent requirements.

Incarceration alone is not the answer to the gang problem. Incarceration almost assures that an individual will not leave gang activity. In order to survive while locked up, the individual must show greater loyalty to his or her gang or form alliances with other gangs in the institution. The prisoner usually develops a stronger affiliation with the gang lifestyle. When released, he or she goes back to the same situation but may now be perceived as a local hero by emerging gang members. Retirement is not an easy option for the gang member who has been in prison, or for anyone.

Those brave enough to attempt to walk away from the gang face possible death at the hands of their former gang or enemies, once the shield of the gang's protection is removed. To leave the gang, a member may be forced to undergo a physical beating more severe than that of initiation. Such beatings have even led to crippling injuries or death.

Throwing Signs:
Communicating Gang Identity

*If someone would disrespect my neighborhood by throwing a sign, I would
have to go over and whip their ass with a crowbar. It didn't matter if I got
my ass whipped. I would go back again for more.*

—Payasa

One warm spring evening a 15-year-old boy was walking home alone from
afterschool activities at about 6 P.M. He had just crossed a major street within our
small town, when a carload of approximately six young males slowed and pulled
along side of him. In his words, they began "messin'" with him. They were making
comments and harassing him. The boy became scared and found himself in a
serious dilemma. He was too far from home to run, and clearly he was outnumbered
and couldn't fight them. He thought perhaps if he could scare them, they would
leave him alone. How could one boy make six boys afraid of him? He got the idea
that if they thought he was in a gang, they would be too afraid to start trouble. He
remembered seeing some kids at school use hand signs to designate their gang
affiliation, and thus decided to "throw some signs at them." He proceeded to
manipulate his fingers in such a manner that it represented a local gang sign.
Unfortunately, the gang sign that he made was the rival gang of the boys in the car,
and upon seeing his sign they pointed a gun out the car window and shot at him.
Fortunately, the boy was not hit, and the car sped away.

HOW GANGS COMMUNICATE

Signals such as hand and body signals, special terminology or codes, dress, tattoos,
and graffiti are used by gang members to advertise their gang affiliation. A gang
can use one or all of these means of communication and may change its signs
frequently. No absolute rule exists, but local choices determine what is in vogue.
While it is imperative that law enforcement and school personnel be able to
decipher these forms of communication, the general public can also benefit from
education about gang communication.

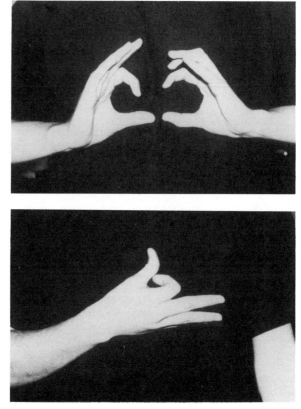

Hand signs such as this one representing the Compton CRIPs in Los Angeles are common indicators of gang affiliation.

Hand signs are used by black gang members. This is a symbol of the letter "b" representing the Blood gang.

Hand Signs

Youth street gangs adopted hand signs as a quick means of identification and as a method to challenge others, but the use of hand signs by organizations as a means to identify members is as old or older than verbal communication. Hand signs range from simple and unassuming to obvious two-hand configurations. Making a rival gang's hand sign backwards or upside down is a way to show disrespect. The practice of displaying hand signs is known as throwing, tossing, flashing, or shooting hand signs. Throwing hand signs can cause a spontaneous fight for which the casual observer sees no apparent reason. Some youth gangs also practice special handshakes to show gang affiliation.

Body Language

Gang body language involves the use of, or preference for, a particular side (right versus left), a style of walking, or even a style of standing. The use of body language is much more prevalent among the gangs of the midwest and eastern states than among those on the west coast, particularly among affiliates of the People Nation and Folk Nation.

The Folk Nation prefers the right side, and shows it in the following ways: members tilt hats to the right, wear their earrings and jewelry on the right side, tie shoes on the right side, roll up the right pants leg, and wear one glove on the right hand. They lean to the right and place their left arm over their right when crossing their arms. Affiliates of the People Nation may demonstrate the same behaviors, but with the left side.

Special hair styles are also a type of body language found among gangs of all ethnic groups. The short cropped heads of Skinheads and Sharps are the most easily recognized.

Language

Street gangs are no different than other subgroups in society that have unique vocabularies. Subgroups use special language as a common bond and as a barrier against intrusion by outsiders. This special gang vocabulary, like the English language, is constantly evolving, and it changes across regions and subgroups. Hispanic street gangs, who speak a mixture of Spanish, English, and street slang, even have a name for their specialized language—Calo.

Tattoos

Tattoos are a popular trend among all young people today. They are especially popular with youth gangs who use them for identification and to bind members closer to the gang. By permanently marking members with a tattoo, a gang has established a lifelong psychological bond. Tattoos also prevent dissatisfied members from joining rival gangs or attempting to leave the gang lifestyle behind. The placement and styles of tattoos vary, ranging in complexity from three dots or a Christian cross to large words or elaborate symbols.

Tattoos may be homemade amateur creations or professionally done and artlike. The amateur variety tends to be done by fellow gang members on the streets or by other acquaintances during incarceration in detention facilities. The homemade tattoo is usually distinguishable by its poor quality. Homemade tattooing is dangerous; infection as well as contraction of the hepatitis and HIV viruses are very real possibilities. Professional tattooing reduces these risks.

The placement of the tattoo is strategically and psychologically important in creating the right effect. Tattoo placement can tell much about an individual and his group. Gang members who don't want their gang affiliation readily known to others will have tattoos placed where they are easily and naturally covered by clothing. These individuals may be hiding their gang membership from family or the general public to avoid recrimination. Self-preservation may also be a reason

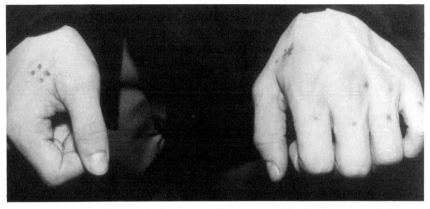

These tattoos show affiliation with the Hispanic Norteño gang. The four dots across the fingers and the four dots clustered in the web of the hand are an abbreviation for the number 14, which symbolizes Norte or Norteños.

Simple tattoos such as this Roman numeral 13 across the fingers are one of the first signs that a juvenile is involved in gangs.

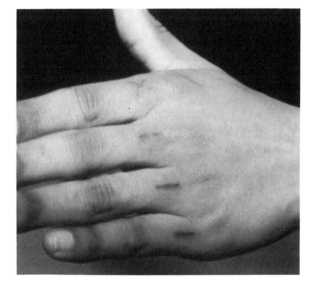

to hide tattoos, since a rival gang's ability to easily identify an enemy can shorten life expectancy considerably.

At the other extreme are gang members with tattoos prominently displayed to demonstrate their hard-core commitment. Such tattoos are meant to intimidate, and are usually placed on the neck, face, and hands so as not to be easily covered up; for example, the traditional teardrop tattoo of Hispanic gangs is placed below the outer corner of the eye. At one time this meant either that the wearer had served one term in prison or committed murder. Additional teardrops were for subsequent jail terms or murders. A tattoo of three dots, usually on the hand, stands for *mi vida loca* (my crazy life).

Asians attribute the same meaning to three dots, which may be scars from cigarette burns or hot coins. Asian gang members believe that burning these symbols on themselves shows greater courage. Asian gangs also use four and five tattooed or burned dots to represent other gang-related ideas. Branding gang symbols on the body is a similar practice found mostly in the southeast portion of the United States, though it is spreading. The recipient has a permanent scar that is believed to show dedication and courage, similar to that of the Asians.

Gang members who wish to leave the gang lifestyle behind them are often hindered by their permanent tattoos. Many former gang members find they are denied employment and social opportunities because of prominent gang identifying tattoos.

Removal of tattoos is difficult and expensive, and therefore a limited option. Several medical professionals and service groups have developed programs to remove prominent gang tattoos from former gang members. They provide this service free or at a reduced cost. Despite these types of programs, many juveniles are still not able to leave the gang lifestyle behind, and are trapped by decisions made without consideration for the total effect a gang-related tattoo can have on their lives. An important component of an anti-gang education program should include information about the impact of such tattoos.

Clothing

Many street gangs involved in drug dealing originally adopted dressing in their flashy colors as a means of helping potential customers locate them on the streets. This also had its drawbacks, since competitors and the police could also identify their adversaries. The more sophisticated street gangs have changed to less conspicuous modes of dress as a means of self-preservation.

Identifying apparel can range from the blatantly obvious to the nondescript. The gang-related apparel gives the individual a sense of being a part of something greater than himself, and boosts self-esteem in the same way that a military uniform can. Consequently, any form of disrespect to the clothing that symbolizes the gang commitment can create a reaction of potentially deadly violence.

A non–gang member may be physically harmed for wearing anything that a street gang considers its trademark. A mere refusal to turn over the offending apparel can result in death for the wearer. Identifying clothing items vary greatly, depending on the gang's degree of sophistication and maturity, and its geographical location.

HEADGEAR

Gangs may use the traditional baseball cap of a specific team. Sometimes the team's logo will be altered. The cap may also have markings on the outside from a permanent marker, especially under the brim, and the color usually reflects the gang's affiliation with a larger gang alliance, such as CRIPs or Bloods. Other types of distinctive headgear are also popular, including the Civil War kepi, a knit watch cap, and even a hair net. Bandannas are a common trademark too. Sometimes headgear is embroidered with the gang name or other affiliation information. Manufacturers' tags may be worn on the caps as a way of proving the cap is an expensive original.

JACKETS

Various types of jackets are worn, but the most popular in recent years have been professional sports team jackets. These jackets make the wearer appear more bulky and menacing, and also provide the wearer with an easy place to hide his weapons. The trenchcoat is another popular jacket, preferably in black; this coat, like the sports jacket, makes it easy to hide weapons, especially rifles and shotguns. A third type of jacket, the jean jacket, has long been popular with teenagers. It is often marked up with symbols or patches.

BEADS

The use of beaded necklaces and/or bracelets as a common gang identifier is a particularly strong phenomenon on the East Coast and in the Midwest of the United States. Street gangs have taken specific color combinations, typically two colors, and arranged them in a pattern of so many beads of one color alternated with another. Within the gangs, the patterns may even vary to designate positions of authority or duties. For example, among the Latin Kings, members generally wear five gold alternating with five black beads, but executive members wear five black with two gold beads. Anyone who is a trigger man or muscle for the group wears all black beads.

SHIRTS

Favored gang shirt styles vary greatly, depending upon local preferences or customs. The traditional khaki or plaid Pendleton shirts have long been popular with Hispanic street gangs. They are often buttoned all the way to the top, and shirttails are worn outside of the pants. This too allows for easy concealment of weapons. Blue work shirts and white T-shirts are also preferred clothing items, and gang members may mark them in permanent ink. Certain buttons may be buttoned from the top of the shirt, with the remainder left unbuttoned as a sign of gang affiliation. An example would be having only the top three or four buttons of a shirt buttoned to show allegiance to the Sureño (13) or Norteño (14) factions. Likewise, only the third or fourth button from the top of the shirt may be buttoned to show the same type of allegiance. T-shirts bearing certain messages, logos, or colors may also be popular with local street gangs. Some gangs have now adopted popular cartoon characters as their symbols.

PANTS

These tend to be baggy, again allowing for ease in hiding weapons. Denim jeans are popular, as are khakis, sweat pants, and long calf-length shorts which may be cut-off pants. Colors vary as desired by the wearers. Bib overalls are also a popular trend. Wearing only one side strapped up can be a sign of gang affiliation, based on the preference for right or left side. Pant legs rolled up on one specific side can also indicate gang affiliation.

SHOES

Brand-name sports shoes are very popular, especially in a gang's preferred color. If the desired color is not available, then colored shoelaces can be substituted. Lacing the shoe up one side or the other is also an identifying symbol of gang affiliation. Certain gangs prefer certain brand-name shoes. Some CRIP sets have adopted the brand British Knights, initials BK, to mean "Blood Killer" in reference to their opposing gang. The recent popularity of construction, military, or high-topped Doc Martens boots is an example of gang phenomena spilling over into the fashion world. In the mid 1990s this type of footwear, most often associated with the Skinheads, became a popular fashion item, worn by a growing segment of young people. Hispanic gangs have long been known for wearing highly polished oxford shoes or "hard shoes." They are a source of extreme pride to the wearer, and scuffing or stepping on them is considered a serious form of disrespect.

BANDANNAS

These are seen in many colors and are used differently by various individuals and groups. The traditional gang-affiliated bandannas of red and blue are now competing with brown, black, green, etc. These may be commercially purchased and altered by gang members with permanent markers or embroidering. Gang members wear them tied around the head, arm, neck, or leg. The side that they are worn on can also indicate affiliation. The bandannas are also sometimes folded and placed in a pocket with only a small portion showing.

This item may appear innocent but has been the cause of numerous violent confrontations. Sometimes an offending street gang member caught in enemy territory may be forced to perform some type of disrespect to his or her bandanna, or observe someone else committing such an act, as a penalty for trespassing. This would probably be in addition to a severe beating.

Schools and public shopping malls, such as in Stockton, California, have developed and attempted to enforce dress codes to curb the violence resulting from perceived slights or insults. Not all gang-styled clothing can be banished through dress codes, but such rules can help reduce gang influence and violence. It is important to remember that, although clothes do not make anyone a gang member, they can sometimes help identify gang members.

Graffiti

*After my jump in, I went into the park bathroom to clean up. One of the
guys handed me a pen and told me to go ahead and write my new placa on
the wall. . . . We had our first big rumble at the park. We tagged on walls
everywhere. We were making a name for ourselves.*

—MASE

The days of "Johnny loves Susie" etched into a tree trunk are disappearing. Though
the average citizen driving down the street thinks graffiti is just nonsense painted
on walls and fences, the majority of all graffiti is gang-related. A trained eye knows
that graffiti tells a story. It is the newspaper of the "hood."

Most people would agree that graffiti is destructive and contributes to the
deterioration of a neighborhood. However, graffiti is also an excellent tool for law
enforcement to keep track of gang rivalries, territories, and members. It is often

*This graffiti was found on a wall of an apartment complex two days after one of the gang mem-
bers was stabbed to death. In addition to the name of the Norteño gang, SSL, members' names
are also listed. In the left portion of the photo are two stenciled Aztec eagles that represent an
association between SSL and the prison gang La Nuestra Familia.*

used in solving crimes. Though gang graffiti is meant to be written in a code intelligible only to other gang members, many law enforcement officers have learned to interpret these codes. In one particular homicide, the responsible party used the victim's blood to write the name of the gang that the murderer belonged to on the pavement next to the body. It is not necessary that citizens be able to decipher the exact meaning of graffiti. It is important, however, that they recognize it as gang-related and take steps to notify the police and remove it as soon as possible.

GANGS USE GRAFFITI

To Advertise

Gangs will spray paint the name of their gang or set/clique to advertise to the area that they exist.

To Claim a Territory

Gang names will appear on walls to let other gangs know that this is their territory or neighborhood.

Common Graffiti Abbreviations and Their Meanings

AOK	Always Out Killing
ATC	Addicted To Crime
LTK	Live To Kill/License To Kill
187	California Penal Code Number for Murder
PSC	Perverted Sex Crew
TWY	Totally Wasted Youth
ITK	Intent To Kill
RTD	Ready To Destroy
916/415	Telephone Area Codes used by gangs to show where they're from
BK	Blood Killer
CK	Crip Killer
BNG	Bahala Na Gang. This is a Filipino gang.
ASW	Asian Street Walkers
SWP	Supreme White Power
XIV	Norteño
XIII	Sureño

This wall is an example of what happens when graffiti is not immediately removed.

To Challenge

Gangs will often cross out or "X out" another gang's name, or write it upside down as a challenge for control of the neighborhood or a challenge to fight. Crossing out a gang's name or *placa*, writing it backward, upside down, or split in two is an insult. Most gangs subscribe to the belief that no insult can go unanswered. Consequently, fights have erupted and, in some cases, gang members have been murdered for crossing out another gang's *placa*. Using the initials CK (CRIP Killer), BK (Blood Killer), LKK (Latin King Killer), VLK (Vice Lord Killer), etc. means that the writer or gang responsible for the graffiti is intending to kill rival gang members.

Graffiti will always contain the name of the gang and may sometimes include the street name (moniker) of the person that wrote the graffiti. Often, a large roster of the gang will be accompanied by monikers. When the *placa* is written in a gang's territory and followed by a roster, the last name on the roster is usually the member who performed the vandalism. Listing his name last is a sign of respect to the other gang members. On a *placa* written in a rival area, the person responsible writes his name first on the roster to take credit for the graffiti.

Graffiti is primarily used by Hispanic, Filipino, black, and white gangs. Recently, however, Asian gangs have begun using graffiti to advertise their presence and claim territory.

TAGGERS

Taggers are another identifiable group on the graffiti scene. Not your stereotypical street gang members, taggers usually operate independently or in small groups of two or three members; however, there are documented instances of tagger groups with as many as eighty members. A tagger will attempt to place or "hit up" their tag on as many locations as possible. This gives the tagger a feeling of importance or notoriety. The most notorious of all taggers was a Los Angeles tagger known as Chaka. Over a period of several years, he was estimated to have caused $500,000 damage and to have marked over 10,000 places before being caught. In another case, two taggers in Davis, California, accomplished twenty-eight hit ups in one night's work.

Tagger graffiti is just as destructive and unappealing as that of more violent gangs, but their motivation is entirely different.

TAGGERS USE GRAFFITI

To Express Themselves Artistically

The individual desires some outlet to show his or her creativity and ability to a large audience, although public acknowledgment of the identity of the artist may not be possible. Graffiti can be classified into three basic types or styles that are known as tagging, bombing, and piecing. Tagging is the simplest and quickest, involving only the marking of a tagger's initials, symbol, or alias. Bombing takes a little more time to complete and may be multi-colored and detailed. Piecing is the highest level, and often takes extensive time and work to complete. Examples of this would be multi-colored murals on walls.

Tagger Terminology

tagger/writer/artist	Someone who defaces property with spray paint, permanent marker, or etching tools.
rack/swarm	Steal graffiti materials from a store.
the heavens	Overhead freeway signs and billboards.
work/hit up/graffiti	What a tagger places on property to get attention.
crew/posse	Group of taggers who work together.
buff/rub out/snuff	Mark over another taggers work.
wild style	Tagging done with the tagger's name or group's acronym as a part of the work.
landmark/monument	A hard place to tag without being caught.

To Gain Notoriety

Satisfaction is derived from the concept that the tagger has placed something long-lasting or permanent in public. Chaka is an example of this type of tagger.

To Get a Thrill

Individual taggers and tagger gangs receive an adrenaline rush when tagging. The more dangerous the act, the greater the thrill. Another tagging fad involves the use of commercial stickers from manufacturers and youth-oriented products, such as skateboards and clothing, that can be placed anywhere discreetly. They are at first ignored, but soon become a real annoyance and are time consuming to remove.

To Vandalize

Taggers wantonly deface public and private buildings for purely destructive reasons. The perpetrator finds the act and its consequences pleasurable or satisfying.

To maintain a personal touch and fulfill their desire for notoriety, taggers like to sign their work using specific personal monikers or their group's designation. This can be either initials or a name with a distinctive spelling.

In order to preserve the memories of their vandalism, many taggers record their work on video camera or Polaroid pictures that they can later show off as trophies. Underground videos and magazines that promote the taggers' activities as desirable

Taggers are always looking for any public place to promote themselves.

and worthy of emulation have appeared. Some magazines that target youth culture even feature sections showing graffiti art. In 1993, taggers adopted a new method of gaining permanence for their work—they began to use glass cutters, chisels, and drill bits to carve into glass windows or walls. This damage is very costly to repair or remove, and therefore stays up longer for the populace to observe.

Tagging for thrill has become a growing problem across the United States. Many taggers have been seriously injured and even killed. Taggers dare each other to accomplish specific feats of vandalism. The more daring the tagging act, the more respect the perpetrator garners from his or her associates. The danger arises when a tagger paints over the graffiti of street gangs that are willing to kill in retaliation for what they perceive as a sign of disrespect. Some taggers in turn have started to carry weapons to defend themselves. Law enforcement agencies are reporting "tagger wars," a fairly new development in 1996. One nearly fatal incident happened in Stockton, California, where a tagger was caught by the opposing group while crossing out the signature of the artist. The group beat him senseless. Another danger in tagging occurs when taggers attempt to place their tags at dangerous places. Many taggers have been killed by trains, automobiles, or falls from structures while tagging. Taggers have also caused extensive damage and danger by painting over traffic signs.

COMBATING GRAFFITI

Communities have developed several approaches to combat graffiti, with varying degrees of success. Providing graffiti zones, areas where taggers and others can express their creativity and desire for notoriety, has had limited success. The area that is designated as a zone is usually removed from public view and provides the graffiti artists an opportunity to pursue their interests without the threat of arrest or community wrath. Communities are at risk of causing gang fights when rival gangs arrive at the same time to graffiti in the designated zones.

The ultimate graffiti zone allows for the creation of murals depicting historical and/or ethnic themes on designated community walls. These are usually commissioned by the community with graffiti artists of proven artistic ability. The risk is that all members of the community may not appreciate the "art."

Another somewhat successful method of graffiti control is to control sales of spray paint and permanent markers to minors. Strategies include recording purchases for later use in identifying vandals, and forbidding the sale of spray paint and permanent markers to minors. This solution has obvious shortfalls too. In order to reduce the consequent high level of theft (racking) of graffiti materials, some stores have placed spray paint and permanent markers in secured cages so that customers must request assistance to gain access to the items.

Eradication, a third approach to graffiti control, seems the most workable. Once graffiti is found, workers photograph and log it for police intelligence files. It is

Graffiti Examples

✡ Norte *Norte*, or North, refers to Northern California Hispanic gangs and a
1 x 4 possible affiliation with the northern prison gang, La Nuestra Familia. Sometimes the star symbol is used to represent the North Star.

NORTE *Mr. Smokey* is a moniker or nickname. *SS Lodi* is the South Side Lodi
SMOKEY (California) gang of which Mr. Smokey is a member. South Side
SS Lodi Lodi, or SSL, is a Hispanic gang. *1 x 4* stands for the fourteenth
1x4 letter of the alphabet, *N*, a reference to the north.

B̶N̶G̶ *BNG* stands for the Bahala Na Gang. This is a Filipino gang.

Sur *Sur*, or South, shows an affiliation with Southern California Hispanic gangs.

A5W *ASW* or Asian Street Walkers is a gang made up of primarily Cambodians.

 VNS or Barrio Norte Stockton is a Hispanic gang centered in North Stockton, California. The monikers that flank the VNS graffiti are a partial roster of the VNS members. Rosters are often included in gang graffiti.

Latin Kings *Latin Kings*   Originally a Hispanic gang but is now multiracial and nationwide.

NSGC *NSGC* stands for North Side Gangster CRIPs. *SSGC* stands for South Side Gangster CRIPs. CRIP gangs are primarily black; however, some white and Hispanic youths associate closely with certain CRIP gangs.

5 W P *SWP* stands for Supreme White Power. White racist gangs often use
this symbol, which is often accompanied by a swastika. *KKK* stands
KKK for the Ku Klux Klan. While the KKK is most active in the southern United States, there are active chapters all over the country, and white supremacist youth gangs often claim affiliation.

AFC *AFC*, or Art Fiendz Crew, is a Portland, Oregon, tagging crew. Note the distinctive spelling of the word *fiends*.

Phyn *Phyn*, pronounced "fine," was the distinctive moniker of a young tagger in New York who was killed when tagging on a subway track.

WxB *W x B* or Woodbridge Boys is a Hispanic gang located in Woodbridge,
—xIV— California.
Norte

✝ This inverted cross is an anti-Christian symbol. The FFF is equivalent
to 666, the mark of the beast, since F is the sixth letter of the
FFF alphabet.

⬠ *Pentagram*   Satanic symbol.

666.999 *Sign of the Beast*   Satanic symbol.

NATAS *NATAS*   Satan spelled backward.

Ⓐ *Anarchy*   Satanic or antiestablishment symbol.

Vice Lords One of many examples. Other symbols used include a half moon, pyramid, *Playboy* emblem, champagne glass, top hat, all-seeing eye, and cane. Note that Vice Lords are affiliated with People Nation, and the pitchfork is therefore pointed down and the stars have five points.

 Black Gangster Disciples One of many types of Folk Nation–affiliated graffiti. Note that the pitchforks are pointed up and that the star is six pointed.

then removed. This approach seems to work best because it limits the amount of time the graffiti is in public view.

Eradication programs assign removal responsibilities in differing ways. Some require property owners to remove graffiti in a specified period of time. Failure to do so results in a fine to cover the costs for removal by the city. Other forms of eradication programs allow volunteer groups or paid services to patrol the community and remove graffiti as quickly as it appears.

One option allows for restitution-based punishment of taggers and others who are mandated by a judge to serve time for their crimes or to perform community service by removing graffiti. One proposed punishment is to suspend the tagger's driver's license for up to one year. Communities have also used specific taxes on spray paint and markers to help pay for graffiti-removal programs.

Some courts have gone after the parents of vandals, arresting them for allowing access to spray paint and requiring them to pay fines as high as $10,000. Monetary restitution by the juveniles, along with their parents, has also been effective in some areas.

Technology has become a factor in the war on graffiti. Scientists have developed special paint that prevents other types of paint or markers from permanently bonding to its surface. The use of a portable laser that can remove one square yard of graffiti in ten minutes is the latest technique being used. The laser costs about $5.00 an hour to operate.

Several specialized businesses that operate profitably in the removal of graffiti have been created in metropolitan areas. Warning signs in graffiti-prone areas that list the penalties for placing graffiti are sometimes effective. However, this strategy may backfire and become more of a challenge than a deterrent. Finally, an abundance of motion sensors, lights, and surveillance cameras can also be effective in keeping graffiti vandals away from potential target areas.

The most effective way to address graffiti problems is to educate the public to the danger and costs of what many consider only harmless pranks. Knowledge is power, and informing parents and youth about the actual financial burden of graffiti to cities, schools, and businesses each year can open some eyes. This money could be better spent on student services than on repairing vandalism, especially graffiti.

To heighten the community's awareness about the growing problem of graffiti, Phoenix, Arizona, conducted a Paint Out weekend to show their support for the eradication of graffiti throughout their city. This program had the added benefit of giving city maintenance workers an advantage in their war on graffiti.

Victims and Survivors

The gangs aren't gonna do nothing but get you killed or get you in prison. All you gonna see is your friends die, even your family members. One thing you gotta remember, it's either your family or your gang. You're gonna substitute your gang for your family. The gang took my mom and my family from me. None of it was worth it!

—Oso

When a juvenile joins a gang, it not only affects him but his family, friends, neighbors, and entire community, as well. When he commits a crime, he leaves behind a trail of victims and survivors. At first, he may not see how anyone outside the gang could become endangered by his gang activities.

THE INNOCENT PUBLIC

When gang members engage in a violent confrontation, innocent bystanders, who happen to be in the wrong place at the wrong time, are often the ones who get hit with a stray bullet. The general community is also victimized, since gang activity causes businesses to lose customers and close their doors. Potential investment in a neighborhood is also obstructed, resulting in lost employment opportunities. Millions of dollars a year are spent on repairing, repainting, and repurchasing merchandise and buildings after gang vandalism. Vandalism, theft, and the devastation of gunfire and firebombs have become community nightmares. Insurance claims spiral uncontrollably in high crime areas, and police cannot guarantee the safety of potential customers. When merchants grow tired of being victimized, they move out of the area, often creating an economic hardship for the residents, who in the end are the final victims.

EFFECTS ON FAMILY

When a gang member becomes active in criminal activity such as vandalism and drive-by shootings, he can expect his home and family to be targeted by the rival gang. His brothers and sisters may be harassed at school and in public, and his home may be shot at or graffitied. A June 15, 1994, report in the *Sacramento Bee* described how one gang targeted the home of a rival gang member's mother.

> Bullet holes ripple across the side of the steel-gray stucco house in the Meadowview area. A shotgun blast punctuates the front, and the place is still charred from an alleged fire bombing attempt last month. In all, Cindy Portillo said, there have been six gang attacks on her house in the past six weeks, since her older son was incarcerated and his gang friends started hanging out to make sure she was okay. The worst was when her 14-year-old was shot in the back while opening the garage door. Police say it's not uncommon for them to see parents stuck in the violent morass of their offspring's gang affiliations, unable to fix the problem themselves and not knowing who to ask for help. "We go into a home where we're going to make an arrest for some serious crime and the parents are dumbfounded and overwhelmed by the whole experience."

Parents often suffer financially when their children become involved with gangs because many states have enacted legislation forcing parents to take responsibility for their child's behavior. If the child is arrested and placed in a juvenile or rehabilitative facility, the parents often must pay for the time spent there. A day's stay in juvenile hall can range from $20 to $100, depending on the parent's income. In some areas parents can be fined as much as $30,000 if their child breaks the law. Parents who cannot afford the fine are required to do community service work.

There is not one standard pattern or background environment that predisposes children to gang involvement. "I'm an ex-gang member," said one woman. "I do not come from a broken home. I do not come from the barrio. I do not come from the ghetto. I come from a middle-class white neighborhood. I became a gang member at the age of 13. I served three years in the state penitentiary for seven counts of attempted murder and was released when I was 21." Indeed, gang members come from all socioeconomic and ethnic groups. And while many parents may abuse, neglect, or ignore their children, causing the youth to seek love and respect elsewhere, other parents are loving, caring individuals who cannot understand what has happened to their children.

Frustrated and not knowing where to turn, these parents have also become victims. In the end, they are blamed for their child's actions by law enforcement, the schools, and the courts, regardless of the fact that they may have tried their best to control the child's actions.

Michael came from a moralistic, loving, hardworking family in San Joaquin County. His two brothers and sister were very popular in school and made good grades, but he always seem to attract the "wrong crowd." He eventually joined a large, active gang. His parents tried everything—counseling, strong discipline, tough love, but he wouldn't listen. At that time, both the local school district and the community were in denial that a gang problem even existed, so no prevention, intervention, or alternative programs had been created. His father later said, "Perhaps, if these had been available, things would not have turned out the way they did."

Through the gang, Michael obtained drugs and an indifference toward violence. One of Michael's friends was jealous of a girl who was dating another guy, so jealous that when the two teens were high on drugs, they kidnapped the girl and viciously murdered her. Although the gang was not involved in this murder, they did everything they could to protect their homies, including threatening the witnesses and members of the victim's family. One of the witnesses, the best friend of the murdered victim, had to move out of the country for the remainder of her school year until the trial because of the danger her family was in over her proposed testimony. During the months of the trial, both the victim's family and Michael's family got to read all the gory details about the crime in the recapped front-page stories that seemed to run daily in the local newspapers. Michael's brothers and sister got harassed at school for their brother's actions. Michael is now on death row, awaiting execution. The other teen got life in prison. How many victims were there to this crime?

In some families, however, joining the gang is just another family tradition. This systematically victimizes successive generations, who are trapped into joining the family gang and participating in its activities. Family support for the gang lifestyle is total, and any alternative lifestyle choices are nonexistent.

Law enforcement officials are now processing third- and fourth-generation family gang members through the judicial system and see no end to the problem. Often teachers and school counselors will come across a youngster who doesn't want to join a gang even though his family is involved. He gets pressure from his relatives, who see it as a fun and exciting club.

The youngster admires the way the girls flock around the gang members and the expensive cars and clothes the gang member owns (if he deals drugs or commits burglaries). Most of time this child has already been typecast by the school or community as a potential gang threat. While it's very hard for the youngster to be different, there are many success stories of teachers, counselors, and other caring non-parent intervention into potential or even active gang members' lives.

Immigration and the Gang Member

Often our laws and policies help to create gang problems in immigrant families. At a 1994 Southeast Asian Conference, the plight of confused immigrants was related. Laotian Family Services explained that many families move to this country thinking that family relationships will remain the same, with the father as the controlling and respected head of the family, while the wife and children remain submissive. The parents soon find that their inability to pick up the difficult language and assimilate into the new society causes a lack of respect from their formerly obedient children. In addition, they are told that they will be jailed if they use corporal punishment to control their troublesome teens, which is their culture's traditional method of maintaining discipline in the home. The only thing left for the frustrated parents is to remove the offending youth from the rest of the family.

At fourteen years of age, the troubled teen often leaves the home and moves into a home with other older Asian youths. The older youths extort money and goods from their own people in brutal home invasions, and the younger ones commit car thefts.

Immigrant families are also threatened with the loss of their visas if a child is involved in criminal gang activity. The law enforcement agency and Department of Immigration and Naturalization revoke the youth's "green card" and, because he is a minor, send the entire family back to the country of origin. Many of these families are already confused and intimidated about their disciplinary roles in our legal system. These problems are enhanced by the memory of abusive and corrupt police authorities in their homeland, which causes them to isolate themselves into small ethnic islands away from the fearful system. In immigrant families, the parents have become the victims as well as the survivors.

Girlfriends/Spouses

Girlfriends and spouses of gang members also suffer. Their boyfriend's gang affiliation determines their narrow lifestyle, dictating the styles and colors of their wardrobe; which friends are "acceptable," and where they can go. Often attending school becomes dangerous because of harassment from rival gang members; even walking to the store without protection becomes a risky act.

The female's role is one of submission. Males feel it is their right to see other girls, while expecting true fidelity from their girlfriends. Commitment and fidelity are not words a male gang member acknowledges easily.

> Yeh, I had a reputation. I was a shooter. I was quiet, but I always handled my business. It was something I liked to do. Getting guns is real easy. You can get 'em from pawn shops or dope dealers. You get to know a girl and see if her dad has any guns around the house. So I would have one of my homeboys keep her busy and I would search the house and take their guns. They were easy to get.
>
> —Flaco

The girlfriends are discouraged from returning to school as they may become more educated than their mate. They are also discouraged from getting a job, partly because of the boyfriend's insecurity and partly because of a fear for her own safety if rival gangs see her. A relationship with a gang member becomes a dead-end existence.

If their boyfriends are incarcerated, these young women are alone. They are not only expected to be faithful but to somehow pay for collect phone calls from the prison, visit the inmate regularly regardless of the cost or inconvenience, and acquire the necessities for themselves and their children—all on a minimum-wage job or welfare. Because of their choice in mates, they are often ostracized by the rest of their family. Many times they turn to selling drugs or prostitution to survive.

As time goes on, these young women get older and wiser and realize this is not the lifestyle they want for their children. They may try to get their mate to quit the gang. Unfortunately, even if he is able to resist the allure of his homies and gang lifestyle, old enemies are not forgiving and his life will be very restricted unless he moves out of the area.

Lack of education and job skills, not to mention being tattooed and having acquired the look and walk of a gangster, make it hard for him to get a job. If he's been convicted of a felony crime, it will be hard to obtain credibility and trust from an employer. He can't even join the armed services if he has a felony on his record. It's a continual uphill fight until he can get his life reorganized, and many times it's a lot easier to fall back into a life of crime. He has become a victim of his own earlier choices.

How Death of a Gang Member Affects His Family

In September of 1994, Eloy Javier Gonzalez, a member of an Oakland street gang, was buried in a grave site next to one occupied by a rival gang member at the Mountain View Cemetery. Since that time both grave sites have been subjected to repeated vandalism by the opposing gangs, causing Eloy's mother constant grief.

When a gang member dies, his family's victimization by gang activity does not cease. Certain gangs have made funerals a gang ritual; members appear, take photographs, and eulogize their fallen comrade. They attempt to make him a martyr and to unify the group in revenge. Gang members create photograph albums and wear shirts known as "funeral shirts," depicting the deceased member's picture and gang-related information. Gang members may wear these shirts to school or when avenging the deceased. Funerals may be targeted for additional gang violence since the deceased member's former associates are in attendance. Drive-by shootings and other violent acts may occur at the funeral. Younger family members may see this whole scene in some romantic or heroic light and vow to join the gang and seek revenge. The cycle of violence and grief then continues.

Two examples of funeral shirts

Rick's Report

LORD HELP ME!

It was August 16, 1994, at approximately ten o'clock at night. Cyco had just been released from two years of incarceration in the deserts of Arizona. He was sitting on the front porch of his house with his brother and a street preacher known as Jose. Jose was explaining to Cyco the evils of gang membership and why he should not renew his relationship with his past homies. Preacher Jose had once been a member of the Norteños and was fully aware of the perils involved in gang banging. He got out of the gang and decided to spend his free time trying to prevent younger guys from making the same mistakes that he had made at their age.

Gangs were nothing new to Cyco. Cyco's brothers had been involved in gangs, and he had joined a gang at the age of eleven. His boyhood idol was his brother, who had been sentenced to prison in 1991 and while there, picked up an additional few years for stabbing an inmate. I once brought Cyco home when he was 11 years old for wearing gang clothing. He was young, but I was the immature one for thinking I could save the world. I was met at the door by his mother, who did nothing to ensure that he stop wearing this type of clothing. She had already lost control of him, and his father did nothing to discipline him. He did as he wished and ignored his parents. Cyco was used to hanging out with the boys and getting into trouble. He thought it was a lot better than going to school.

On this particular evening after Cyco's release, he sat with his brother and Preacher Jose in a circle on the front porch, trying to escape the late summer heat. It was hot and miserable inside the three-room house. No one on the porch noticed when the black, primed Monte Carlo with the red vinyl top drove past the house without slowing. Within minutes, the car reappeared at the end of the block, and once again drove up the street. The car slowed in front of Cyco's house just long enough for him to see the barrel of a shotgun come from the passenger window. Before he could yell, there was a blast from the gun, and he felt a burning sensation in his arm. Everyone on the porch was up and running when the second blast fired from the vehicle. This time it wasn't Cyco, but Preacher Jose who was shot in the legs and feet. The Monte Carlo sped away. Cyco's brother had also been hurt by a scattered lead shot.

When a neighbor came out of his house next door to Cyco's to investigate what sounded like a gunshot, he saw a black, primed Monte Carlo speeding away. He couldn't believe what he was seeing. The speeding car was the same car that he had sold the previous night to a guy from a nearby town. Less than 24 hours later, the buyer was using the car to shoot at a friend and fellow gang member.

All three victims were taken by ambulance to the hospital. Cyco and his brother were treated and released, and Jose spent the night before being released the following day. It only took two days before all three people in the Monte Carlo were arrested and in custody. The three suspects and occupants of the car were Norteños with extensive criminal histories as juveniles. The driver and the shooter had each turned 18 a few months prior to the shooting, making them adults. The third person, who sat in the back seat, was 16 years old. Upon his arrest, the 16-year-old convinced himself that he had done nothing wrong. In his mind he was just the passenger and therefore was not guilty of any crime. The 16-year-old was tried as an adult and all three were charged with attempted murder, street terrorism, armed with a firearm during a felony, and shooting a firearm from a vehicle. If convicted, all three were looking at life in prison.

Six months after the shooting, the three suspects were still in custody. Two days before the trial was to begin, all three pleaded guilty to the shooting. The driver and the shooter were sentenced to eight years in the state prison. The passenger in the back seat was convicted as an adult and sentenced to one year in the county jail.

Since that shooting, Cyco has been the victim of two more drive-by shootings and is now 14 years old. He can be found hanging out with the homeboys every night of the week, drinking, smoking, and fighting. Preacher Jose only preaches indoors these days and is rarely seen on the streets.

Everyday Life: Gangs in American Culture

I've thought about it a lot. I know now that whatever you're exposed to, that's what you become. When kids get exposed to violence, they think it's the right thing to do. In the projects, kids have to fight every day. If you don't fight, people will mess with you. I had older brothers and cousins who made me fight. Then it was just like, forget it. I joined the gang. I was just out there, shooting up everything and everybody.

—California Youth
Authority Inmate
Corey Shaw, 23 years old.
Stockton Record, Nov. 5, 1993

DOES GANSTER RAP AFFECT KIDS?

Sandra Davis, founder of Mothers Against Gang Wars, relates the following incident:

"We were having a 209 (area code for San Joaquin County, California) Party, which had been planned for a long time. Getting several rival gangs together in a neutral setting had taken a lot of hard work. But, here we were. Everyone was having a good time dancing when the music was changed to some gangster rap. All of a sudden the atmosphere in the room changed. It was filled with agitation and anger. The crowd in the room separated into two groups. A line was formed down the middle of the room and the male members of rival gangs stood across from each other and to the beat of the music began to throw signs at each other. The tension grew and I knew we had to change that music. So, I hurried over to the DJ and put a different popular song on. Within a few minutes the atmosphere returned to a neutral setting and the guys wandered back to their friends and dates. People have told me that music makes a difference, but until that moment I hadn't believed them."

Gangs in the Boardroom

This bitch comes walkin' through our block wearing her Cowboys jacket. We got her good. Made her take it off and spit on it. Then we beat her ass good so she'd remember us. I got the jacket now in my room.

—Female gang member

MAKING A PROFIT FROM THE GANG LIFESTYLE

Selected businesses have profited considerably from the growth and popularity of modern street gangs. Millions of advertising dollars are aimed at large groups of young people who want to wear what is "in" for that season, and often what is "in" originates with the street gangs. For example, the loose, baggy, low-hung pants and long T-shirts worn by gang members for several years became a fad when the media caught on. Suddenly, well-known retail stores were carrying these clothes, and many non-gang youths were happily buying the same apparel. Often an individual wearing this baggy look is mistaken for a gang member by both the authorities and gang members with disastrous results. This is especially true if the individual favors certain colors.

Athletic and Logo Apparel

The most obvious profiteers, in the general public's view, are shoe and sports apparel manufacturers, whose name brands and styles are worn by street gang members across the nation. At one time, wearing a sports team logo on a hat or jacket implied following and supporting that team. Generally such affiliations were regional, and the majority of children and teenagers in a given area supported one team. Liking another team might be considered somewhat deviant, so one would keep such an opinion private. Today that philosophy is out of tune with the street gang mentality. The most important aspects of sports apparel tend to be color and/or the letters and symbols in the team logo.

According to the Sporting Goods Manufacturers Association, the average American spends $193 per year on sports apparel. Broken down by age group, those between the ages of 13 and 17 spend the most, averaging $311 per year. This number diminishes steadily with each successive age group, with the lowest spending group being those over 55, who spend an average of $155 per year. Obviously, marketing will focus on the youngest consumers—those who are purchasing the most product.

The amount of profit to be made on the sale of officially licensed professional sports team merchandise is increasing at a tremendous rate. According to Major League Baseball, the National Football League, the National Basketball Association, and the National Hockey League, combined sales of their officially licensed merchandise rose from $5.5 billion in 1985 to over $12.1 billion in 1992. This doesn't account for unofficial products with team logos.

Manufacturers recorded domestic sales of over $5.5 billion for athletic shoes in 1990, and an additional $2 billion for the sale of related apparel with affiliated logos or brand names on them. Advertising expenses for athletic shoe manufacturers in that same year amounted to more than $200 million, with Nike spending the most at $60 million.

Although the manufacturers of athletic shoes and clothing are not responsible for the misuse of their products, logos, and/or brand names by gangs, these companies do market to youth, and there is a need for greater social responsibility on their behalf in this marketing. *Sports Illustrated* published an exposé on the athletic shoe industry in its May 14, 1990, edition, revealing several disturbing stories about the marketing of these shoes to inner-city youth. The magazine reported on several sales representatives of major shoe manufacturers who wanted to use youthful drug dealers and street gang members as walking advertisements.

Such promotion of the images of drug dealers and street gang members brings into question the true motives of corporate salesmen. Marketers hope that youth who see these "role models" wearing the latest athletic gear will want to purchase the same item to emulate that successful, bad, and/or dangerous image. One sporting goods store owner, who questioned the practices of his athletic shoe suppliers, was told to enlist the local drug dealers as marketing tools by supplying them with free shoes. He refused to name manufacturers directly, fearing they would retaliate by damaging his credit.

Another indicator of the marketing strategies targeted at youthful gang-oriented buyers is the appearance of team hats in the wrong colors. This new trend is quite disturbing. A visit to a well-stocked sporting goods store may surprise the average person. Several team hats now come in colors totally unrelated to their official team colors. Explanations from salespeople vary, but the bottom line is that they sell. Street gangs no longer need to mark over the logos because the manufacturers do it for them.

Professional sports teams are not the only benefactors of the street gang dress code. Many major college teams also take in gang-related revenues resulting from the increased sales of their licensed team products. The apparent widespread popularity of several teams across the country is not always attributable to their athletic success; often the appeal is in the teams' colors, initials, and logos. For example, many gangs who favor the color blue and may use the word *gangster* in their gang name, such as the Black Gangster Disciples or the Eight Tray Gangster Crips, wear the blue Georgetown hat. There are numerous variations of this example, but one can readily surmise the direct relationship of sales of specific teams in an area to gang activity.

Fresno, California, has been plagued for many years by the increasing violence of its many ethnic street gangs. Several street gangs claim the Fresno State University mascot, the bulldog, as a symbol, and they use it to promote themselves in the community and vicinity. The university administration discussed the possibility of changing school colors and mascot in order to distance the university's image and that of its teams from the gang violence in the community. Additionally, it was considered potentially dangerous for students to wear clothing printed with school colors and logos. School officials backed down from considering the change after influential alumni protested, and the administrators realized that the misuse issue was not really under their control.

Teacher Mike Miller has one explanation for students purchasing team apparel that is not in official team colors.

> One day while teaching, I noticed several students in class who had purchased L.A. Dodger caps that were not in the official team colors. I was very curious as to why a cap with the obvious L.A. logo on it would be made in maroon and dark blue until I thought about my own knowledge of gang colors and the use of sports caps as indications of gang affiliation. I was even more curious when I thought about the how students wearing these caps were not, to my knowledge, involved in gangs and seemed to have no desire to join one.
>
> I decided to ask several of these students, and others that I came across, the reason for the caps in such odd colors and why they had bought them. Surprisingly, I found several students who had bought the caps because they believed that the colors would make them appear neutral to any potential gangs they came across, and they wouldn't be bothered. Some others purchased the same hats because they had seen them at school and thought that they looked good, and wanted to wear what others were wearing. It made me start to take notice of the hat and jacket selections that students were wearing, and wonder what might have started making certain colors and teams popular with the students on our campus. After thinking about this for awhile, I began to ask students randomly why they bought certain items. Most would reply that they just liked the team, but occasionally some would admit that they bought it to be safe. Wearing the wrong color and/or team could, they felt, get them hurt.

The appeal of popular sports gear to street gangs is relatively easy to understand. Street gang members often lack maturity and self-esteem. Advertised by the nation's best athletes, the image promoted by the marketing campaigns of most popular athletic apparel is one of success and talent. On the street, this may provide the only identification outside of the street gang. The high cost of these items also promotes self-esteem and a successful image. To lack any of these material representations of success can harm an image or reputation. The incomes derived from gang activity can help members attain these items along with the positive feeling of immediate gratification. Stories abound in which gang members have several pairs of expensive shoes and/or clothing items but own nothing else of monetary value. They place the highest value on these items.

Graffiti Removal

The plague of graffiti on buildings and cars throughout American cities has created a demand for new products and profitable opportunities for entrepreneurs and large corporations. Inventors at Dow Chemical developed a surface coating for buildings and walls that causes paint sprayed on them to bead up and be easily washed off.

Another approach is the creation of anti-graffiti businesses that will paint over graffiti given 24 hours notice. These have been popular in larger metropolitan areas. One such company in the San Francisco Bay area has opened three outlets to service customers needs.

Electronic Devices

The image of the drug dealer in constant communication with his clients has created a demand for pagers and cellular phones. Although most juveniles have no use for these devices, they have become popular status symbols in many areas of the country. Some parents use them to stay in contact with their children during the day or evening and to monitor their whereabouts. Many students like bringing them to school to provide distraction and achieve notoriety. As a result, most electronic communication devices are banned on school property. One specific problem arises when actual drug dealers perceive the owners of such devices as competing dealers; the individual carrying such items may be targeted for robbery or elimination.

Safety Products

The tragedy of innocent bystanders caught in the crossfire of drive-by shootings has influenced the development of several new products. A contractor in San Antonio, Texas, developed a bulletproof home insulation. This material is promoted as a means of saving lives and energy at the same time.

Children's manufacturers are now designing and marketing bulletproof vests to be worn inside clothing. Parents who fear that their children may be caught in gang crossfire coming from and going to school can purchase these special vests for protection.

Recently the city of Los Angeles tested a bullet resistant shield for streetlights and found it impervious to most gunshots. Street lights are routinely shot out by street gangs and drug dealers and the replacement cost is $500 per light. The shield costs approximately $130, but the savings for replacement costs should easily offset the initial costs for the city's Bureau of Street Lighting.

In response to the frequent occurrence of patrol cars being shot at by gang members, the Los Angeles Police Department has begun protecting officers with vehicle armor plates. At a cost of $1,000–$1,200 each, the department will begin installing plates in the front doors of its vehicles. The estimated cost to armor over 900 patrol cars is nearly $1 million.

Even in the area of gang prevention there are many companies making a large profit providing posters, videos, and seminars for communities in need. Many nonprofit organizations and government clearing houses will provide the same material for free or at a much lower price, but communities are often unaware of these services.

Even in the political arena, one of the buzz words for election and reelection is crime, especially juvenile crime. As more and more cities acknowledge this growing gang subculture, numerous politicians will most likely jump on the bandwagon. In the fall of 1994 many politicians campaigning to win or keep office used the cry "build more prisons" at the expense of proposing alternative-based prevention programs.

Stockton, California, claimed a 30 percent rise in juvenile crime after many prevention programs were slashed in 1994. Logically, the $32,000 spent to house one juvenile in a California Youth Authority facility for one year could go a long way in supporting more effective gang prevention, intervention, or suppression programs.

ADVERSE EFFECTS OF GANGS ON BUSINESS

The crimes and problems associated with street gangs can severely effect business profitability. Many businesses consider themselves to be waging economic war with street gangs because of the gangs' negative influence on customers. Customers who perceive dangerous street gangs in an area will change their shopping habits, possibly avoiding a particular neighborhood completely.

A 1994 poll of 1,000 people by the America's Research Group revealed several important consumer attitudes about crime:

1. In the last year or so, have you changed the way you shop due to a crime problem?
   Yes: 37%   No: 63%
2. If you changed, how?
   Don't shop after dark: 44%   Don't use cash: 8%
   Keep doors locked: 24%   Carry security device: 4%
   Shop with someone: 15%   Other: 5%
3. What types of stores are you shopping at less due to crime?
   Convenience Store: 41%   Drug Store: 10%

Department Store: 21%   Mall: 8%
Grocery Store: 12%   Other: 8%

The results of this poll indicate that over one third of consumers surveyed are changing their shopping habits due to crime. Nearly one half are declining to shop after dark, which impacts considerably upon retailers who depend upon steady customer sales throughout a shopping day. Many shoppers are fearful of large groups of rowdy, potentially dangerous teenagers. Businesses face the dilemma of keeping older customers and also attracting the teenage shoppers, who alone account for over $30 billion a year in retail sales.

Gang-related crime has forced the business community and local authorities to examine their attitudes and reactions. Street gang activities have become so prevalent that many people no longer find them unusual. As gangs proliferate, they tend to increase their range of criminal activity as they search out new territory and opportunities for exploitation.

Many street gangs practice extortion, taxing their victims to guarantee themselves a steady source of income. Street vendors in downtown Los Angeles have been required by street gangs to pay "rent" to ensure continued health and safety. Many of the vendors are afraid to inform police of the shakedown, and some even feel that the gangs are providing more protection than the police. Vendors have stated that gang members will settle disputes for them and have even come to their assistance when they're being robbed. The 18th Street gang, a Hispanic street gang that claims a large amount of territory in downtown Los Angeles, has boldly established Sunday as their regular collection day for rent payments. Asian street gangs are notorious for forcing protection payments from Asian businesses. The victims rarely report the problem; there is a traditional mistrust of law enforcement authorities based upon experiences in their countries of origin, as well as a feeling that the police cannot provide adequate protection.

Shoplifting, also known as boosting or racking, has been a traditional street gang enterprise, useful in demonstrating bravado and stealth as well as in obtaining minor trophies. Shoplifting is sometimes used as an initiation requirement. Most often gang members commit this crime to entertain and test themselves, or to lift such items as alcohol, cigarettes, spray paint, and marking pens that they cannot purchase legally. The crime is usually nonviolent but can quickly turn violent and even deadly if a gang member is caught.

Incidents of assault, hostage taking, and murder have occurred when store employees have confronted gang members over shoplifting. Aggressive and violent street gangs have targeted convenience stores for armed robbery because they can make an easy and quick profit. Shooting even unresisting customers and employees is considered part of the robbery scheme; this eliminates potential witnesses. Convenience store owners and managers are increasingly aware of how such robberies impact profit, as well as customer and employee safety.

Many communities are now requiring convenience stores to have two or more employees working during certain hours as well as improved visibility from the outside. Additionally, new stores cannot be built in remote locations; police and customers must be able to view the stores clearly from populated areas. Video games, a high profit resource, are being removed from stores to discourage juveniles from congregating.

The city of Gainesville, Florida, enacted a model ordinance in 1987, incorporating several of the above-mentioned strategies. This helped reduce convenience store robberies by 80 percent, and has been adapted for use in the state laws of Florida and Virginia to help reduce convenience store robberies.

"Swarming" is another gang phenomenon. Caravans of cars, full of gang members and associates, will target a specific convenience store, arrive at one time, and literally ransack the store, assaulting employees and customers. After vandalizing the store, gang members flee in separate directions, making it difficult for law enforcement to track them. During the summer of 1993, caravans of up to 100 vehicles were cruising around Sacramento, California, swarming several stores in an evening. Police used aerial surveillance and attempted ticketing caravan vehicles for dozens of traffic violations.

Victims Who Sue

The growing trend of crime victims suing businesses on whose property they've been victimized has led merchants to attempt to reduce their liability and vulnerability. Businesses in shopping malls must both attract customers and maintain a sense of safety and security. Unfortunately, street gangs have used malls as a battleground to establish themselves and build reputations; consequently, there have been frequent confrontations between rival gangs in shopping malls, with resultant shootings endangering innocent shoppers.

The management of a mall in Newport, Virginia, had severe problems with juveniles and gangs congregating every evening. These groups were driving away customers with their unruly and violent behavior, and mall security regularly confiscated weapons from them. In response, the mall manager implemented a 6 P.M. curfew whereby anyone under 18 years of age would not be admitted into the mall unless accompanied by an adult. The result was an 80 percent decrease in security incidents within the first 90 days.

Many shopping malls across the country have used similar enforcement techniques to keep gangs and violent juveniles from deterring customers from shopping on their premises. Highly visible security officers, once thought to have a negative influence upon customers, are now seen as giving a more positive and reassuring impression. The use of dress codes and rules that forbid the congregation of large groups on mall premises also help to prevent trouble. However, several retail malls have been sued for discrimination over their dress codes, and they have lost the cases or settled out of court. A 1991 lawsuit brought against the Great America theme park by the American Civil Liberties Union found that dress codes using a standard "gang profile" were discriminatory. Most businesses have since corrected their security policies to reflect a focus on behavior rather than appearance.

Gangs and the Military

Socially, my life revolved around a group of eight guys called the "Hoods."
Teenage gangs were big in the United States—we'd seen them in movies.
And though there was nothing criminal about us—we were all athletes, letter-
men, and good guys, and considered ourselves the junior class elite—we
loved the gang trappings. We had a Hood's nickname: there was Baby Face
and Chopper, and the Chief. I was Cuddles, as a result of having smooched
with one of my girlfriends on a city bus. We had a gang uniform: a white
dress shirt with the sleeves rolled up and a pack of cigarettes in the pocket,
white socks, loafers, letter sweaters, and Levi's.

—General H. Norman Schwarzkopf,
It Doesn't Take a Hero

MILITARY DEPENDENTS AND GANG INVOLVEMENT

Street gang violence and related incidents have been cropping up at military installations in the United States and around the world at least since the 1940s. Far too often there was a lack of concern about gangs, and due to the constantly changing military life, they didn't appear to have much of an impact. The most often seen cases involve military dependents who have a very mobile lifestyle, changing their home station at least every two years. These delinquent kids coming into the military housing areas don't have much time to establish themselves or their gangs before they and the entire gang membership move on. Most often, they become involved in some type of minor criminal activity such as vandalism. Before becoming sophisticated enough for the local authorities to bother with, the gangs break up due to family relocation to other installations. More serious problems occasionally erupt when gangs of military dependents fight with local youth groups over control of school areas or popular hangouts. Fortunately, these are kept to a minimum, as the military dependents have access to their own facilities at their home installation, which helps keep the groups separate. Smart installation commanders always insure that they have recreational facilities and programs available for youthful dependents so as to keep them from becoming a major headache to them and local law enforcement. This has been especially important since the 1970s when the U.S. military became an all-volunteer force, and most of the volunteers who stayed had families.

In 1994, the Defense Department estimated that it had 1.4 million children of active duty members who lived on or near military installations in the United States and overseas. Out of this number, they estimated that 400,000 were between the ages of 10 and 18, just the age for gang involvement. What worries military officials the most is the mobility of the dependent population. A youngster may become involved in gang activity at one installation and bring that knowledge and influence with him to a new facility. For this reason, a problem at one installation cannot be considered in isolation.

The impact of street gangs increased at many military installations during the 1980s, as it did in other locations. Many military installations are located close to high-crime areas, which has directly influenced the behavior of some military dependent children. Gang-style graffiti appears regularly near or on some installations, along with an increasing number of incidents of vandalism. Parents in the military have become concerned about the gang activity in local schools, where they have to send their children. The old animosities between locals and military dependents are now becoming more serious as the locals form street gangs that do not disappear when military dependents move on. Assaults at schools and drive-by shootings occur in local civilian communities, and even at installation housing areas, causing military parents to become more vocal. The Defense Department, at the urging of installation commanders, has begun to organize conferences to discuss these common problems. It has provided increased funds for additional programs aimed primarily at the 10- to 18-year-old age group. Training of military law enforcement on street gang crime and community policing techniques also has become more widespread, as well as better coordination with local police agencies. Commanders of installations now encourage new programs whereby service members volunteer their time and talents in the local civilian community to help in schools and assist in recreation programs. In Europe, the army even went as far as creating a command level task force specifically to help them address the prevention of youth violence. This is seen as especially important since increasingly violent confrontations have occurred between German and American gangs. One incident is known to have involved a gun. Although these coordinated efforts have been in place for only a few years, their positive impact should soon be apparent.

GANG MEMBERS IN THE RANKS

In addition to gang members among the children of enlisted military men and women, there have always been some gang members in the ranks of the armed services. From the 1940s on, the military draft has caught a large number of juveniles from street gangs and given them a taste of the world. In the past, as these street gang members entered the military, they could leave their gang affiliations behind and start anew. This was sometimes the easiest pathway out of the street gangs.

However, starting in the 1960s with the Vietnam War, some former street gang members saw little or no future in the military and, after doing their time, got out and brought their military skills back to the streets. These returning prodigal sons were eagerly welcomed back to the street gangs, as their technical and combat training could be very useful. It is also important to remember that during this time, many street gangs were becoming politicized and active in civil rights causes, which at times erupted into urban violence. Gang members trained to make bombs and use automatic weapons fit nicely into the scenario.

With the elimination of the military draft in the early 1970s, the forced exodus of juveniles from the streets into the armed services no longer existed. At first, in order to fill its needs for manpower, the armed forces lowered the standards for potential recruits and readily accepted almost anyone they could enlist. As the image of the U.S. military rose from its post-Vietnam low, and service conditions improved dramatically, the standards for recruits became more stringent. The services are now more selective in accepting recruits, but with quotas to meet, some recruiters still lower themselves to some unusual tactics to lure potential recruits. An example of this is a recruiting ad placed in the street gang magazine *Teen Angels* in the 1980s, which directly solicited street gang members to join the California National Guard. The ad played upon the desires of its intended audience to handle and shoot guns, and emphasized the access National Guard members have to ammunition and weapons. Despite these types of drastic attempts to recruit street gang members into the military, it has become more difficult for the gang bangers to enter the armed forces. Academic standards are more stringent, and criminal backgrounds also make it difficult for many to be considered acceptable for military life. Despite this, some are still able to enter the military and supposedly escape the streets.

In the early 1980s, the military encountered gang activity among enlisted white supremacists. The military, by its nature, is very attractive to these types of individuals. A sense of patriotic service and a desire to obtain training in combat-related skills is a common trait. Many enter the services with their preconceived racist ideology, and despite mandatory military training in equal opportunity as well as exposure to members of all races as peers and leaders, they retain their twisted beliefs. Some individuals were even able to actively recruit new members in the service. Several white supremacist organizations, such as the Ku Klux Klan, were successful in recruiting members of the armed services, especially the army and navy. Military authorities have tried to suppress these organizations within the respective services, but they continue to appear occasionally.

The dangers that extremist gangs pose to good order and discipline in the military is obvious. In 1985 Libya's Colonel Muammer Gaddafi, in a live satellite broadcast to a rally attended and supported by members of Chicago's El Rukn gang, urged black servicemen to desert and bring their military skills and knowledge to Libya. Although there were no known takers, the scenario exists for gang members to purposely infiltrate the military. What is sometimes overlooked is a service member's ability to serve illegally as a conduit of weapons and supplies to groups outside the military. The loss of large amounts of military equipment, especially from the National Guard and Reserves, has long been a closely guarded secret of the Defense Department. Weapons and supplies are often lost despite security measures to prevent such losses. Many times, investigations of the losses show that they were the result of deliberate actions of individuals in the military or by civilian employees of the military. The gift of antitank rockets, claymore mines, plastic explosives, and other light weapons to members of the local White Patriot Party in Fort Bragg, North Carolina, in 1985 was the result of collusion between soldiers from the post's 18th Airborne Corps and the white supremacist gang. The soldiers even helped to train the gang in how to use the weapons.

Military law enforcement authorities began to acknowledge the problems of street gang members entering the military in the late 1980s. During the spring of 1988, sailors at an enlisted men's club at the U.S. naval base in Long Beach, California, had to be restrained after waving red and blue gang bandannas, claiming to be rival Crips and Bloods. Naval Investigative Service officials downplayed the incident as just an attempt to imitate what the sailors had seen about gang lifestyle in the film *Colors*. Other incidents have occurred on or close to military installations, especially in southern California. Most involve local street gangs coming onto installations and becoming involved in confrontations with dependent youth, but service members themselves occasionally appear as subjects in incident reports.

Military officials have sought to develop liaisons for training on street gang crime, sending their law enforcement personnel on ride-alongs with Los Angeles Police and Sheriff's Department gang units. Military law enforcement personnel now attend seminars on street gang crime conducted by civilian law enforcement agencies. Military leaders' primary concerns are the possibility of gang members becoming active in the armed services and maintaining their allegiances to the gangs, creating a pipeline not only for stolen weapons but also for drugs. The potential for military vessels and aircraft being used to help smuggle drugs and weapons is also seen as a very real danger. Though there is a need for domestic intelligence gathering on local gangs and membership, the military has been forbidden by law to do this since the early 1970s. They must rely upon local, state, and federal law enforcement agencies for information of this nature. Without the cooperation of these agencies to share information, military law enforcement would be forced to operate in the dark in trying to combat gangs in the military.

In 1991 the commander in chief of the Pacific Fleet issued a warning to his commanders that the threat of gangs in the military was real. An investigation, ordered by the chief, revealed that sailors and marines had been joining street gangs based in southern California. The investigation reported an incident of a drive-by shooting in front of a navy enlisted men's club, as well as fighting taking place between ships' crews involving sailors who were rival gang members. Still, the military continues to have problems with gangs, both in the service and with dependents.

In July 1995 a *Newsweek* article reported on gangs in the military. Its investigation revealed that gang activity had been documented by all four services at over 50 major installations around the country. Pictures taken during Operation Desert

Storm showed service members flashing gang hand signs. The article also revealed that the documented crimes associated with gangs in the military now include drug trafficking, robbery, assault, and at least ten homicides.

In December of 1995, an incident involving three white soldiers from Fort Bragg, North Carolina, served as a rude awakening to the American public about gang members in the military. The three soldiers, who had openly espoused white supremacist sympathies, were arrested for the random murder of a black couple. They were members of a group of soldiers at the post who believed in Skinhead ideology but had not previously acted on it. The Army quickly reacted to the incident with an investigation that became worldwide in scope. Although limited to white supremacist groups, the investigation showed the Army that gangs in its ranks were becoming an increasingly severe problem.

The *Newsweek* investigation found out that a U.S. Department of Justice street gang symposium in 1994 advised attendees that street gangs were now becoming more sophisticated in weapons technology. The gangs are known to be receiving training in the use of grenades, rocket launchers, and explosives by gang members who are or have been in the military. These gangs were cited as having the ability to take terrorist-style warfare to the streets.

The availability to street gangs of massive firepower and illegal weapons is not the only concern. Manuals written by former members of military special operations units, such as the Army's Green Berets and the Navy's SEALs, are easily obtained through any bookstore today. These books illustrate how to make explosives out of ordinary household chemicals and materials, and methods of setting booby traps. Many of these military techniques are useful in an urban environment as well as in rural settings.

In fact, law enforcement authorities are coming across these techniques in their activities against drug operations. Many crack houses and gang hangouts have been designed not only to slow down police during a raid, but also to injure or kill any intruder. Marijuana-growing operations and methamphetamine labs in rural areas use booby traps frequently as a way of slowing down or stopping law enforcement officers from entering the area too easily. Military close combat skills are also being adopted by street gangs. The U.S. army Military Police School was warning its trainees in the late 1980s of street gang members practicing a specific technique to disable law enforcement officers who were armed with the new Beretta 9-mm pistol that the military was then issuing to all units.

THE ROLE OF THE MILITARY IN FIGHTING GANGS

The United States military has escaped the negative image of serving as a federal police force. But this status may change due to current political pressure. Many countries have occasionally had to use their national military forces to maintain order and keep the government in power. The United States has had similar incidents whereby federal troops have been used to enforce laws and restore order.

The Whiskey Rebellion during George Washington's term of office was likely the first major incident requiring the use of federal troops to enforce unpopular laws. During the Civil War, federal troops had to be used to put an end to the draft riots plaguing several major northern cities. The army, under then Chief of Staff Douglas MacArthur, handily dispersed World War I veterans in 1932 who were demonstrating in Washington, D.C., for a desired bonus payment for past services rendered. Modern-day examples are more apparent with federal and state troops being used to enforce desegregation orders during the 1950s and 1960s, and to quell race riots that began in the 1960s and continue today in places like Miami, Atlanta, Detroit, Chicago, and Los Angeles.

In most instances, state National Guard or federal troops have been called in to assist local law enforcement personnel in restoring order. This has created a perception with some citizens and political leaders that the National Guard should be used to help defeat gangs and crime in our urban war zones. In March of 1993, the mayor of Washington, D.C., Sharon Pratt Kelly, requested that Congress authorize her to mobilize National Guard units to help local law enforcement fight crime in the nation's capital. Although not successful in her bid to gain that authority, her request did put a spotlight on the issue of using National Guard and federal troops for such purposes. Already National Guard troops have been used in Texas to demolish crack houses, and California's National Guard works with state and federal law enforcement authorities in drug suppression and border surveillance. In Sumter, South Carolina, National Guard troops supported a massive three-day sweep of the community's high crime areas, assisting in more than 80 drug-related arrests and the confiscation of illegal weapons. In October 1995, U.S. National Guard troops in Puerto Rico were used extensively to help raid a 494-unit apartment complex in San Juan that had become a haven for drug dealers and gangs. Additionally, the military is being used to help staff and organize boot camp–style correction and education programs in various states. The drawback to these types of operations is the increasing dependency on the use of state and federal troops to fight domestic crime, which takes the military out of its true constitutional role of national defense and turns it into a national police force.

The Los Angeles Riots

The Los Angeles riots in April of 1992 made many leaders and citizens realize the danger that gangs now pose in profiting from urban disorder. These riots shut down Los Angeles and created a national panic. Unchecked fires set by rioters resulted in so much smoke that authorities were forced to close Los Angeles International Airport.

Street gangs were most apparent in their activities on the second day, as they organized looting runs to specific businesses. They were even credited with random sniping at innocent targets, such as a church meeting where ways to control the rioting were being discussed. The influence that the street gangs had on the initial flare-up of disorder at the intersections of Florence and Normandie Streets in Los Angeles should not be underestimated. Police at this intersection were attempting to disperse a crowd of people when they came under attack by rocks and bottles. In the back of their minds, they knew that the drug-dealing gangs in the area were well armed, and that gunfire was surely to erupt next. The officers used the only option available to them by leaving the area when the crowd grew large and started to swarm their position. The result was unexpected mayhem as riots broke out in south-central Los Angeles in response to the impression that the police had given up control of the streets.

Television reporting of the rioting was thought by many to be promoting the violence. Mayor Tom Bradley of Los Angeles asked local stations to return to regular programming on the second day of riots to help calm the city. Media coverage was even blamed for causing simultaneous riots in Las Vegas, Nevada, which also had National Guard troops on the streets, as well as San Francisco, California; Madison, Wisconsin; Atlanta, Georgia; and Toronto, Canada.

The L.A. police had been unprepared for such an event. Despite several warnings from community leaders, no effective plan was in place to deal with the situation, especially during the first few critical hours when control was still possible to maintain. After four days, order was finally restored, but not until state and federal troops had been brought into Los Angeles to help.

The aftermath of the riots caused a review of state and national civil disturbance plans and training. The State of California commissioned a study of the State National Guard during the riots. It found itself severely behind the times in training and planning for such events. It was later stated by the Adjutant General of the California National Guard that what helped make his troops effective during the rioting was not the information from the army's Field Manual 19-15 based on 1960s-style civil disturbances, but the urban-combat training they had received for their wartime mission. The after-action report specifically pointed out the need for preparation in confronting gangs during future civil disturbances, especially the more than 100,000 gang members residing in L.A. Many countries throughout the world have already seen the evolution of street gangs into organized crime syndicates or revolutionary movements. The possibility is always there for the United States to follow that path, too.

Gangs in the Schools

There was one person that I'll never forget. It was a schoolteacher who had a lot of interest in kids. She took me under her wing. She taught me how to read and write. She was probably the most important person in my life.

—Former gang member

According to the 1991 National Crime Survey, approximately 3 million thefts and violent crimes occurred on or near public school grounds during that school year. This means that a crime is committed in or near schools every six seconds for a total of 16,000 incidents per school day.

Each school system is more or less a reflection of its community, and the gang problems of the community will usually be centered in the schools. In the 1991 National Crime Victimization Survey, 15 percent of students responding to the survey acknowledged that street gangs were present on their school campus. Over one-third, or 35 percent, stated that they feared being attacked while in school and almost one-fourth, or 24 percent, feared attack while going to or from school.

Schools have responded to this threat. A more recent 1993 survey conducted by the National School Board Association of 729 school districts nationwide, representing 5 percent of all districts, found that 15 percent of the districts now use metal detectors to screen for weapons at school. Half of the districts searched student lockers on a routine basis as a preventative measure to keep drugs and weapons out of their schools. Almost one quarter, 24 percent of the districts, reported using drug-sniffing dogs as a part of their efforts to decrease school crime and violence.

Despite these measures, students assaulted other students in 78 percent of the school districts, and 60 percent of districts reported students assaulting teachers in the past year. The incidence of weapons being confiscated on school grounds was reported by 61 percent of districts, with 31 percent reported a shooting or knifing, and 23 percent reporting at least one drive-by shooting.

Schools throughout the nation serve as communication centers for communities; they are also the recruiting grounds for future gang members. By effectively combating gangs in schools, communities can greatly reduce gang power and influence.

SIGNS OF TROUBLE

Graffiti

Graffiti is the newspaper of the neighborhood for the streetwise. As previously explained, graffiti is an important tool used by gangs and taggers to communicate their existence and intentions. With graffiti, they advertise themselves and attempt to intimidate others even when they are not present. By not challenging its existence and quickly removing graffiti when it first appears, school administrators allow it to increase. A gang will place graffiti anywhere that it can and will continue to search out new and highly visible targets.

The first appearance of graffiti in the school may be in the bathrooms and other seldom monitored areas. School books are also common targets and are frequently being vandalized if there is no appropriate system checking for damage. Graffiti vandals will next move to more open targets such as notebooks, furniture, and outside walls. They begin to get more brazen about placing their trademarks in public when they are not being challenged by authority. The placement of the graffiti can indicate the claiming of territory on campus by rival groups and should be noted for future reference. Immediate removal or covering of graffiti on all surfaces is important to keep it from proliferating. Even graffiti that may appear innocuous should be removed.

Students in possession of spray paint, permanent markers, or etching tools are likely to be involved in gang or tagger activity. Many schools across the country

Trends in School Violence Over a 5-year Period Ending in 1994

Small cities (pop. under 50,000)		Medium cities (50–100,000)	Large cities (100,000 +)	Average cities
Increase	31%	46%	55%	38%
Same	47%	44%	35%	45%
Decrease	6%	5%	8%	6%
No problem	16%	5%	2%	11%

Are student/neighborhood gangs a factor?				
Yes	27%	52%	72%	39%
No	73%	48%	28%	61%

Nearly 25% of school dropouts cite "trouble with gangs" as the primary reason for leaving school.

Gang involvement is admitted by 43% of males and 21% of females who drop out of school.

Source: Survey of police and city officials in 700 U.S. cities conducted in August and September 1994 by National League of Cities.

Gangs

Letters are applied to hats to display gang names. The letters LK, meaning Latin Kings, have been ironed onto this cap.

now prohibit such items on their campuses, and possession of them is considered a serious breach of school rules.

Clothing

Certain styles of dress do not necessarily indicate gang membership, but they can influence the beliefs of others. Many current fashion trends are influenced by the clothing of gang-associated rap artists and musicians sporting the "grunge" look. This blurs the distinctions between gang identity and normal current fashion. Certain trends, such as specific colors, team names, or logos being worn by identifiable groups, should be noted by school officials. Sometimes the most unlikely items, such as a colored rabbit's foot or colored shoelaces, may indicate some group affiliation. Students belonging to gangs and attempting to conceal their activities from parents at home may change clothes after leaving in the morning.

Clothing bought by parents can also be altered or marked to indicate gang affiliation. Caps may have logos crossed out and may be marked or embroidered with the street moniker of the wearer. Sometimes the gang name or other information is written underneath the brim. Many times jackets and/or jeans have cryptic graffiti written all over them. Additionally, clothing worn in some unusual way often indicates gang affiliation, such as one pant leg rolled up or a bandanna tied around one arm. A heavy coat or jacket worn at inappropriate times or places may also indicate an attempt to conceal something.

Schools across the country have developed dress codes to handle the problem of students being mistakenly targeted by rival gangs. Many students and parents feel this to be an infringement of their individual rights, but the safety of the majority of students needs to be considered above all else. In 1994 the state of California enacted a law giving each school district the legal right to establish and enforce dress codes, even allowing the option of mandatory school uniforms.

Tattoos

Gang tattoos identify an individual's gang affiliation and may also indicate the street name or moniker. Often the tattoos mirror local graffiti. Individuals most commonly have tattoos placed on their body where they can be easily shown but still concealed. Some students draw tattoos on their hands and arms with an ink pen to show off and get approval from their peers. This is a way for gang members to demonstrate their dedication to the gang. As students get more involved in gangs, actual tattoos replace these penned-on versions; members receive tattoos from other gang members or professionals who will tattoo minors. Generally, the more obvious the placement of the tattoo, the greater the gang involvement of the owner. An increasing number of gang tattoos on campus most likely means that the number of gang members is increasing, along with their commitment to the gang.

Territory

The selection and claiming of certain common areas in school by an easily identifiable group can be a precursor to gang activity. When gangs lay claim to areas of a school, they often defend them with violence. Teachers, administrators, and students should take note of areas where certain groups tend to congregate before, during, and after school. If most students tend to avoid certain areas, this may indicate claimed locations where violence is feared. For example, if students are waiting until class time to use the restrooms, it may be because a gang occupies them at all other times, prohibiting normal student use.

Hand Signs, Vocabulary, and Nicknames

Hand signs are popular due to their appearance in rap videos and on advertisements. The fact that a gang or a group of potential gang members has acquired a hand sign is not a significant indication of activity, but it does show some formal identification. The use of and response to hand signs can demonstrate the members' degree of commitment to their gang. The failure to respond to any sign of disrespect by another group "throwing" their hand signs means a loss of status. Teachers at schools with a high degree of gang involvement note that whenever gang signs are flashed, bystanders generally scramble to safe territory to await the mandatory retaliation.

The "show-by" in which gang members drive past another gang is another way for a gang to demonstrate its presence and challenge rivals. Gang members cruise through the rival's neighborhood or past its school, flashing hand signs and verbal taunts. The show-by can be a precursor of escalating violence.

The use of gang terms and nicknames for individuals and groups is another indicator of increased gang activity. Although many young people are exposed to gang terms and names via music videos, the flagrant and consistent use of these terms should be readily noticeable. Their appearance in gang graffiti should also alert administrators to increased gang activity and sophistication.

Appearance of Unusual Wealth

The sudden display of wealth by students in school may indicate gang involvement. Although the image of the gang member with a lot of gold jewelry and cash, conducting business with a pager or cellular phone, may not apply to the average gang banger, there are other more subtle signs. Gang members may at times accumulate large amounts of cash if they are involved in drug sales, burglaries, or auto theft. Their maturity level may often lead them to spend their cash profits on items that they believe will gain them status, such as clothes, athletic shoes, team jackets, etc. Additionally, those involved in household robberies may show off stolen items as trophies. The sudden possession of expensive electronic devices, such as video camcorders, laptop computers, and cameras, should alert school authorities to the possible off-campus activities of the individual claiming to own them. Administrators should notify law enforcement authorities when expensive items appear on campus unaccounted for.

Increase of Crime and Vandalism

Increased crime and vandalism at school and in the surrounding community may indicate gang activity. Crimes may include damage to public property, aggravated assault, burglary, auto theft, rape, arson, and even murder. The increase in crime may also be a secondary result of other gang activity.

Initiation into many gangs now requires the commission of some type of crime. These initiation crimes may be committed at or near school since this locale provides many convenient targets. A perpetrator can also demonstrate bravado by committing a crime in closely supervised school surroundings, protected by other students' "code of silence."

By targeting the school and terrorizing students and staff, the gang can quickly establish itself as a force. The gang's reputation will generally spread throughout the community as it expands its activities. Often school administrations attempt to handle problems in-house, for fear of being seen as weak or incompetent.

Seeking help and combining anti-gang strategies with groups outside the school is the only way to build a coalition to control the gangs. For example, filing civil charges against students for crimes committed on school grounds will immediately focus attention on the serious consequences of their actions. A teacher in West Palm Beach, Florida, personally filed criminal assault charges against a student who punched her as she attempted to break up a fight. The school administration had punished the student with a ten-day suspension, a weak penalty for the offense and one that sent a weak message to other students.

Declining Attendance

Low or declining school attendance signals danger. School districts often receive funds based upon daily attendance; absences mean lost funding. It is important to know that even good students will avoid coming to school if they fear gang violence or are being pressured to become involved.

Early warning signs may include students arriving late and leaving early or as soon as school dismisses. Students may also be habitually tardy in the attempt to change classes when there is the least movement and potential for conflict. Gangs recruit new members early and late in the school year in order to replace others who may have been killed or incarcerated. During this recruitment period, attendance may decline when students feel the pressure of active recruiting. Additionally, attendance may drop considerably during periods of growing tension between gangs. Students not wanting to be caught in the crossfire of the coming confrontation will skip school until they feel the danger has passed.

Gangs may also affect attendance and participation at extracurricular activities. Some schools have noticed a decline in student attendance at athletic events and even dances as many students avoid potentially dangerous situations. In October 1995, a football game between two rival California high schools was canceled due to officials' fear that students would be injured in gang violence.

What do truant, suspended, and expelled students do with their time? They may become a problem for law enforcement and the community. Often these individuals become involved in such crimes as burglary, disorderly conduct, and other mayhem, since they are unsupervised for most of the day. In 1994, San Jose, California, decided it was not cost-effective to pursue truant youth, and the rate of daytime burglaries rose immediately by 12 percent. In three years of experience with its anti-truancy program, Charleston, South Carolina, has reported a drop of 37 percent in daytime burglaries. Oklahoma City, Oklahoma, has had a similar program for five years with a similar drop of 30 percent in daytime crime.

Alternative discipline programs, such as in-school suspension, prove more effective and less costly alternatives in the long run. Some communities have taken the parents of truant students to court, charging them with child neglect. A police phone call to parents is about 90 percent effective in preventing further truancy, according to the San Jose, California, Police. Another unanticipated benefit to cities keeping students in school has been a declining dropout rate.

Weapons on Campus

A 1993 survey by the Centers for Disease Control and Prevention indicated 11.8 percent of students surveyed said that they had carried a weapon in school within the previous month. The problem of students bringing weapons to school is of growing national concern. The November 8, 1993, issue of *U.S. News and World Report* featured a cover story about the level of violence and the alarming number of weapons-related incidents occurring in our schools every day. Most often, students are bringing weapons to school to protect themselves from others.

School districts have responded to this issue in a variety of ways. The use of metal detectors at school entrances is on the rise nationally. Some schools have removed lockers and force students to use clear plastic or nylon mesh book bags. They even require coats to be checked in at the beginning of the school day.

Intelligence Gathering

Students want to feel safe. An unwritten "code of silence" exists in all schools that students should never turn in their peers. Administrators and teachers must counter this by nurturing in their students a sense of responsibility for their safety and that of others. Students need to learn that they can inform on peers in order to protect them and others from potential injury and even death. Often when students do attempt to approach school staff about a dangerous situation, they want assistance or intervention. The staff member needs to be sensitive to the situation and the possible repercussion for the student providing the initial information.

The Antelope Valley Union High School District north of Los Angeles established a program in November of 1994 rewarding students for information about classmates who bring drugs or weapons to school. In the first three months of the program, tips provided by students resulted in 38 arrests and 5 handguns being confiscated. The important point to understand is that students, if properly supported, will break the code of silence to ensure their safety and that of others.

Schools with crime, violence, drugs, and gangs are not only an urban problem; many rural and suburban schools are faced with these problems daily. Schools like Central High in Rapid City, South Dakota, close to the Mt. Rushmore National Monument, report students staying home or leaving school due to gang presence. School officials add that students have stopped wearing red and blue because of the colors' gang association.

Gangs in the Media

If it bleeds, then it leads.

In April 1992, 18-year-old Ronald Ray Howard killed State Trooper Bill Davidson when stopped for driving a stolen vehicle in Houston, Texas. Howard, a crack cocaine dealer, later attempted to blame the influence of gangster rap music and an unhappy childhood growing up in the inner city for the shooting. The jury found him guilty as charged and sentenced Howard to death by lethal injection. A juror stated that although music can have a strong effect, people are ultimately responsible for their actions.

The influence of street gangs on our daily lives is best exemplified by the appearance of stories or urban myths based on gang culture. Several of these stories appear in media periodically as factual, as part of a news story, or as a story in itself due to the need for official denial by local authorities. These stories are now being posted on the Internet as a part of an urban myth Web site that portrays them for what they truly are. Although several myths may have at one time or place been based in fact, most often they are now too distorted to take seriously.

An example of this type of urban myth being circulated is the rumor of gang initiation requiring the murder of the occupant of the first vehicle to flash their headlights at a gang initiate's car. An incident similar to this occurred in Stockton, California when a woman driving through a shopping mall parking lot flashed her headlights out of courtesy at a car with dimmed headlights that contained members of a local street gang. The gang members took this as a challenge or show of disrespect and killed the woman. Most peculiar is that most of these urban myths involving street gangs concern membership initiation.

MEDIA INFLUENCE ON SOCIETY

The entertainment, news, and advertising media exercise a powerful influence on society, and they have played a major role in the public's growing awareness of street gangs. Since the 1970s, newspapers and national magazines have carried stories on youth street gang problems, and such attention has increased exponentially during the 1980s and 1990s. A 1988 shooting outside a Stockton, California, theater may have been a turning point in the national media attention given to street gangs. Patrons waiting to buy tickets outside the theater were caught in the line of fire when a gang member committed a drive-by shooting, targeting a member of a rival gang who was standing in line. The people in line were waiting to see the film *Colors*, one of the first hit films about gang life and violence.

In such cases, the film celebrities become intimately connected to the gangsters firing shots. Entertainment media merges with the news media, and a relationship is established. The entertainment celebrities are sought to promote themselves and other products through advertising. However, this type of association may also backfire for the celebrity, as in the case of actor Edward James Olmos. He revealed in 1993 that he was being targeted for death by the Mexican Mafia due to his realistic, unflattering portrayal of the organization in the film *American Me*. As a result, he moves on a restricted schedule and in the accompaniment of bodyguards.

Often, the public has a difficult time separating the celebrity's image of gangster violence from the reality. The difference between image and reality is even harder to grasp for young people growing up with a barrage of images and ideas that are contrary to accepted public values.

Many fear that the antisocial values promoted in various media have created skewed attitudes and expectations of behavior for the nation's youth. Because of the tremendous influence media exercises, there is a national outcry for greater responsibility in the media today.

Guns, gangs, and juveniles capture the headlines throughout the country on a daily basis.

Gangs

News Coverage

Media decisions are motivated by complex forces. Television news reporting is no longer just the factual presentation of events. Most news producers feel a certain amount of sensationalism is necessary to gain viewers. More viewers result in higher ratings and, thus, greater advertising fees, which produce more revenue for the station. The story is very much the same for newspapers and magazines who need to maintain a level of readership that will guarantee continued advertising. The nonprofit Rocky Mountain Media Watch Group surveyed 50 newscasts in 29 different cities on the night of January 11, 1995, and found that crime, disasters, and war made up 53 percent of the stories, with a high of over 70 percent in some cities.

Gang activity is easily exploited by news organizations as an attention-getting story. Most often, responsible journalism has prevailed with stories designed to inform the public about gangs. Occasionally, some news organization fails to be responsible and attempts to manipulate stories for increased sales or television ratings.

A case in point occurred on the February 16, 1993, front page of *USA Today*, when the newspaper ran a story about the potential violence after the Rodney King trial controversy. Under the headline "Sooner or later, justice will happen," was an attention-grabbing photo of five young black men brandishing weapons and giving the camera a mean stare. The true story was that these five young men were part of an effort to promote a "guns for jobs" program that was organized by the community activist and singer Cashears to create positive alternatives for inner city youth. The young men believed, as did Cashears, that the photograph would be used as part of an article about their attempt to start a "guns for jobs" program in the South Central Los Angeles community. Tom Bradley, then mayor of Los Angeles, and Representative Maxine Waters, whose district includes South Central Los Angeles, were outraged at the paper's inappropriate use of the incident to sensationalize violence.

Readers wrote letters to the paper and severely criticized the blatant exploitive nature of the photograph. *USA Today* ran an apologetic editorial about accuracy and attempted to explain the misplaced photo as a bureaucratic mistake.

Gangster Rap

The music most often associated with street gangs is a form of hip-hop music commonly known as *gangster rap* or *gangsta rap*. The origin of rap can be traced to the east coast of the United States in the late 1970s. Artists appeared on street corners, in underground clubs, and anywhere else an appreciative audience could be found. Commercial recordings of rap artists were few and far between until 1979, when the Sugarhill Gang released an album called Rapper's Delight, marking the commercial emergence of rap.

Throughout the 1980s rap became more popular, moving quickly across the country. Groups using mild lyrics and themes gave way to groups whose hard angry raps were laced with profanity. The trend continued through the early nineties with few restrictions on the vulgarity of rap lyrics. As the image of the gangster rapper became more closely tied to rap, rap lyrics talked more about life in the inner city and the social conscience, or lack thereof, of the artist.

Despite gangster rap's popularity among youth, radio stations across the country have called the music "socially irresponsible" and have edited offending lyrics, limited play, or refused to play it at all. Such actions were the subject of many feature news stories in 1993. Protests by several groups against gangster rap's derogatory portrayal of women and blacks became national news. Despite these objections, the saga of gangster rap continues. The tragedy of this situation is the failure of rap artists and recording companies to responsibly address the influence that their music has on young listeners. In September 1995, as a public response to outcries about the negativity and violence espoused by gangster rap, Time Warner divested itself of Interscope Records, which distributed its rap artists' music.

Sales analysis indicates that gangster rap is popular among blacks, Asians, Hispanics, and whites. Fascination with the "gangsta" image is creating a cult following for the "gangsta rap" stars, who cultivate an image as drug dealing gang bangers because that is what their fans admire.

The death in March 1995 of rapper Easy-E, a former member of the early rap group NWA (Niggaz With Attitude), forged the connection between image and reality. Easy-E, whose real name was Eric Wright, was only 31 at the time of his death from AIDS. Wright was born and raised in Compton, California, a gang-infested area of the Los Angeles metropolitan area.

A former drug dealer, Wright was a member of a notorious Compton-based street gang and used his gang credentials to promote the authenticity of his music. Wright even bragged about having fathered seven children by six different women, part of his image as a ruthless womanizer.

By having lived the life he rapped about, Wright promoted an image as an authentic gangster rapper. He was not a "studio gangster," as fans have labeled many rappers. Wright and NWA had a big impact on rap culture with the release of their 1988 album, "Straight Outta Compton." It depicted vividly the lifestyle of street gangs, with lyrics about drive-by shootings, drug dealing, and confrontations with police. Its depiction of violence helped to sell over 2 million copies of the album despite the lack of radio play due to graphic contents.

Wright's life and death supported the negative messages of gangster rap—to live life fast and hard before dying. By dying young, Wright's immortalization as a rap star was ensured among young hip-hop followers.

Several other rap stars have also demonstrated that their art mirrors their life. Dr. Dre, another product of the Compton, California, gang scene, has a police record that helps to promote his gangster persona. He lives as though adhering to his own lyrics—"Rat-a-tat and a tat like that/Never hesitate to put a nigga on his back." Even after achieving celebrity as a rapper, Dr. Dre beat a woman in a Los Angeles night club.

The ongoing saga of Calvin Broadus, known more popularly as Snoop Doggy Dogg, is another example. He's been arrested for possession and sale of cocaine, charged with a weapons violation, and linked to the murder of a rival gang member by his bodyguard. Broadus followers believe these incidents help legitimize his work. The incidents do not seem to have hurt the sales of his 1993 release *Doggy Style* and the 1994 album *Murder Was the Case*. Despite this popularity, Snoop Doggy Dogg said, "As far as my acting career, I want a role of an attorney. I don't want to be remembered as a gang member."

Tupac Shakur, another successful actor and rapper, is also known for his scrapes with the law. In 1993, he was arrested for allegedly being involved in the shooting of two Atlanta, Georgia, police officers. Within three weeks, while he was out on bail, he was again charged as an accomplice, along with two associates, to the forcible sodomy and sexual abuse of a woman in a New York City hotel, a crime for which he received a sentence of four and a half years. Although he was imprisoned at the time and unable to promote or make a video, Shakur's latest album release, *Me Against the World*, was *Billboard* magazine's number-one album for several weeks during March and April of 1995.

Shakur's short span of stardom came to a halt when he died on Friday the 13th of September 1996. Six days earlier Shakur was the victim of his image after being shot several times by unknown assailants while riding in the car of Marion "Suge" Knight, the president of Death Row Records. This undoubtedly would raise his gangster image to an even higher level of reality and sell more albums.

Another rap artist, Christopher Wallace, known as the Notorious B.I.G., a.k.a. Biggie Smalls, was gunned down in March 1997 by unknown assailants. Wallace was known as an East Coast–style rap artist in contrast to Tupac Shakur's West Coast style. Rumors began to fly about a feud between gangs on each coast of the United States being responsible for the deaths of both rappers. The truth, however, is probably that each was a victim of his own hyped image that he created for himself, and it just got out of control. Gangsta rap may have reached its peak as record sales have begun to slow for the genre. Even Dr. Dre has softened his image and is said to be going back to a rhythm-and-blues style of music.

Music recording companies have not been shy in attempting to exploit gang rivalries and interest in gang lifestyle. In 1993, Dangerous Records released an album titled *Bangin' on Wax*. Sixteen supposed members of various Blood and CRIP gangs from the Los Angeles area who were amateur rappers were featured on the album. To enhance the mystic image of the rappers, their faces were covered by bandannas in the appropriate blue or red colors, and they were listed on the album only by their street monikers. The album's producers claim their intent was to bring rival groups together to show them their similarities. Such peaceful intentions, however, were not evidenced in the album's selections, with such titles as "I Killed Ya Dead Homies" and "Another Slob Bites the Dust." The album producers also attempted to claim community responsibility by donating a percentage of the album's profits to recreational facilities in Compton and South Central Los Angeles.

Music, as an influence on gang violence and image, is not limited to the black rap artists who have received the most media and public attention. Several bands popular with Skinheads and white racist groups do not get equivalent coverage and are therefore largely unknown to most people. The groups' albums are not carried by most music stores as a result of their limited appeal. Some such music is only available through bootleg tapes passed around at meetings of white hate groups. These groups, including Screwdriver and White Rider, may appear to the uninformed as two more malevolent heavy metal rock groups, but careful listening reveals lyrics as vulgar, racist, and violent as those of the gangster rappers.

Gangs Portrayed in Books

In 1991 Léon Bing, a journalist who had written cover stories about Los Angeles gang life for *L.A. Weekly* and *Harper's* magazines, wrote a book titled *Do or Die*. The book sold many copies, introducing many readers to the attitudes and behavior of South Central Los Angeles street gangs. It described the difficulty its young characters faced living in the urban war zone created by street gangs and their violence. Bing recorded the actions and statements of both Blood and Crip gang members in a factual, enlightening presentation.

Bing's book introduces readers to street gang "hero" Kody Scott, known on the streets as Monster Kody. Scott joined his street gang in 1975 at age 11, and despite several gunshot wounds has survived life on the streets. He served time in the security housing unit of the California State Prison at Pelican Bay and is known as a ruthless killer who admits to participating in drive-by shootings from the age of eleven. At age 13, he acquired his street name, Monster, based on a brutal beating that he inflicted upon a robbery victim.

Scott, despite his lack of formal education, has educated himself. His 1993 book, *Monster: The Autobiography of an L.A. Gang Member* has sold over 75,000 copies in both hardback and paperback versions, earning Scott at least $200,000 in royalties.

While in prison, Scott took on the guise of a revolutionary and continues to portray himself and those who follow his beliefs as soldiers who are fighting an unjust system. His book is laced with references to the revolutionary ideology he promotes in the attempt to create a new-found image of himself as a guerrilla fighter. His ideology has resulted in a name change to Sanyika Shakur. Scott has also become a member of the Republic of New Afrika, an organization that advocates the takeover of five former slave states as a new homeland for American blacks.

Gangs on Television and in the Movies

Television and films have been a very popular and influential medium for transmitting information about gangs. The weak portrayal of L.A. gang life in the 1988 film, *Colors*, preceded several better and more realistic film representations. The primary focus of these films has been the L.A. gang scene, resulting in a predominance of knowledge across the nation about CRIPs and Blood.

The 1992 film *American Me* told the story of the origins of the notorious California prison gangs La Nuestra Familia and the Mexican Mafia. Actor Edward James Olmos portrayed one of the founders of the Mexican Mafia who was killed by his own gang. Shortly after the film opened, two consultants for the film were killed in gang-style executions, and Olmos believed himself to be in danger. He hired bodyguards and changed his normal activities accordingly. Suspicions about the wrath of the gang were confirmed when Joe Morgan, the godfather of the Mexican Mafia, filed a lawsuit against Olmos. Morgan claims that his life story is portrayed in the film without his consent. As of this writing, Olmos continues to worry about a possible contract on his life.

The 1994 HBO documentary *Gang War: Bangin' in Little Rock* gave a fresh view of gangs outside of L.A. Its portrayal of black and white gangs in Little Rock, Arkansas, showed the national migration of gang activity and the influence of popular music and film in promoting youth gang culture.

The 1994 film *Mi Vida Loca* presented a different angle on gangs. Following the lives of several Hispanic female gang members from the Echo Park section of Los Angeles, the film presented the impact of gangs from a female perspective. Although not a commercial success, the film did try to promote some understanding of gangs without gratuitous violence to make its points.

Gangs in Periodical Publications and Advertising

Gang lifestyles and values have been introduced to young people across the country through a variety of periodicals. Most music magazines today cover the hip-hop scene with interviews, articles, and news about the stars and their latest escapades. Such articles may be mild, but they often include profanity, as well as talk of gangs and tagging.

Several youth music magazines, such as *The Source* and *Street Beat*, contain pictures to accompany their articles, including specialized graffiti sections that credit the creators of the graffiti and have tips on graffiti art, as well as interviews with some of the top graffiti artists. They provide a far-reaching billboard for taggers to display their work and promote their reputations.

One of the most interesting gang-related periodicals is *Teen Angels Magazine*. Published since 1981, this magazine is aimed at young Hispanic youth involved in the California gang culture. The magazine combines Hispanic pride in heritage, anti-Japanese rhetoric, and patriotism with warnings of government conspiracies. Featuring letters, drawings, and pictures by young Hispanics, it covers a variety of themes including gangs, prison, religion, and love.

Teen Angels invites readers to submit items for publication along with payments to "guarantee" their publication. Any criticism by media or community leaders of the magazine's contents is met with cries of racism in the magazine's editorials, although a cursory check will find flagrant anti-Japanese comments throughout the magazine.

Teen Angels Magazine also sends mixed messages to readers by publishing pictures of babies in gang regalia next to pictures of a gang member's funeral. Stores have refused to carry the magazine, citing its promotion of antisocial values among young readers in articles and photos comparable to those found in racist white hate group publications.

The street gang image plays a significant role in advertising, too. Mervyns, a major family-oriented department store, advertised a new line of clothing, using a photograph of a young boy wearing his jeans low enough to show the top two inches of his underwear. The style followed the trend set by Marky Mark, a popular rapper known for showing his underwear.

Numerous callers to the store's headquarters did not like the fact that the store made this style of dressing appear acceptable by using it in its advertisements. Store management apologized to irate callers and promised to monitor future advertising more carefully for subtle messages.

A 1993 Nintendo advertisement showed a line of young boys attempting to appear menacing while performing drill team moves. To the casual observer the ad did appear very provocative, as the young boys wearing the video-game guns looked like idealized gang members. This ad became known in the advertising world as one of the worst ads of the year, as a result of its violent undertones.

Gang terms are even creeping into computer software. One children's writing program, My Own Stories, uses an example of a group of kids who call themselves the Mall Posse because they hang out at a local mall. Although the program's publishers may not have intended to refer to gang violence, My Own Stories is just one example of the extent to which the language of the street gang has become acceptable to the mainstream.

Meanwhile, the image-conscious National Football League has questioned players who wear bandannas or do-rags on the sidelines during games. Owners brought the subject up at the league's annual meeting in 1995, fearing that the players appeared too gang-like and could be misconstrued by young viewers as endorsing gangs.

Gangs in the Courtroom

I went to school until I hit juvenile hall. That was my last schooling. I went to juvenile hall because a lady wouldn't sell me cigarettes. I got mad and my friends and I got together and blew up that lady's car. I did a year for that. I was 15 at the time. I never went to school when I was in a gang. We would go just to wait outside school to jump them. That was my hobby.

— Payasa

A PATH THROUGH THE CRIMINAL JUSTICE SYSTEM

To many street gang members, a run-in with the law is a means to gain respect and prestige among peers. Multiple and increasingly serious offenses boost the offender's status. Street gang heroes are not traditional movie stars and sports figures but OGs (old or original gangsters) who are doing, or have done, time in prison. Many street gang members are indoctrinated into the system early, listening to the stories of prison life as told by the OGs. The film *American Me* offers an excellent portrayal of a typical gang member's path through the criminal justice system.

Probation

The first encounter with the criminal justice system usually involves a probation. A minor with a first offense will probably face a judge who generally provides a stern lecture and returns the offender back to the custody of a parent or guardian. After the next offense, the youth may be placed on a probation officer's caseload. At best, this results in infrequent contact.

The youth may find that misdeeds have lent him notoriety among his peers. Finding no compelling reason to curb criminal activities and receiving what seem to be positive reinforcement, he may continue to commit crimes.

Juvenile Detention

After exhausting the patience of the juvenile court judge and/or probation officer, the youth may be placed in a juvenile detention facility or group home. The youth now has an opportunity to network with other youths from differing backgrounds. They begin to compare notes and learn more about other gangs and methods of operation. This level of corrections is relatively relaxed compared to other facilities. Youths often form alliances with others in the detention facility to avoid being victimized or pressured, and the concept of the prison gang is born. The alliances in the juvenile detention facility are usually informal, even when based on necessity. The inmate often attempts to seek out those who are familiar or from the same area. Former enemies may even unite to fend off others if they have no one else; however, these informal alliances formed in juvenile facilities may endanger a gang member's standing with his original street gang.

Inside the juvenile detention facility, fights are frequent and erupt over the most minor confrontations. Failure to defend or stand up for oneself and one's allies will encourage the label of coward and reflect badly on the outside gang.

Once released from the juvenile detention facility, a youth may be placed in a group home or returned directly home, with increased attention from the probation officer. Most likely the youth associates with gang affiliates and may find that he has gained new respect as a result of his time in detention.

The next step in the system is usually a state facility for juveniles. Here the process resembles that in the juvenile detention facility, but the inmates are more dangerous; the hard-core criminals may share their mentality and values, which the newcomer may attempt to emulate. At this level of incarceration, the youth gang member must continue to prove himself through defiance of authority and violent physical confrontations with staff and other inmates.

Alliances with members of other groups are more formalized, and failure to conform to these allegiances can cause serious physical harm in and outside of the institution. While at the state juvenile facility, the youth will learn new criminal techniques and obtain additional ideas and contacts for unlawful activity.

On release, the youth may be returned home or placed in another group home facility during the transition back into the mainstream. The same negating criminal behavior is likely to continue as before, with the exception that the youth is now older and wiser in criminal methodology. Upon returning to the streets, the youth has gained more respect for and recognition of "hard time" and can tell more elaborate "war stories" to younger gang members. Small petty crimes no longer suffice to maintain his reputation, and his level of criminal activity escalates until the offender, who may no longer be considered a juvenile, is sentenced as an adult to a county jail or state prison.

Prison

Increased gang sophistication and street training ease the transition to an adult prison facility. The harsh system of proving oneself still exists, but years of training in the juvenile institutions prepares the newcomer. Once a gang member has reached this level of imprisonment, a cycle of parole and recommitment tends to develop since the individual usually has minimal educational and vocational skills and cannot adjust adequately to society outside the prison environment. The end of the cycle occurs only with a lifestyle change or death.

PROBLEMS WITH THE CORRECTIONS SYSTEM

The public and media consistently criticize the juvenile and adult corrections systems for their handling of criminal offenders. These systems deal with offenders who have failed to respond to preliminary levels of correction. According to correctional officials, inmates today are more violent and sophisticated than any group before them. They require more special services related to drug abuse, educational deficits, and the psychological problems of abuse and depression.

The financial cost of meeting all these needs is tremendous and constantly growing. Many voters and taxpayers who are unwilling to support programs that will keep potential inmates out of correctional facilities are also adverse to providing the same services to convicted felons. Failure to address adequately the rehabilitation needs of inmates during incarceration and parole only leads to a continuation of the cycle of crime and imprisonment.

Recidivism rates at this level of corrections are usually very high; successful programs are generally treatment-based. Data on this is difficult to obtain, but most people involved in the study of corrections programs feel that a success rate of 50 percent is indicative of a good model program. These successful programs combine academic education, individual and small group counseling, and vocational training. These types of programs, properly maintained, cause a 40 percent drop in recidivism rates, according to Vanderbilt University's Center for Crime and Justice Policy.

As of 1995 the New York Department for Youth was spending $80,000 a year per juvenile committed to its care and had a recidivism rate of 86 percent according to Judge Judith Scheindlin of New York City Family Court. The Center on Juvenile and Criminal Justice cites an 88 percent recidivism rate at a cost of $32,000 per year for wards of the state in the California Youth Authority.

Obviously, in these two examples, the disproportionate amounts of money spent on incarcerated juvenile offenders did not help them avoid further incarceration. Any type of treatment program for criminal juvenile offenders will be costly, but effectiveness is determined by how the money is spent. As the public becomes increasingly frustrated with the growth in violent juvenile crime, voters and legislators tend to be in favor of a more punishment-oriented program, at the expense of rehabilitative treatment programs in juvenile facilities.

ADDRESSING THE GANG PROBLEM

Three approaches to confronting the street gang problem through law enforcement and the court system are prevention, intervention, and suppression. Prevention involves those measures taken to eliminate the potential for joining and being recruited into street gangs. These are usually educational programs to inform young people and the general public of the dangers and consequences of gang membership. Such programs include police presentations at school safety fairs, assemblies, safe school programs, and other public forums. Prevention programs should start in the lower grades of elementary school. However, the success of this approach is difficult to measure and, therefore, hard to promote as effective.

The second approach, intervention, takes place in communities that have emerging and obvious gang activity at a level manageable for local authorities. The strategy is to redirect the street gangs and peripheral groups away from negative criminal behavior and pull them back into the mainstream of the community. Examples of this type of approach are court-directed, restitution-based sentencing for minor offenses. Mandatory attendance at counseling and supervised visits at jails or local prisons are known as the "scared straight" method. Police may be involved, through a Police Activities League (PAL), in directing young people into positive interaction with law enforcement personnel. In many communities, both local-government sponsored and grass-roots groups run successful programs.

The third approach, generally the first choice of the community legal system, is suppression. Examples of suppression include maximum sentencing, pressure on gang leadership for any infraction of the law, sweeps of gang territory, and extensive patrolling of gang territory. This method of confronting street gang activity is designed to put pressure on the most active and high profile gang members. Suppression is intended to make examples of gang leadership and demonstrate to the community that gang activity will not be tolerated.

Suppression policies can be effective. In 1994 Fort Dodge, Iowa, convicted 88 hardcore gang members on drug and weapons charges: the result was a drop of 33 percent for assaults in the community. Similarly, in 1994 Shreveport, Louisiana, arrested 13 members of a local drug gang known as the Bottoms Boys on drug and murder charges. Violent crime in the community decreased by 34 percent following the arrests.

Although the immediate reaction to the increase in violent criminal acts by juveniles has often been to create more laws, which citizens believe will deter criminal behavior, many of these laws fail to have the desired impact because they lack an understanding of the underlying issues. The "get tough" approach is intended to deliver a message that often is not received or has negligible meaning to juveniles. These laws are often used by politicians to make themselves appear to be doing something about juvenile crime. For example, in 1995 Governor Pete Wilson of California signed a bill intended to deter drive-by shootings, even though existing laws already covered the criminal act. The bill serves only political (and public relations) goals.

Furthermore, suppression policies can be used by the gang as a unifying tool in recruitment, thus increasing the level of gang activity and membership. Communities with full-blown gang problems need to combine the suppression with prevention and intervention programs.

Rick's Report
THREE STRIKES AND I'M OUT!

It was shortly after the "three strikes" law passed (1994), when the deputy district attorney assigned to our municipal court visited our gang office and began explaining the benefits of the new law. We were excited by the possibility of finally locking up our local criminals for more than just a meager three or six months. The county jails were overcrowded, and despite the sentence given by a judge, the sheriff usually released convicted criminals within a couple of weeks.

The new law was going to insure that career criminals spend 25 years to life in prison when convicted of a third felony. Gang members are, in fact, career criminals, and I was quite certain that within two years, our streets would be empty of the hardcore gang bangers.

It was a Friday night and the local skid row was starting to bustle with the familiar prostitutes and drug dealers. The big gang hangout was just two blocks away in a city park, but nothing was happening there. When the park is quiet, my partner and I drive down skid row looking for an easy arrest. There is always someone with a warrant out for their arrest, and we are always happy to transport them to our jail.

On this particular night we turned onto the street and saw Bulldog standing in front of a cantina, speaking to another man. Bulldog is in and out of prison on a regular basis and is associated with La Nuestra Familia. His nephew followed in his footsteps and went to prison after shooting Preacher Jose, who was sitting on the porch of a house telling a juvenile parolee to stay out of gangs. Bulldog's sister is 32 years old and still dresses in her gang colors when she isn't incarcerated.

Bulldog and the man talked for a few seconds and then the man crossed the street and got into a parked car. As the man crossed the street, Bulldog saw us and ran into the bar. We parked our car and walked up to the man who was now sitting in the driver's seat of his car. I shined my flashlight at the man through the car window and saw that he was in the process of unwrapping a small cellophane package that contained heroin. On the seat next to him was a syringe, a spoon, his water and cotton. He had just purchased the heroin and was getting ready to use it.

He was arrested and taken to the police department. I had never met the 21-year-old man, who was covered with gang tattoos, but I soon learned that Carlos had been released from prison two months ago after serving three years on a robbery charge. This would explain why neither my partner nor myself had seen this guy in the past. He had a large tattoo of the Aztec Bird on his hand—a symbol of La Nuestra Familia. This explained his association with Bulldog. We filed our case charging Carlos with a new felony and went on with our jobs.

Two weeks later we were notified by our district attorney that this was Carlos' third strike and he would be the first one from our city to get 25 years to life for his new crime. The preliminary hearing came, and the judge found there was ample evidence to hold Carlos until a trial date could be arranged. A week later the Deputy District Attorney telephoned me to let me know that the charges were being dropped against Carlos in the interest of justice.

According to the district attorney, his supervisors thought that it wouldn't be prudent to sentence a 21-year-old to life in prison for merely possessing a $20 piece of tar heroin. It would cost the state too much money to keep Carlos in prison all those years, and according to the new law, the judge had no discretion in the sentencing of third strike criminals. Carlos would have to do at least 25 years in prison. Due to this mandatory sentencing, the District Attorney's Office thought it was appropriate to drop all the charges. It was Carlos' third strike and he walked!

Working Toward Solutions

All the gangs respect us because we are straight with them. I am down-to-earth with them because I know what they are going through. I have been there myself.

—Sandra Davis, former gang member and founder of Mothers Against Gang Wars

VOICE FROM THE FRONT

SURVIVING THE GANG LIFE

I was going out with a guy for more than a year when he got locked up in juvenile hall. When I heard he got locked up, I started to cry. I cared for him a lot. I loved him so much that every day I would talk to him and tell him to leave the gang, but he wouldn't listen and got into more trouble. Finally, he was sentenced to California Youth Authority for two years. I was heartbroken. We wrote each other every day, and I would hurry home from school each day to get his collect call.

Then the phone bill came in and my mom was mad because it was so high. So I just wrote him. When I didn't have money to buy stamps, I thought he would be mad at me for forgetting him, so I stole some money to buy the stamps and envelopes. I would cry every night because he wasn't there with me. After a while I couldn't take it anymore and went out with someone else.

Right now, I'm trying to get back into school and get a job so that I can help my parents. I started going to church and that has helped me a lot because the people are so nice and supportive. It has really changed my life. Before I thought gangs, drugs, getting tattoos, and drinking was everything I needed but I was wrong. It only kills or hurts you. That's why I told myself I was going to change. I've learned that my family, school, and church should come first. I just hope that when my boyfriend gets out, he gets his life straight.

—Dimples

A United Front: Enlisting the Help of Community and Service Groups

What I was looking for in a gang, I already had and didn't know it. I lived for support, money, for belonging. I had my family there and my positive friends. Everything I looked for I had.

—Huero

COMMUNITY-BASED CONTROL

The idea that communities can put in place barriers to prevent gang activities is naive. Gang activity can be controlled but not eradicated. The socioeconomic factors that cause gang activity are much too complex and pervasive to be eliminated through local programs.

Factors that Promote Gang Activity Include

Peer group pressure
Need for recognition
Low self-esteem
Parental neglect
Low academic achievement/ability
Poverty
Need for protection
Poor role models
Lack of opportunity
Lack of recreational social options

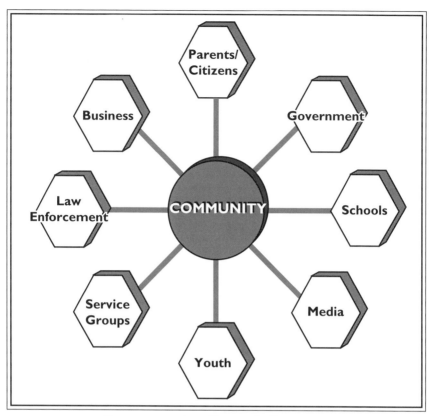

Community-Based Control

No single group or organization has the scope to prevent all of these factors, but combined with other organizations, some degree of control can be exercised over gang activity and growth. Many anti-gang programs around the country do succeed in reducing and controlling gang problems. The most successful programs tend to be:

1. *Community-based*, involving up to eight "special interest" subgroups: Service groups, parents, youth, schools, business, government, law enforcement, media.
2. *Long-term*. These programs are not short-term or dependent upon discretionary annual funding.
3. *Need-based*. Programs should address and meet the realistic needs of youth in the community and be inclusive of all groups and activities.

Each of the eight special-interest subgroups has been a critical element in contributing to successful gang suppression programs. A truly effective program to control gang activity and growth must bring together as many of the eight groups as possible and allow their individual efforts and contributions to develop into a pervasive and coordinated program. Too often a good idea founders because of a lack of time, personnel, facilities, and/or knowledge. By bringing the resources of the eight community subgroups together, many pitfalls and roadblocks can be overcome.

What Communities Should Look For

1. Movement of businesses out of town.
2. Declining property values or lack of development.
3. Graffiti on buildings and fences.
4. Increase in crime and the sale of drugs based upon police statistics.
5. Juveniles out on the street late at night or hanging out late in parks, parking lots, and fast-food stands.
6. Gang colors and dress being worn on the streets and in the schools.
7. Rumors of gang activity.
8. Young people frequenting certain houses or motels that may indicate drug sales.

What Communities Should Do

1. Acknowledge gang activity.
2. Form a community anti-gang task force (long-term commitment) with representatives of the eight major groups (parents, government, business, youth, law enforcement, service groups, schools, media).
3. Prioritize the gang problems and pick specific goals.
4. Identify available gang prevention, intervention, or control resources within the community.
5. Develop a plan of action based upon the community's needs, desires, and available resources.
6. Formalize a community anti-gang program.
7. Assign responsibilities and coordinate efforts and resources.
8. Continue to meet *regularly* and review progress and take actions when and if necessary.
9. Remember this is a long-term battle and cannot be resolved quickly.
10. Don't expect positive signs of improvement in the short term.

The U.S. Department of Justice, Office of Justice Programs, publishes a book on promising prevention, intervention, and suppression programs in existence throughout the United States: *Partnerships Against Violence: Promising Programs—Resource Guide*. Another good source is *What Works: Promising Intervention in Juvenile Justice*, published by the Office of Juvenile Justice and Delinquency Prevention. (See Resource Section).

ALBUQUERQUE, NEW MEXICO: CASE STUDY OF A SUCCESSFUL COMMUNITY-BASED PROGRAM

Information is used with permission from the Mayor's Council on Gangs in Albuquerque, New Mexico.

Albuquerque, with a population of approximately 550,000, had 5,000 documented gang members as of October 1995. The term *documented* means that the gang members are well known to the police and usually have arrest and conviction records or "rap sheets" detailing their criminal activity. Often the police have pictures of the individuals or groups dressed in their gang clothes and "throwing" hand signs. The number of documented gang members does not usually include wanna-bes or associates, who are often more active and dangerous than initiated members because they will do anything to impress the hard-core gang members.

In 1993 the local government decided to create a coalition to control the rapidly growing gang problem, and the Mayor's Council on Gangs was organized. It consisted of a policy steering committee, which would establish policies for the development of a community-wide strategy to combat gangs and youth violence and make sure that this strategy was carried out in a coordinated manner by local government, schools, law enforcement, business, religious, neighborhood, and community organizations. The strategy would encompass prevention activities, intervention activities, and suppression or enforcement activities.

Another section of the Mayor's Council on Gangs was called the working groups. This consisted of three committees—prevention, intervention, and enforcement—each with expert representatives from major segments of the community, including law enforcement, education, the courts, neighborhoods, etc. The job of each committee was to study the situation, process its findings, and provide recommendations based on facts and research about youth violence and gang problems in Albuquerque. Their work concluded with a series of meetings between steering committee members and the chairs of each working group to review and design a document of final recommendations for presentation to the mayor. Information gathered from town hall meetings and youth speak-out sessions also contributed to the contents of the final document.

Findings of the Working Groups

The prevention committee found three areas that have a direct relation to youths' predisposition to and/or involvement with gang behavior.

1. Truancy (missing school without permission). This could be addressed by a strong collaborative effort of the public school system, the city, county, and community in working on developing and enforcing more stringent policies.
2. Lack of organized recreational and academic extracurricular programs. After-school programs needed to be expanded to vacation periods and should range from sports and recreation to skills-building and academics to help enhance self-esteem and a sense of belonging.
3. Ineffective programs for dealing with troubled youths. Pertinent alternative programs in current educational settings and alternative schools needed to be created. This would increase the capacity of existing schools to deal with "difficult" youth, to improve student retention, to minimize risk to other students, and to provide education and opportunities for youths who have been given long-term suspensions and should not be put on the streets.

The intervention committee found a need to develop a standardized assessment tool to accurately determine the level and type of intervention needed by youth at risk.

A second key strategy was the creation of a crisis intervention team and a 24-hour crisis hot line to provide immediate response and referrals for youths leaving gangs and finding themselves and their families in danger. There was a strong recommendation for developing jobs and related job training programs by means of a comprehensive, collaborative effort.

The enforcement committee did not see the juvenile justice system and the children's code as fully prepared to deal with hard-core criminal gang members. First time and/or nonviolent offenders intermingle with hard-core violent offenders, effectively raising the level of criminality of the nonviolent offenders. The committee recommended the expansion of both the police and sheriff departments with administrative support, equipment, and additional police officers, especially on the gang unit.

The committee also recognized that a strong effort is required to develop and implement a relevant curfew that can be enforced. This will reduce the possibilities and opportunities of youth involvement in gang activity during the hours proven to be high-violence periods.

The committees working in the Mayor's Council on Gangs found many crossover problems in their research. Truancy enforcement, curfews, youth activity programs, and the overwhelming need for jobs and job training emerged as keys to mitigating the gang problem.

One key prevention strategy involves the community and the parents. Parental responsibility and accountability are vital. Means must be made available to promote the stability and well-being of families, as well as to assess and provide appropriate services. The committees recommended:

1. Training and education for parents of all backgrounds, beginning with affordable prenatal care that links up with school and community programs.

2. Training in the development of independent living skills and family skills for teenagers through the schools and public service agencies.

3. Promoting healthy families and availability of services to the community through public awareness campaigns and public service announcements. Providing a toll-free service number to distribute general information and make referrals.

4. Finding ways to stimulate and interest parents in their kids, e.g. offering family activities at hours when parents don't work, involving both kids and parents in programs at community centers.

5. Making parents responsible for fines, restitution, or community service as part of sentences given to kids.

6. Encouraging the public sector to take a leadership role in implementing a plan to create family-friendly workplaces so that it is easier to be both a good parent and a good employee.

7. Fostering economic growth in the community to help families improve their quality of life and create a level playing field for more children. Parents and kids both need jobs.

Community Outreach Centers

Community life as a whole must be nurtured and developed. Kids need to live in neighborhoods where they enjoy the basics of life—safety, shelter, nourishment, and sense of belonging. All members of the community must find ways to interact and combine resources.

One thing a group can do to nurture the community is create an outreach center. These centers should be hospitable, open, friendly places where youth can feel comfortable enough to play games, express creativity in some form, or expend energy in a physical activity or sport. The most important aspect is to create an atmosphere where youth feel comfortable enough to talk about their problems and seek help with pursuing their education, job training, or counseling. Having tutors and mentors available is essential.

Culture is an important aspect in dealing with ethnic gangs, and volunteers from the specific culture should be available. Feeling safe is extremely important, and the concept of "neutral territory" should be enforced: the wearing of gang clothing, or exchange of threatening gang signs or language is forbidden in or around the center. Churches, park departments, and schools often have buildings or halls that could be used as a full- or part-time outreach center.

Once an outreach center is established it becomes a focal point for resources and information as well as specific program activities. It is important to keep regular and consistent hours as participants will rely on that schedule. Often, these centers become the only real home the children and teens have, and the committees in Albuquerque determined the following basic needs in terms of these centers:

1. Make existing centers more interesting and inviting to youth.
2. Make sure programs are affordable to kids with little or no money.
3. Use schools and community centers to provide a wider range of activities and classes for youth and families, such as ESL (English as a second language), GED (general education diploma), parenting, and arts and crafts.
4. Recommend a policy that future community centers are combination senior and youth centers to create intergenerational mentoring relationships.
5. Open schools to serve as community centers in areas where none exist.
6. Instruct staff and volunteers in gang awareness and prevention, as well as in developing positive attitudes toward youth.
7. Work with community centers and schools to facilitate community activities.
8. Bring more police officers into the community and help make them involved members of community life.
9. Encourage local businesses to be members of the community in which they conduct business.
10. Persuade organized religions and groups to participate in community activities, and view churches as a resource for youth development, mentoring, and counseling services.
11. Develop and implement programs addressing cultural and heritage values and diversity.

SERVICE GROUPS

Almost every community, despite its size, possesses service organizations whose purpose is to promote and support the community with the philanthropic efforts of its members. The interests and dedication of their members will vary, but these groups can be a valuable resource for volunteer personnel, facilities, and in some cases financial support. No group should be overlooked, due to size or current activities, as a potential contributor in the community anti-gang efforts. Many of these groups are eager to focus their work on community needs if asked. Additionally, a local service group may have a powerful national organization whose more extensive resources can be brought to bear on a local problem when requested by its local chapter.

Other important community groups that can be considered service groups are the grassroots volunteer groups that are formed for the express purpose of providing a key program in prevention, intervention, or suppression. These can range from a strong neighborhood anti-gang, anti-crime, anti-graffiti, or anti-drug partnership to a specific group, such as Mothers Against Gang Wars.

While a youth prevention program is aimed at preventing youth involvement in gang activities and related violence, a youth gang intervention program targets youth who are already gang members or who associate with gang members. The goals of such programs are to prevent further involvement with gangs, assist youths in leaving gangs, reduce delinquent behavior, and improve school attendance. In this category we can list specific youth clubs such as Boys and Girls Clubs, YMCA, Boy and Girl Scouts, 4-H agricultural associations, and other similar youth programs.

Volunteers

Volunteers are the most practical, and usually most available, resource that service groups have to offer. They exist as a combined resource of expertise and experience in promoting special events and activities, as well as their own individual skills and abilities. Many of these people are more than willing to assist when asked, especially in a community need–based project. The local chamber of commerce can provide a listing of community service groups, but these groups must be contacted individually for assistance. They provide excellent opportunities for networking of information on community projects through presentations that can be made at the groups' regular meetings. Coalitions made up of private and public groups can create needed outreach or teen centers.

Other Assets

Facilities, transportation, and equipment are also available from service groups and can be used for community projects free or on a cost basis. Programs need facilities in which to operate, and many service groups are willing to provide that support if called upon. Using these resources can reduce the overhead costs of running some anti-gang programs, which may at first appear too expensive to attempt.

Financial Support

The financial support that these local service groups can provide may seem minimal upon first consideration, but a more careful evaluation reveals that these service groups are very good at fund-raising and can help provide this type of expertise. They have successfully conducted fund-raising activities in the form of raffles, direct sales, special events, and appeals for donation for many years. These groups, if mobilized in their community, could raise funds to help finance the community's anti-gang project or support specific programs that are part of it. Finally, regarding finance, these groups can appeal to their national organization for special grants or assistance to help a community establish and operate an anti-gang program or special project.

Recognition of Volunteer Efforts

Service groups need to be recognized by the community for their efforts. This can be easily accomplished through media reports in television, radio, and the newspaper. Recognition by the local, state, and federal government also provides a great deal of goodwill.

Letters of appreciation from elected officials can be easily solicited from the local level all the way to the federal. Presidential recognition is also possible for outstanding support provided to the community by an individual or group. Failure to recognize and show appreciation to individuals and/or groups for their efforts will discourage support for future projects.

How to Work with Service Groups in the Community

WHAT TO DO

1. Identify what support needs can be met by service groups, both as organizations and individuals.
2. Identify all the service groups in a community (religious, business, social, educational, etc.).
3. Identify all the resources of the community's service groups (facilities, volunteer personnel, expertise.
4. Ask the service groups to volunteer available resources for assistance in the community's anti-gang effort.
5. Recognize the group's support activities in the media and through government declarations, letters, and awards, etc.

WHAT NOT TO DO

1. Ignore the valuable potential contributions that community groups, with their assets, can supply in supporting the community anti-gang effort.
2. Fail to recognize individuals and service groups for their support.

In the strictest sense, a youth gang suppression program uses the criminal justice system to combat gang-related crime, including arrest, gang prosecution units, gang probation supervision, and parole. But suppression can also be used by volunteers to control a budding problem. Many cities have encouraged police senior volunteer programs with such names as Partners, VIPs, and STARs. These nonconfrontational groups cruise neighborhoods, parks, and schools, radioing in to the police if they find any problems that are brewing. Also, many parents and service groups help patrol school hallways during breaks and lunches. Just the presence of adults often deters trouble.

Neighborhood watch groups contribute to both prevention and suppression, as they give control back to the neighborhood. Making neighborhoods safer, better places to live is a challenge. One of the better prevention strategies neighborhoods can use is to clean up the problems that breed crime and a gang environment. Following are a few examples of how neighborhoods can contribute to the community.

THE GREAT SAN JOSE PAINT OUT

On May 14, 1994, San Jose, California, received a fresh coat of paint. Supplied with paint and graffiti remover, approximately 600 volunteers came out to tackle graffiti. Driving through the city and seeing volunteer crews cleaning and painting walls, one could sense the community pride. There were volunteer groups, ranging from 20 to more than 100 people, in each of the twelve police districts. One of the most impressive things was the number of children and teenagers who participated in this event. This large youth turnout sends a clear message to the taggers that their peers won't tolerate graffiti. After the Paint Out, there were celebrations in each of the twelve police districts. There was plenty of food and drink to go around. In some cases, there were raffles for prizes.

SOUTH CENTRAL L.A. FOLKS TURN ALLEY INTO SANCTUARY

Fed up with garbage, graffiti, and loitering gangs, a South Central neighborhood turned a "nuisance alley" into the city's first alley park, complete with apple and peach trees, shrubs, and blooming flowers. Since seizing control of the alley, residents no longer have to worry about the drug addicts and winos or the people who used to shoot guns and start fires just behind their houses.

APARTMENT TENANTS PROTEST—LODIANS HIT STREETS TO STOP GANG VIOLENCE

A 17-year-old gang member was arrested at an apartment complex in the Lodi neighborhood and charged with the attempted murder of an apartment complex resident. Because of the violence, 50 residents of the 110-unit complex withheld rent until the apartment complex was made safer with on-site armed security guards. They also took turns walking a protest march in front of the apartment.

Home Work:
Parents and Youth Get Involved

Drugs weren't a big deal in my house. Both my parents used them.

— Juvenile street gang member

PARENTS

The most critical people in the anti-gang effort are the parents and guardians in the community. Our short list of contributing factors in promoting gang activity lists several factors that are directly connected to the home. Parental neglect, the absence of recognition, and poor role models are known to have a large impact on gang recruitment.

Many parents give lip service to anti-gang efforts, but what must they do to support the community?

1. *Accept responsibility.* Parents must be parents. They should know what their children are doing in and out of school. Who are their friends, where do they go, and what do they do there? They should respond to notices of unexcused absences from school, have their children at home by a reasonable time, be a role model and demonstrate genuine concern about their children, and teach their children to respect themselves and the community.
2. *Be knowledgeable.* Parents need to know the signs of gang involvement, as well as the services available in the community to help when they suspect trouble.
3. *Support and participate.* Parents should get involved in the community anti-gang programs and offer support by volunteering time and money if possible.

Those citizens who are not parents still have a responsibility to become involved and support the three criteria listed above. No one should be sitting on the sidelines. There are those recalcitrant parents who will need to be encouraged to participate. This can be done through community effort. Parents of students with unexcused absences could serve detention and/or community service with their offspring. Failure to respond to school requests for a conference could be handled by the courts as a case of parental neglect. Placing legal pressure upon the parents to be responsible is a last resort, but one that needs to be considered. Additionally, parents of known gang members could be held accountable for their children's activities, and sent to anti-gang education programs with their children.

Following are several specific examples of how parents and others can make a contribution to the community's gang control program.

Kennedy High School in Sacramento, California, started a program known as Parents on Campus in November of 1992 after another local high school experienced one in a series of school shootings. The parents volunteer their time to help school security patrol the campus, and are additional eyes and ears for potential trouble. Since the program started, the school has seen a 24 percent drop in reported cases of injury, while the school district had a 20 percent increase overall. Suspensions have also decreased by 28 percent compared to the district's increase of 38 percent.

Like Sandra Davis of Stockton, California, Joe Debbs of Sacramento decided to become a community activist when his nephew was assaulted and beaten in a savage gang attack. Debbs formed A Guard Against Narcotics and Gangs (AGANG) as a neighborhood watch program to counter the spread and influence of street gangs. Despite his efforts, his own daughter was seriously wounded in a drive-by shooting in May of 1994. The attack may have been revenge motivated.

Debbs volunteers his time to work with the Sacramento Police Department in a conflict resolution program at area high schools. He also works with youngsters one on one to help them with problems. The violence that continues to afflict his family appears only to encourage him to continue his work.

In Jackson, Tennessee, Shirlene Mercer grew tired of the gang violence that claimed 19 deaths there in 1993. She decided that community action was the only way to put an end to the violence and began weekly marches that attract between 50 and 350 participants. The community has responded, and as of September 1994 the city had recorded only four murders.

Another individual attempting to make an impact is Dave Brown in Boise, Idaho. He publishes a monthly magazine, *Wanted by the Law: America's Monthly Crime Report!* It promotes positive stories about police officers and ordinary citizens whose heroism is an inspiration to everyone. As the magazine's title proclaims, photos of the nation's most wanted criminals are also featured.

Signs of Gang Involvement

Parents or guardians should look for the following signs of their children's involvement with gangs:

- Declining grades and/or attendance problems.
- Friends who are constantly in trouble at school or with the police.
- Appearance of tattoos or graffiti on clothing, books, or in their room.
- Use of unusual nicknames.

- Appearance of unexplained items or money.
- Preference for specific colors or type of clothing.
- Practice and use of hand signs.
- Staying away from home and out late, without permission or explanation.
- Withdrawal from family.
- Increase in vandalism and/or violent activity in the community, school, and neighborhood.
- Use of drugs and/or alcohol.
- Friends who use drugs and/or alcohol.
- Possession of permanent markers or spray paint cans.
- Possession of pagers by friends of children.
- Unusual handwriting or drawings on books and homework.
- Increase in accidents as evidenced by injuries

What Parents and Guardians Can Do to Prevent Their Children's Gang Involvement

- Spend time with your children.
- Learn the signs of gang involvement.
- Know who your children's friends are and contact their parents occasionally.
- Know where your children go and what they do for fun.
- Go to school meetings with teachers and administrators.
- Establish and *enforce* acceptable rules and expectations for your children's behavior.
- Do not tolerate the use and/or presence of drugs, alcohol, cigarettes, or gang involvement by your children or their friends.
- Talk to your children about alcohol, drugs, and gangs.
- Listen to and respect the feelings and attitudes of your children.
- Help your children to become knowledgeable contributing citizens.
- Find or form a parent support group if you find your child involved in gangs.
- Contact school officials and police about your children's involvement.
- Check your children's rooms for drugs, money, and weapons.
- Ensure that your community provides adequate and appropriate recreational activities for youth and families and participate in them.
- Be a role model.
- Help your children develop regular study habits and show interest in their schoolwork.
- Give your children praise or encouragement; don't allow yourself to become too judgmental about their choices, and allow for mistakes or disagreements.
- Teach your children how to deal with peer pressure and how to say no to friends.
- Volunteer, if possible, to participate in and promote the programs that support the community's anti-gang program.

YOUTHS

The youths of the nation have not been silent on the issue of street gangs, drugs, and violence. They are more than willing to take a stand and work to remove these threats to the community. Some have even given their lives. We hear about stories of young people killed, shot, and/or beaten for refusing to join or give into gang intimidation. Many have called hotlines to inform authorities of potential hazards and criminal behavior. Others provide positive role models in their communities and remain to help others when no alternative help is available. Even gang members themselves have become sick of the constant violence and have asked local authorities to help them call a truce between rival factions and find a peaceful way to resolve their problems.

The following are examples of how youths across the country are taking charge and attempting to make a difference.

In separate, unrelated cases, members of street gangs in Sante Fe, New Mexico, and Lima, Ohio, have asked community leaders to help them keep a truce in an attempt to stop the senseless killing. Significant is the fact that the gangs are initiating the pacts and are trying to change.

Jesse Atondo, a 16-year-old student in rural Kern County, California, gathered over 300 signatures on a petition to the board of the local elementary school district requesting them to consider and adopt a school uniform policy. Atondo's petition drive resulted in California State Senator Phil Wyman sponsoring a bill in the legislature to legally support local school districts adopting school uniforms to help keep their students safer from gang violence. The bill became law in August 1994, and many districts across the state began planning for implementation in the following school year.

In February of 1994, over 100 students staged a two-hour protest over the adoption of a dress code by Highland High School in Sacramento, California. The dress code banned hats from being worn indoors and shirts that portrayed drugs, alcohol, smoking, or sexually explicit material. Baggy pants and gang-related clothing were also banned. District officials met with the students and agreed to conduct weekly meetings and to publish a newsletter informing all district students on progress in discussion of the policy. What may have appeared to be open defiance was actually an attempt by students to have some input into the decisions affecting them directly. Better communication and student involvement would have prevented this embarrassing situation for the district and resulted in a more effective student dress code.

In Nebraska, plans for organizing youth councils in communities across the state were presented by the Cornhusker Youth Leadership Council. The council intends to travel throughout the state and help youth in individual communities set up similar councils that can give them a voice in solving problems and other community affairs. The council believes that the more that youths are involved in community affairs, the less likely they are to become a problem.

Locking up youthful gang members has not resulted in any long-term reduction in crime, only temporary reprieves while offenders are off the streets. These offenders return to the same community environment that they left, and soon pick up their old ways unless they have gained insight while incarcerated. Such insight is rare unless the juvenile has participated in education and treatment programs during incarceration. To combat this cycle, we need to refer to its causes: poverty, need for recognition, peer group pressure, poor role models, lack of opportunity, etc. We must counter these factors, which lead to gang activity, by providing education and positive alternatives.

Factors Leading to Gang Involvement

- Lack of personal identity
- Lack of appropriate alternatives and/or activities
- Peer pressure
- Need for safety/security (protection)
- Absence of parental involvement or demonstrated concern
- Membership by other family members or friends
- Substance abuse by youth and/or parents
- Lack of opportunity for recreation or employment
- Poor academic achievement
- Sporadic attendance at school
- Rundown physical environment
- Inappropriate, or lack of, role models
- Feeling of hopelessness
- Limited education opportunities
- Lack of knowledge of the consequences of gang involvement

Consequences of Gang Involvement

- Risk of physical injury, disabling injury, or death
- Constant fear of physical danger
- Probability of committing a crime as an initiation rite
- Obtaining a criminal record
- Incarceration in a juvenile and possibly an adult institution
- Permanent tattoos
- Financial hardship, emotional distress, physical injury and possibly death to family members
- Risk of AIDS from homemade tattoos

What Youths Should Do

- Accept personal responsibility for your safety and others by informing officials of potential danger
- Support the community's anti-gang effort
- Suggest and participate in community activities to combat gang activity
- Don't pretend to be a gang member; it could get you killed
- Tell the truth to parents and adults about activities. If you want trust and respect, then you must earn it
- Keep your family informed about your activities and friends
- Remember that adults and parents make mistakes too

Classroom Strategies for Teachers and Administrators

What public school teachers see as the cause of most disciplinary problems in schools:	
1940	**1990**
Talking out of turn	Drug abuse
Chewing gum	Alcohol abuse
Making noise	Teen pregnancy
Running in hallways	Teen suicide
Cutting in line	Rape
Dress code violations	Robbery
Littering	Assault

Source: *Congressional Quarterly Researcher*

CLASSROOM MANAGEMENT

It was a hot sultry day in August as Frank Johnson hurried down the graffiti-marked hallway of Seniors High School. Warnings about this particular math class exploded through his brain. He entered the noisy classroom. Groups of boys clustered around a porn magazine, snickering at the pictures. Girls with frizzy, over-permed hair giggled, popped gum, and talked rapidly, letting out a squeal of delight every so often over some boy.

The room smelled of unwashed bodies, sweaty socks, cheap perfume, and smoky clothes. Feeling the urge to gag, Frank bolted over to the paint-stuck window. After working it loose, he lifted it, breathing in the warm sticky air. A slight breeze moved through the room. Frank stood silently in front of the room and thought about the best way to control this group. Leaning on his prior military experience, he applied the following rules.

Get their attention. He dropped a book loudly on the desk. They looked up startled. Who was this?

Let them know who is the boss. "I'm Mr. Johnson. Sit down and be quiet."

Establish the rules. "In this classroom there will be no gum chewing, magazine reading, or talking out of turn. We will be covering pages 64 to 75. When we are

217

done, you may leave. Anyone having problems with this schedule may leave now, after giving me your name, which will be turned into the vice principal at the end of class." During the long silence that followed this statement, a girl with blue-tinged frizzy hair spoke in a loud whisper. "This man means business. I'm not messing around with him."

Acknowledge their efforts. After the session ended, he praised the class for their attention. The same girl stopped for a moment by his desk. "You know, this is the only time that no one was kicked out of class. I hope you come back tomorrow." She smiled as she left. Frank let out a breath, one day down . . . four to go.

The Teacher's Job

Teachers have a difficult job: oversize classes, multicultural and language problems, drug and alcohol abuse, weapons in schools, and gang fights, combined with a lack of parental, community, or authority support. The teacher is expected to be a social worker, counselor, security guard, and parent stand-in. Because each class has its own set of unique problems, it is impossible to find one overall solution that will work in all cases.

A combination of gang identity and anger at the system is shown by the ongoing vandalism and graffiti on books, materials, walls, and furniture. A shortage of money to make needed repairs and purchase materials is also apparent. Students often display disrespect for themselves, their peers, and adults. They appear to lack motivation and a desire to succeed. The teachers are consistently breaking up fights or verbal confrontations, and are the targets of violent threats. To add to this list of problems, teachers are expected to follow a curriculum that meets the diverse needs and abilities of students, many of whom have learning disabilities, language deficits, and emotional problems.

Several approaches can be used to attempt to contend with gangs in the classroom, but it ultimately comes down to the individual teacher and his or her ability and experience. Teachers are usually the best judge of what is needed in their classrooms and must be given assistance and support by the administration in a cooperative effort to combat gang activity. The classroom management of gang behavior will be much more effective when integrated with the overall school gang management plan.

To achieve an effective classroom management plan for gang control, teachers must accept two basic premises. First, they are not alone in the battle with gangs on the school campus and in the community. They must network and communicate with other staff about what works and what doesn't. School administrators need to assist in this sharing of techniques and include it in their overall school gang management plan.

Teachers must also decide whether the glass is half full or half empty. The glass in this case is the available resources to combat gangs in a community, school, and classroom. If looked at negatively, the glass is half empty, and the teacher in question definitely is in the wrong career, or needs to change his/her attitude. There are tremendous resources available to both teachers and administrators. They must work together to make everyone realize that the glass is half full, and rising.

HOW TO HANDLE GANGS IN CLASS

As previously stated, only the teachers on the spot will know what may and may not work for them in the classroom based upon their ability, experience, and knowledge. Provided here are basic concepts that have worked in various forms and situations and are intended to be adaptable to any classroom environment or teaching personality. The one immutable concept that must be stressed, however, is that control of the classroom must occur if any learning is to be accomplished. Also remember that gang control programs cannot be a quick fix, but take effect over a long period and must be planned for with short-term goals leading toward a long-term objective.

WHAT TO DO

1. Rules should be clear, concise, and relevant. Post them for all to see. Students should review and acknowledge understanding them. Those that are general usually work best. The use of the single word "respect" was very effective for Susan Johnston in her Palo Alto, California, classroom (see *My Posse Don't Do Homework*, the book made into the movie and television series *Dangerous Minds*). The consequences for violation of them must also be clear, concise, and *carried out*. Meet with your administration and obtain their backing.
2. Evaluate what you're teaching and why. Is the curriculum relevant and appropriate? Do students have the necessary background to accomplish the work and, conversely, do they already know what is being taught? Develop systems in your curriculum that promote student success, starting small with a long term goal being greater.
3. Use humor if possible, but don't make students the object of the joke.
4. Expectations should be a part of your rules. Failure to live up to them should have the consequences stated also.
5. Show that you care about student achievement and progress. Use the telephone regularly and/or computer system to maintain parent/guardian contact on a regular basis.
6. Become knowledgeable of gang activity in your school and community.
7. Network information and ideas with other teachers.
8. Do not overlook gang activity in class, and call attention to it as an endangerment to the students.

WHAT NOT TO DO

1. Don't blame administrators or others for your problems. Instead, encourage them to join you in working to control the gang problems cooperatively.

2. Don't adopt the attitude that it is not your problem, because then you are a part of the problem.
3. When confronting a student, do not do it in front of a group, but take him aside and discuss the problem privately.
4. Don't be negative or hostile towards gang members in your class. The classroom may be the only place they feel safe and comfortable. If they show you respect as a teacher, return that respect to them as students.
5. Don't limit student options during any confrontation. Remember that they have their own code of conduct and feel that it is important. Give them several options so that they feel in some control and can make a choice.
6. Don't side with any group or factions. You must always be seen as a neutral party, and failure to do so will jeopardize your ability to teach and your safety.

WHAT TO DO IF CONFRONTED WITH POSSIBLE ASSAULTIVE BEHAVIOR BY STUDENTS IN CLASS

1. Remember that you are the authority figure present whether the assaultive behavior is directed toward other students or you.
2. Safety of your students and yourself is the most important concern.
3. Send for assistance immediately or as soon as possible. Don't try to be a hero.
4. Communicate with the potential assailant. Keep him/her talking to distract him/her from harming others until help arrives.
5. If you are the only one involved, leave the scene, but not if others are present (i.e., students under your supervision).
6. Watch the hands of the assailant and any others who may be involved.
7. Use force only as a last resort, and only the amount necessary to subdue the assailant and guarantee safety.
8. Allow assailant an escape route. They can easily leave and later be apprehended by school security and/or police.

Gang Awareness Training

An important component of any school program to combat gang activity is a gang awareness curriculum. Many programs have been created across the country to address the specific needs of the community and school system. One such program in Paramount, California (pop. 48,000, 20 miles outside of Los Angeles), successfully deterred the recruitment of future gang members. The Paramount schools implemented a 15-unit anti-gang curriculum for fifth graders and saw the number of local gangs drop from six to four. This kind of success has been dependent upon factors not always related to the program itself, including follow-up efforts and the program's connection to community anti-gang efforts. An effective school program must address the needs of students, parents, and school staff and link that knowledge to the community anti-gang program, if one exists.

Gang awareness training has been most effective when conducted in a progressive and coordinated program, such as in grade levels 3, 5, and 7. This provides a sense of continuity without overkill and reaches students prior to the prime recruiting ages for gang membership.

GANG AWARENESS TRAINING FOR ALL LEVELS

1. Determine group's knowledge of gangs and terminology.
2. Define the history of gangs—locally and nationally.
3. Define and clarify gangs and gang-related behavior.
4. Discuss the present and future personal costs of gang membership.
5. Address the connection between gangs and drugs.
6. Discuss the family costs of gang activity.
7. Discuss the community effects of gang activity.
8. List the reasons for gang activity.
9. Provide alternatives to gang membership.
10. Teach conflict management.
11. Provide resources for help.

Each level should have a focus and depth that is appropriate for each grade.

SCHOOL MANAGEMENT

According to a January 1994 report by the National School Boards Association, 15 percent of school systems in the nation are now using metal detectors and 11 percent are using video monitoring to help control violence in schools. Of the 729 school districts responding to the survey, one half of them conduct searches of student lockers. Additionally, many schools use photo IDs to exclude nonstudents from their campuses. Despite such precautions, violence still occurs in the schools.

In Richmond, California, a student with a handgun at Kennedy High School opened fire on an outside PE class, wounding two students. This happened despite the school's use of metal detectors, a single entrance, and mandatory ID badges for students. The young gunman escaped through a hole in the school fence. Obviously, the school's attempts at security were not realistic in view of its lack of comprehensiveness.

Several television reports have shown how easy it is for youths to defeat the security systems set up for schools when they are not well thought out and maintained. The removal of lockers as a haven for contraband has been tried in schools throughout the country, but its effect is negated by the use of backpacks, which can easily hide the same contraband items. Sam Houston High School in Houston, Texas, has taken this a step further and required the use of clear plastic backpacks by all students to reduce the likelihood of drugs or weapons being carried in the school.

Interestingly, 61 percent of the schools responding to the National School Boards Association's 1994 survey said they use conflict resolution and peer mediation programs to help curb student violence. These programs exist under many names and slightly different ground rules, but all have the same basic objective of reducing student violence on campus. Usually, students are chosen or selected to become peer counselors and are given responsibility to assist school administrators in preventing minor incidents from becoming violent.

Peer counselors are seen as less threatening and can more easily break down barriers in communication between adversaries. The quick and immediate intervention by the mediators has been very effective according to many school administrators across the country. They usually cite a decrease in the number of fights once this type of program is in place. The New York State Board of Regents' response to increasing school violence in 1994 was a recommendation to spend $5 million dollars of the state education budget for conflict resolution programs.

Anonymous hotlines are potentially effective tools for schools when used in conjunction with law enforcement. Callers can provide information to authorities about possible problems. Their effectiveness is limited, however, in many communities by the lack of publicity and community orientation training. Many students fear using these hotlines, and perceive it as "snitching," which can be as deadly as direct confrontation in some cases. Proper training in community safety and social responsibility is needed to establish confidence in the use of such systems.

School Site Control

The appropriate use of a school system's facilities, staff, and programs can be one of the most effective means of combating gang activity in a community. Schools already have the framework on which to build an effective anti-gang program, but must first identify and acknowledge the degree to which their problem exists.

Although simplistic in design, this assessment attempts to give educators a frame of reference for identifying the level of gang activity in their school. Of particular note is the differentiation of levels. By their own standards, educational leaders in some areas of the country may feel that scoring in even the lowest category poses as much of a problem as scoring in the highest level. However scores are viewed and interpreted, attempting to quantify and evaluate gang activity will raise awareness and initiate more dialogue on the problem.

As previously stated, no community can shut itself off from outside influence, and gang activity is no exception. The range of activity can be divided into three categories.

DEVELOPMENTAL

No outright gang involvement or organized group. Individuals may claim membership (wanna-bes) in a gang, or have been a member in another community. No incidents attributable to a gang have occurred, but some of the signals have started to appear.

EXISTING

Specific groups are identifiable, and incidents occur that are directly attributable to these groups. The problems could be minor to serious in nature but are a concern to the community. Gang members openly attempt to demonstrate their existence.

OVERRUN

The school has lost control of its campus, and gangs are a dominant force. They control the area of the school, openly defy authority, and flaunt their lack of respect.

This is a very simplistic division, but schools all over the country can be placed in one of these categories. Schools in any one of the three categories can fight back. The amount of effort required, however, will be greater with increased gang infiltration.

The existing structure of the school provides the following three support areas upon which to build an anti-gang program:

Staff. Includes administrators, teachers, support staff, and volunteers.

Physical environment. This includes the campus building, schedule, and organizational structure.

Rules/procedures. Includes federal, state, district, and local school site policies, regulations, and laws.

School management must effectively orchestrate the development of an anti-gang program by insuring that coordination and mutual support are possible between these areas.

Tasks

SCHOOL MANAGEMENT STAFF

- Invite local law enforcement to the school campus on a regular basis for bonding between school staff and students.
- Acknowledge the problems. Don't deny that a gang problem exists. They're in your school. Don't be secretive about the issue. You are only allowing the problem to continue and grow.
- Develop and provide a gang awareness education program for *all* school personnel, parents, and students. Teach staff about gangs in the area and trends throughout the area and country. Develop and train staff in dealing with gangs at school, and especially in the classroom.
- Develop and maintain quick communications between the school, parents, police, and community.

- Do not acknowledge gangs as a viable representative group. This will only enhance their status and power.
- Share information with staff, even rumors, since they tend to be based upon some fact.
- Create an intelligence network about what is going on in and around your school. Know who the gang members are, and where they hang out. Remember that the school is only a part of the total community, so share information with the police and other community schools and groups. Implement an anonymous hotline, if possible.
- Have a student communication channel with administration via regular meetings in homerooms or special sessions.
- Have crisis plans that address a variety of scenarios including gang incidents, especially violent ones.
- Be proactive, not reactive, in dealing with gang problems. Focus on prevention.
- Maintain a useful database that correlates the time, place, and individuals involved in each incident.

PHYSICAL ENVIRONMENT

- Control access to your campus. Know who is there and why. Maintain a closed campus during the day to reduce unnecessary traffic.
- Keep rival gang members, especially leadership, separated through controlled scheduling. This can be accomplished through coordination of school administration and law enforcement in identifying potential troublemakers.
- Reduce crowds whenever possible. Stagger release times and lunch periods.
- Insure quick, if not immediate, repair of vandalism, especially graffiti. Prior to removal of graffiti, be sure to photograph it for police intelligence use.
- Assign staff to monitor areas of responsibility on campus, such as hallways, loading zones, and main entrances, so they know the normal routines and can become suspicious when routine is disturbed. Recruit parents and/or service groups to volunteer as monitors to increase your supervision force during the school day, especially in the morning, during lunch, and at the end of the day.
- If need be, schedule activities such as athletic competitions with major rivals for school hours.
- Network information with parents, police, and the community.
- Assign roving school security staff and administrators who have radios and do not establish regular patrol patterns that become predictable.
- Implement and enforce a pass system.
- Maintain communications with every classroom.

RULES/PROCEDURES

- Have policies clearly explained and acknowledged by each student regarding gang activity, drugs, weapons, and the consequences for violations. Insure that these are maintained and enforced.

- Punishment for violations should be restitution-based. Coordinating these with the local courts could be a real benefit. Students found guilty of vandalism should be given the task of cleanup and repair.
- Deal quickly with violators of school policy, and bring the parents into the loop.
- Punish individuals, not groups, for violations. Punishing an entire group or class makes them martyrs or heroes and can antagonize those not involved against the administration.
- Establish a clear, easily interpreted dress code policy. Have significant student, parent, and staff input and consensus in its development and implementation. Be aware of ethnic and cultural differences.
- Remember: gang membership is not a crime. It's the activity that the juvenile may become involved in that is criminal.
- Report crimes to the police. Follow up by filing charges and prosecuting. This "zero tolerance" option is effective for maintaining control of your schools and notifying gangs about their limits. Staff will also feel that they are being backed by administration.
- Develop and utilize peer counseling as an effective and immediate method of diffusing potentially violent situations. This allows students to take responsibility for their actions and establish ownership of the school and its programs.

Gang control programs need to start in elementary schools. As previously stated, kids as young as eight years old some times start in gangs. This is where organizations such as parks and recreation departments, Boys and Girls Clubs, and the YMCA can contribute. They can offer alternative after-school programs such as sports, creative activities, and field trips. Police-sponsored programs to educate teachers, parents, and students about the rising incidence of gangs in schools should be developed and implemented. Gang prevention is the key term in elementary school, where the kids imitate the gang activity of their older brothers and sisters and neighbors.

At the middle school and high school levels, a "zero tolerance" policy adopted by the school administration and supported by the community requires that, on school property and at school functions, no gang colors, clothing, drugs, weapons, or anything related to gang affiliation be allowed. Violations of this policy should be punished swiftly and substantially. The obviously serious offenses should be dealt with as criminal cases through the juvenile justice system and vigorously pursued by the school administration. Lesser transgressions should also be dealt with swiftly and appropriately.

Too often students have been suspended or expelled inappropriately due to a school administrator's belief that a tough approach to discipline would discourage future problems. The reality is, however, that students expelled or suspended are free to roam the streets and create additional problems in the community. More effective and creative are in-school detention programs and restitution-based discipline that keeps students within the school system. Examples of such alternative discipline would be campus cleanup projects, participating in gang awareness programs, or assignment to a community service project.

At-Risk Youth

A large percentage of teens who get involved in gangs have learning disabilities and very low self-esteem. Danny was one of these kids. Unusually strong for his age, he was also very immature, had learning disabilities, and needed glasses—only no one suspected these problems. Ridiculed by both his teachers and classmates, he fought back the only way he could. He became a bully. Now he had power and self-esteem. He was someone to be feared. Danny began to associate with other outcasts, and they formed a gang that plagued the community. At fifteen, he found himself in front of a tough juvenile judge who promised to throw the book at him if he ever showed up in his courthouse again. The judge ordered him into counseling, special school classes, and placed him under house arrest. Only then were Danny's other problems discovered. After years of pain and suffering, he was able to turn his life around.

When youths like Danny hang around with similar kids, who not only accept them for what they are but treat them like a respected family member, they become a powerful, destructive force. These at-risk kids need to have their problems accurately defined and addressed early in life so that they can be kept in the educational mainstream. Once they leave the school system, the chances are not good that they will ever come back.

Assessing the Gang Problems in Your School

The following Gang Assessment Tool, developed by the National School Safety Center, was created to raise awareness of gang problems and to provide community leaders and school administrators with a guide for evaluating the level of gang activity in their locale. Answering the following questions may help a school system overcome denial about gang activity and begin successfully addressing the problem. A "yes" response to any question earns the number of points indicated after the question.

1. Do you have graffiti on or near your campus? (5) _____
2. Do you have crossed out graffiti on or near your campus? (10) _____
3. Do your students wear colors, jewelry, clothing, flash hand signals, or display other behavior that may be gang related? (10) _____
4. Are drugs available near your school? (10) _____
5. Has there been a significant increase in the number of physical confrontations/stare downs within the past twelve months in or around your school? (5) _____
6. Is there an increasing presence of weapons in your community? (10) _____
7. Are beepers, pagers, or cellular phones used by your students? (10) _____
8. Have you had a drive-by shooting at or around your school?(15) _____

9. Have you had a "show-by" display of weapons at your school? (10) _____
10. Is the truancy rate of your school increasing? (5) _____
11. Are there increasing numbers of racial incidents occurring in your community or school? (5) _____
12. Is there a history of gang activity in your community? (10) _____
13. Is there an increasing presence of "informal social groups" with unusual names like the "Woodland Heights Posse," "Rip Off and Rule," "Females Simply Chillin'," or "Kappa Phi Nasty"? (15) _____

TOTAL _____

Total the points and compare them to the following ranges, which indicate the possible level of gang activity in and around the school.

0–15 points:	No significant gang problem.
20–40 points:	An emerging gang problem.
45–60 points:	A significant gang problem for which a gang prevention and gang intervention program should be developed.
65 + points:	An acute gang problem that merits a total gang prevention, intervention, and suppression program.

26

Protecting the Bottom Line: Business and Media Solutions

BUSINESS

The purpose of commercial enterprise is to make a profit and provide income for the owners or stockholders. Any business that fails to earn a profit will soon close its doors out of necessity. Communities with gang problems know firsthand the impact of gang violence on business. They have witnessed the decline of their business sector and with it the slow death of the community, which cannot thrive without a strong economic base. The commercial business sector of any community needs to insure that the community anti-gang program is successful because its own continued livelihood depends upon it.

Businesses can contribute many things to the community's anti-gang efforts. Key contributions include providing services and stable employment in a safe environment, training citizens in the community, donating resources to anti-gang programs, and engaging in responsible advertising.

Safety

A business that does not provide a safe environment for customers will soon find itself without customers. Businesses are caught in the difficult position of needing to lure teenagers, who spend the largest amounts of money shopping but who also tend to drive off other more mature customers with their sometimes menacing appearance or rude behavior. Such conflicts have led to the use of shopping mall curfews during school hours, dress codes, and anti-loitering and anti-cruising ordinances invoked by municipal authorities. These have met with varying degrees of success, though at times they have created bad public relations for the businesses concerned. Businesses should thoroughly consider the ramifications of such actions and work with community anti-gang programs to devise effective strategies.

The mall at 163rd Street in Miami, Florida, decided to take a stand on students from area schools who were skipping classes and loitering on its premises. The mall management banned school-age children from its premises until after 6:00 P.M. on school days unless a parent or guardian accompanied them. Students who worked at the mall were given work permits so that they could continue their employment. The ban was a result of students coming to the mall for lunch and staying, instead of returning to school. Many became a nuisance and disrupted other customers shopping at the mall.

Banning certain businesses or activities that attract large numbers of youth can have an impact on customer safety. Video game parlors are a magnet for juveniles who tend to loiter around them and socialize. Many shopping areas have found that by removing these from their vicinity, the number of criminal incidents involving juveniles decreases dramatically. Placing video game parlors in heavily trafficked areas, instead of tucked away in corners, can also reduce incidents due to the increased presence of the public. Convenience store chains are finding that the removal of video games from their stores also helps to decrease loitering and increases sales volume due to an increased customer base.

A visual increase in security personnel and security devices also provides a greater sense of comfort for customers worried about safety. Businesses often employ off-duty law enforcement officers to help boost their regular security measures. The benefit of such extra security can be hard to measure, but many businesses have found that using off-duty law enforcement officers helps to decrease crime and improve customer perceptions about safety. Although such measures appear expensive, the loss of a solid customer base due to safety concerns can be even more expensive.

Employment

By providing stable employment opportunities in the community, businesses are making a significant contribution. The jobs they provide are important in maintaining avenues of opportunity for young people so that they can have some path to upward mobility. Many times juvenile offenders in gangs claim, with some justification, that they had no other alternatives to crime since there were no legitimate employment opportunities in their community. They may see gang members selling dope as their only successful role model and soon become jaded to the "straight" lifestyle. Lack of good role models even extends to their immediate families who, without job opportunities or an ability to provide adequately for their dependents, become despondent and survive only on public assistance. The attraction of the gang can be very easy to understand when placed in these circumstances. Minimum wage positions may not provide the means to an end for many, but entry-level training and experience is better than none.

Training/Mentoring

Another important contribution that businesses can make in developing an aggressive community program to control gangs is joining with schools to develop internship and mentoring programs. These programs do not require significant monetary resources but contributions of personal time. The exposure to positive, successful role models in business is intended to help juveniles look to the future and establish some goals.

Learning and developing job skills is also a vital component of these programs. Businesses offer unique opportunities to provide the training necessary to help at-risk youth obtain these vital skills. Additionally, lifelong relationships and professional references can be obtained by participants. Minority participants who have a chance to work with and observe successful minority role models get an added benefit they probably wouldn't receive if it weren't for such programs.

Other Resources

Businesses can donate resources within reason toward combating gangs. They should look upon this as more of an investment than a donation. Examples of businesses contributing towards community anti-gang efforts are plentiful.

The National Rifle Association has received a lot of negative publicity for its stand against gun control laws, but it has developed a program to teach weapons safety to elementary school children. The pilot program, started in Wyoming, uses a character known as Eddie Eagle to make children understand that guns are not toys, and how to be safe around them. No guns are used in the program, and the need for constant adult supervision around weapons is stressed. The program is being expanded and made available to schools nationwide.

The Burger King Corporation has sponsored a unique dropout prevention program known as the Cities in Schools/Burger King Academy. It is available in only 40 schools across the country, and uses financial support from local businesses and Burger King to provide a specialized two-hour daily program to 50 students who are dropout risks. The students receive extra attention and help from a staff of two teachers and six part-time social workers who assist them in career planning, choice of role models, and normal school assignments. The program also provides a computer lab for student use.

One successful business cooperative program is in Rancho Cordova, California, at Cordova High School. Its mentoring program teams students who are gang members, or potential recruits, with adults at the state Franchise Tax Board. The mentors provide guidance and assistance to their students by serving as successful role models. The school district has other mentor partnerships with local businesses, such as Intel Corp., Bank of America, Aetna Insurance, and several small businesses.

On the marketing side, several corporations are becoming more responsive to the negative images that their products may invoke, and are making adjustments so that the wrong message isn't delivered. Converse, whose Chuck Taylor basketball shoe made the company famous, was caught in an embarrassing position when it was preparing to market a new shoe line. The new line was to be known as "Run 'n Gun," after a style of basketball offense played by some schools. It was quickly pointed out, however, that it appeared to many to be a reference to drive-by shootings and could be used by kids as a new street gang symbol. The company was very quick to change the new line, demonstrating an admirable example of corporate responsibility.

Another corporation that became aware of the misuse of its products through negative association was Timberland. Their products, especially their military-style boots, are popular with Skinhead gang members. The company obviously couldn't discontinue its popular product line due to this embarrassing association. Therefore it took an innovative approach in positive marketing by offering a free T-shirt with every purchase of its footwear. On the T-shirts the company had printed, "Give Racism the Boot." The message was obviously intended to demonstrate the company's disapproval of the Skinheads and their agenda, while maintaining a positive market image for its products.

The removal of gang-related tattoos by members of the professional medical community has become a popular and important contribution towards helping communities battle street-gangs across the country. Gang tattoos, which members place on prominent locations of their bodies, demonstrate dedication to the gang. Often members get tattoos when they are young and naive, high on drugs, or intoxicated. The sad reality becomes apparent later, when the gang tattoos they have placed on their arms, hands, neck, or face become a barrier to joining mainstream society. Despite their vocal denials, the tattoos represent a brand of shame for many former gang members. The presence of their tattoos is a psychological and physical hindrance. Many medical professionals understand the barriers that the gang tattoos represent and have supported community efforts to help gang members change their lives by providing tattoo removal, free or at cost, to groups and organizations that are working to control gangs in their community.

Many local businesses have offered positive reinforcement to students for years. The most popular contributions are discounts or prizes for good grades and/or attendance. Some communities underwrite these discounts and certificates through the chamber of commerce or another business group, recognizing that it is cheaper to reward good behavior than to punish the negative.

MEDIA

As a society, we are easily influenced and molded by the images we are given via the television, radio, and print media. Because of this influence, it is imperative that the media be responsible when choosing the messages they present. Sensationalism in reporting the news for the sake of increasing ratings or circulation is irresponsible, does not speak highly of the professionalism of the reporters, and undermines any community service work done by the media.

The images presented when reporting on gang and drug activities should be in the context of community efforts to control these activities and provide a safe living environment. Portraying gang members and drug dealers as victims, or glamorizing them, does a disservice to the community. Portrayals should emphasize the negative impact on the community and the individuals who are victimized.

Promoting the Positive

The community's anti-drug and anti-gang programs should be given more attention. The media today tends to dwell on the negative and highly dramatic stories and use the positive just to fill time and space or as a special feature. The community's media resources need to mobilize as part of the anti-gang and anti-drug effort and promote the positive role models and efforts of community members and organizations. This can be done as part of an ongoing public service program, with service announcements and regular reports. Examples of this include the 10 P.M. announcement "Do you know where your children are?" Other ongoing programs include follow-up stories on the victims of gang and drug violence, and regular features on positive role models and programs.

Educating the Public

Special reporting on gang activity and sharing knowledge with the community is important. The public must be informed as to what gangs are doing, where they are, who is involved, and how to identify gang members. Encouraging people to be the eyes and ears of the community through neighborhood watches and by becoming "news hounds" will help to keep the police informed and improve their ability to cover the community more thoroughly. The consequences of involvement in gang and drug activity should be reported on and followed through the judicial system.

This type of helpful media coverage encourages an open dialogue about youth problems in the community. Through radio talk shows, public forums, and television specials, young people can communicate their fears and ideas and not feel out of touch. The radio talk show *Street Soldiers* on Oakland, California radio station KMEL is a good example of how communication can start when youth are given a forum, where they can freely talk and remain anonymous.

Anonymity is important at first to many young people until they realize that many others feel as they do about violence, crime, and drugs in their community. Open forums can then take place to discuss the issues concerning youth in the community and to bring youth into the decision-making loop with policymakers.

In Folsom, California, the Police Department's gang coordinator uses a regular weekly newspaper column as a positive step toward passing on information to youth in the community who normally won't talk to the police. The public can now get the story straight on incidents involving juveniles without relying on the grapevine, where stories often get distorted. Many times juveniles are distrustful of the intentions of law enforcement and resent their presence at school campuses and community events. Speaking to them through a newspaper column may help them begin to understand that the police are really there for the safety of all.

Many television stations and newspapers across the country are currently promoting regular features on achieving citizens and programs, giving long over-due recognition to the positive aspects of their communities. Since these are done on a regular basis, people begin to look for them and start to realize the good things going on around them.

The reporting on violent gang activity in her community was of enough concern to the mayor of San Diego, California, Susan Golding, that she called a special forum for media and city government officials. Her intent was to have repre-sentatives of the print, television, and radio media in town sit down and coordinate with the community's law enforcement and social service officials in charge of the community's anti-gang programs. They were able to discuss what impact reporting had on the efforts to control gang activity. Media members found that they could improve their coverage, and not provide the type of reinforcement that gangs crave through recognition, by refraining from naming specific gangs involved in violent crimes along with the penalties handed out. The concept that gangs use the publicity from news stories to promote their image and to recruit new members was eye-opening to some in attendance.

HBO's documentary series *America Undercover* produced a factual and dra-matic representation of the street gang problem in the city of Little Rock, Arkansas. Titled "Gang War: Bangin' in Little Rock," this one hour documentary portrayed how the gang scene has migrated from America's major metropolitan areas to its smaller communities. It exposed the negative influences of violent gang rap videos and music, and traced the story of one L.A. Crip gang member who moved to Little Rock and built a small empire based on drug sales.

The CBS and Fox networks simultaneously broadcasted an hour-long special called *Kids Killing Kids*. The commercial-free simultaneous broadcast of this documentary special by two television networks was extraordinary, underscoring the serious nature of youth violence in this country. It focused on the results of gun violence in conflict situations as compared to conflict solutions in which alternative resolutions were used.

What the Media Can Do

- Follow up on gang violence, especially criminal prosecution and victim aware-ness.
- Develop an ongoing community service program in conjunction with the community's gang control plan.
- Monitor, and refuse, advertising that promotes street gang lifestyles.

What Not to Do

- Glamorize gang violence in portrayals and reporting.
- Fail to report gang activity due to its bad reflection of the community.
- Give notoriety to specific gangs and gang members by identifying them by name when reporting stories.

A Checklist for Business Contribution to Anti-Gang Efforts

1. Provide entry-level, apprentice-type positions for youths under a cooperative work/study program with the schools.
2. Donate facilities/equipment/time to the community anti-gang effort.
3. Promote community service, academic achievement and leadership through advertisement and by offering discounts or awards for these activities.
4. Refuse to use advertising or promotions that positively portray gang lifestyles.
5. If possible, do not carry products that local gangs use as a means of identification.
6. Provide a safe environment for all customers. Enforce parking ordinances and employ adequate security patrols so that no one group is allowed to take over the area.

Curfews and Community Policing: Laws that Work for Everyone

. . . community policing is more than the deployment of police officers and is really a philosophy of law enforcement. It is two words: police and community.

—President Bill Clinton, 1995

NEW APPROACHES IN LAW ENFORCEMENT

We are living in a time when the courts and jails cannot keep pace with the gang criminals. Law enforcement is being forced to take a new approach in the suppression of street gangs, stretching already-tight budgets. Police officers have become targets of shootings, district attorneys have been deluged with gang-related crimes, juvenile halls and youth authorities are overcrowded, and witnesses are reluctant to testify. Safety can no longer be left to the justice system, but rather the entire community must regroup to take back control of their streets.

Many of the smaller and rural police agencies are seeing the preliminary signs of gang activity in their jurisdictions. Many agencies are untrained in the methods of dealing with gang subcultures. Children continue to die at alarming rates and therefore it is illogical to take the stance that this is a phase that our youth will outgrow. It is necessary for even the smallest of law enforcement agencies to assign one or more officers to learn and track gang activity.

Documenting Gang Members and Their Activities

One of the first steps police departments must take when fighting street gang crime is identifying the opposition. Gangs must be documented and this can be done by interviewing gang members and non-gang members alike. Juveniles may not admit their own membership, but most are willing to reveal the names of their rivals. Another means of collecting this data is by reading graffiti. As discussed in the graffiti chapter, gangs will always include the name of their gang or a symbol representing the gang when writing graffiti. A third option is contacting the local school administrators and discussing which gangs are active on their respective campuses.

Once the gangs are documented, the police department must document the individual members. Gang membership criteria may differ from city to city and state to state. The object of documentation is to ultimately use this information in court to enhance sentences or simply prosecute offenders.

Sharing Information

Once the gang members have been successfully documented, including information such as moniker, gang affiliation, associates, and criminal history, it is time for the police department to use and share this information. Information collected but not disseminated is useless. Police departments throughout the country have been gathering to exchange information among fellow peace officers on local, county, state, and national levels. Information on trends in crime, alliances, dress, and rivalries are necessary when combating gangs.

Gang members have become extremely mobile in recent years. This mobility has necessitated that law enforcement agencies establish communication networks to track gangs. The fact that the same gang member can commit a crime in Stockton, California, one day and commit a similar crime in Houston, Texas, the next has made it imperative to maintain a system for exchanging information about gang crime and violence.

The Gang Reporting, Evaluation, and Tracking (GREAT) System can be used to share gang-related information among law enforcement agencies. The system was developed by the Los Angeles County Sheriff's Department and is currently being used by over 100 agencies in California and other states. The system allows users to gather information about gang members, such as physical description, gang affiliation, monikers, tattoos, and associates.

It is critical for law enforcement agencies to share gang information among each other and it is also necessary for officers assigned as gang investigators to share information within their agencies. Training is most important when combating gangs. The signs of gang affiliation can change on a weekly basis, and it is important to keep abreast of these changes. Even the smallest of police departments can assign an officer a collateral duty of monitoring gangs and their membership.

Community Policing

Police officers may say that the police department is the last line of defense against street gang crime and that parents and the community must work together to prevent juveniles from joining gangs. The Office of the Attorney General in the state of

California has promoted the concept of "Community Oriented Policing and Problem Solving" (COPPS) in the public safety arena. COPPS is a model for dealing with gang activity and other problems and is generally defined as a philosophy, management style, and organizational strategy that promotes proactive problem solving and police-community partnerships to address the causes of crime and fear, as well as other community issues.

COPPS supplements traditional enforcement tactics with additional tools to make police more effective. It mobilizes the community to address the problems of gangs and drugs without burdening the public safety budget. In short, it offers a better way of resolving community problems with existing resources.

The 1995 May/June issue of *Community Policing Exchange* discusses programs like the one started in a small town in Arizona, when they invited the community to help design a curfew rewards program. The article showed how the community and police department launched "a curfew incentive program that allows youngsters who play by the rules to earn points toward a bicycle." According to the Police Executive Research Forum and the National Center for Community Policing in conjunction with the FBI, roughly two out of three police agencies in major jurisdictions have adopted some form of community policing or plan to in the near future.

Throughout the nation citizens are performing duties that have traditionally been done by sworn personnel. Port St. Lucie, Florida, now offers a 40-hour Citizen Police Academy taught by the city manager, police chief, and department heads. The curriculum includes topics such as neighborhood policing, code enforcement, community relations, criminal investigation, and disaster preparedness, among others.

Lodi, California, established a PARTNERS program in 1994 employing the services of retired citizens. PARTNERS assists the gang unit by photographing gang graffiti, documenting its location, and making arrangements for its removal. The time-consuming collection of this important information by PARTNERS allows the investigators the opportunity to spend more of their time investigating crimes. PARTNERS performs other duties within the department in addition to assisting the gang unit. Their numbers in 1996 exceeded that of sworn personnel within the department.

Communities working alongside police departments have been responsible for creating several new anti-gang programs. One such program in Los Angeles is Civil Gang Abatement: A Community-Based Anti-Gang Weapon. This program facilitates the use of an injunction from a civil court prohibiting specific gang activities that are deemed public nuisances. Violations of the injunction's order can result in arrest, incarceration, or even banishment of some gang members from the community. The community meets with the police department to highlight what is unacceptable activity. This civil process allows police to assume a proactive role. Police may take action for what would otherwise be considered noncriminal activities.

Improved Relations Between Police Officers and Juveniles

Police departments are attempting to bridge the gap between officers and juveniles. The community benefits from improved relations between these two groups. One method of bridging this gap is through the use of cop cards in the style of baseball cards. Police departments have begun printing cop cards featuring photos of police officers. On the back of the card is biographical information about each officer. These cards are handed out to school children who are invited to collect all the cards and may even be offered a prize if they achieve this challenge.

A similar program involves the printing of stick-on Junior Police badges. These badges are given to children to wear on their clothing or place on their bicycles. It doesn't take long for children who were once afraid of the police to approach them without hesitation, looking for a badge and conversation.

In June of 1995, Roseville, California's police officers participated in the department's fourth annual Cops Care Kids Camp which was held for two weeks at the local high school. Students attending the camp were taught about gangs, drugs, peer pressure, and the consequences of making wrong decisions. SWAT demonstrations including rappelling, and hostage scenarios were played out for the students. In an interview with the *Sacramento Bee* newspaper on June 29, 1995, Sgt. Rocky Rockholm said, "Often our police work is based on negative contact with kids. This camp is a positive contact."

Along the same lines, the Lodi Police department gang unit implemented both a "Late Nite Basketball" program and an in-line street hockey organization. During the winter months the police department sponsors the basketball program which starts at 9 pm and continues until 2 A.M. The supervised setting offers juveniles a safe place to participate in healthy, gang-free activities. The hockey program runs during the summer months and is designed to offer younger children an early evening recreation without the risk of being confronted by street gang members.

There will be times when police department and community programs prove ineffective in preventing gang crimes. When this occurs it may be time for the police to suppress gang activity rather than prevent or intervene. In December of 1994 in Fresno, California, the police and community were outraged over the separate shootings of an 8-year-old boy and an 11-year-old girl. Police officers in conjunction with SWAT, gang specialists, and probation and parole officers unveiled a show of force in crime-afflicted neighborhoods. The police department unleashed a special 30-man Violent Crime Suppression Unit that scoured the streets, cracking down on weapon and narcotic violations.

In the March 6, 1995, issue of *U.S. News and World Report*, author Gordon Witkin wrote an article entitled "Enlisting the Feds in the War on Gangs." He stated that since 1992, an army of federal agents has joined forces with the Connecticut U.S. attorney and with police to inflict a series of blows against gang members involved in drug trafficking. As a result, crime in Bridgeport was down 21 percent in 1994. Federal agencies, such as the Drug Enforcement Agency; the Bureau of

Alcohol, Tobacco and Firearms; and the Federal Bureau of Investigation have all supplied funds to attack street gangs on a federal level while assisting municipalities.

NEW APPROACHES IN GOVERNMENT

With the onslaught of juvenile and adult crime, state and federal governments find themselves with too few prisons and too many convicted criminals. They wonder if incarceration is the appropriate solution to criminal activity, and many would argue that prevention, not imprisonment, is the answer to combating crime in the 21st century.

Local Government

Citizens across the nation are demanding that the federal government decentralize and give more power back to the people on the state and local level. A lack of state legislation in many areas has resulted in city ordinances to deal with juvenile crime and street gang activity.

One of the more popular policies passed by municipalities is the juvenile curfew law. Some cities such as Portland, Oregon, enacted a juvenile curfew as early as 1906; however, it was during the early 1990s when cities began reconsidering their curfew laws and enforcing them.

Curfews

Many cities across the country are returning to a traditional remedy for curtailing juveniles' movement in the late evening and early morning. Critics cite the uselessness of this method of controlling juvenile crime as creating only another law for already overworked police to enforce. The reality of this situation, however, is that it gives police and parents more leverage in keeping kids at home and off the streets during hours when much violent gang crime occurs. A curfew provides a means and a reason for parents to restrict their sons and daughters without becoming overly protective.

In May 1994 the U.S. Supreme Court let stand a curfew law in Dallas, Texas, that had been opposed by the American Civil Liberties Union. Many cities intend to use their curfew laws as a legal means of escorting juveniles home and keeping them off the streets, while others are more aggressive, imposing fines of up to $500 for violation of curfew. In New Orleans, the juvenile crime rate fell 38 percent and the overall crime rate dropped 7.8 percent from May through August of 1994, when a new curfew law was instituted.

Curfew restrictions vary from city to city. These variations are all part of local government deciding what is best for its citizens and enacting laws to protect citizens from themselves as well as outsiders. On July 10, 1995, Baltimore, Maryland's juvenile curfew was suspended. According to *USA Today*, the curfew was suspended because the state supreme court recently struck down a similar curfew in Frederick. The city council and mayor's office worked together to alter the law so that it could be reinstated. On July 12, *USA Today* reported that more than a dozen people had been wounded and three people killed in Baltimore in the three days since the teen curfew was suspended. All the victims but one were under 20 years old.

Curfew laws enable police officers to take a preventive and proactive role in society when dealing with juvenile crime. The mere presence of juveniles on the street after curfew entitles law enforcement to detain children and require their parents to take custody of them for the remainder of the evening. Curfew laws are most effective when used as a selective enforcement tool. Most cities have formal or informal exceptions to the curfew law for juveniles attending special events, such as homecoming dances or proms. Gang members loitering on the same evening would not be exempt from the curfew law.

Cities have begun fining parents for allowing their children to violate curfew laws. California penal code section 272 states that "every person who commits any act or omits the performance of any duty, which act or omission causes or tends to cause or encourage any person under the age of 18 to commit a crime is guilty of a misdemeanor and shall be punished by a fine not exceeding $2,500 or imprisonment in the county jail for no more than one year or both." This section is commonly referred to as "contributing to the delinquency of a minor." Cities in California have used this section for prosecuting parents whose children are continuously in violation of curfew laws.

Restitution for Vandalism

In addition to curfew laws, cities may adopt laws governing restitution for vandalism and malicious mischief. In certain cases gang members and their parents would be required to perform community service as part of the punishment. Juveniles arrested for writing graffiti could be forced to either paint over the graffiti or pay for the repainting by city staff.

Charging Juveniles as Adults

This popular approach has been tried in many states and receives high approval ratings from the electorate. No one under 16 years of age can receive the death penalty, according to a 1988 ruling by the U.S. Supreme Court. In addition, juveniles tried as adults usually receive much more lenient sentencing and are also required by law to be housed in juvenile correctional facilities until they are old enough to transfer to an adult facility.

Since most juveniles who have committed violent crimes say that they did not consider the penalties prior to or during the commission of their crime, the deterrent effect of this type of sentencing is negligible. In November of 1995, Wisconsin governor Tommy Thompson signed a bill that allowed children as young as 10 to be tried for homicide as adults. The fact that any 10-year-old committing such a crime probably would not be aware of the legal ramifications of being tried as an adult did not seem important.

Beyond the scope of municipalities is state government. The state is capable of imposing a vast array of laws governing street gang crimes. Enhancements on existing laws seem to be on the upswing. As described in the law enforcement section, California has a section that enhances the sentence for those crimes committed by gang members. States should implement laws that severely penalize those criminals found guilty of participating in street gangs. Included are laws that would require minimum sentences for crimes involving dangerous weapons and drive-by shootings.

Enhancements and special laws governing gang crimes near schools have become popular. In the late 1980s, schools began establishing "drug-free zones." This meant that any person found guilty of a narcotics offense within the zone received a harsher sentence and, in some jurisdictions, the district attorney was unable to plea-bargain. Schools have expanded on that idea and formed gang-free zones. Like the drug-free zones, any person found guilty of participating in a gang-related crime within 1,000 feet of a school or designated zone would receive a stiffer penalty than a person committing the same crime that is not gang-related.

Some states have chosen to mandate trying juveniles as adults if they commit a serious and/or violent crime, despite evidence that such action has little or no impact as a deterrent. Moving juveniles to an adult venue has several potential benefits. Longer sentences are possible in adult court, but historically adult judges are reluctant to give juveniles lengthy sentences due to their inexperience with juveniles. Longer sentencing would allow more time for juvenile offenders to be exposed to treatment programs, providing they are available and effective. Greater latitude in parole considerations can also be tied to successful completion of treatment.

State government should take an active role in the education of law enforcement, communities, schools, and parents. The state needs to establish databases for information on gang members within the state. This computerized program would link law enforcement throughout the state to a central system that disseminates member information. Seminars should be held at various locations in the state to inform the public about gangs and possible solutions to gang activity. Finally, states need to be willing to take a strong law enforcement stance if intervention and prevention programs fail.

School Suspension and/or Expulsion

In 1995, a federal law was enacted requiring that schools must expel any students who bring weapons to school. Failure to comply with the law would cost the school district the loss of all federal funding.

School administrators and districts have long preferred the policy of removal or transference of problem students. This practice, when overused for minor problems, can create greater difficulties for the community.

Students need to be in school and provided the opportunity to learn. Whenever a student is expelled or suspended, he is given freedom to roam the town all day long and become a potentially greater hazard for law enforcement to manage. Students who are guilty of committing offenses that endanger themselves or others should be dealt with through the legal system.

Minor infractions of school rules need to be handled by school authorities. Blind adherence to get-tough policies like "zero tolerance" alienates students and causes a lack of respect for the system. For example, students who are chronically late should not be suspended, but counseled and placed in some type of restitution program.

A student at Mount Zion High School in Jonesboro, Georgia, was expelled for violating the school's "zero tolerance" policy for weapons on school grounds. The student in question had driven his brother's car to school; in the car there was a realistic-looking black plastic toy gun. This was definitely an example of a good idea being poorly applied.

Charging Parents for the Actions of Their Children

New legislation is being attempted to make parents more accountable for their children. Some laws involve restitution through payment for damages or participation with their child in community service projects as part of the juvenile courts sentencing. Family counseling may also help families develop better support mechanisms.

Some parents may require a court intervention to focus their attention on their children's behavior and its impact has on others. The juvenile court in Hamilton, Ohio, works closely with the school district to identify chronically truant students, serving summons that require parents to attend hearings with their child. The parents are then informed about the child's attendance problems, and the parent must post a $100 bond, refundable if attendance improves. If the situation doesn't improve, the parents may be charged with contributing to the delinquency of a minor. Police in the community have noticed a significant drop in juvenile related calls and criminal gang activity since the program went into effect.

Realistically, parents should know about their child's attendance problem before being brought to court. School districts should make direct contact with the parent or guardian in a face to face meeting before the court needs to become involved. Oregon adopted a state law in 1995 that penalizes parents for failing to supervise their children. Fines can be up to $1,000, with up to $2,500 in additional charges for restitution.

Similarly, parents are once again being held responsible for their children's conduct. Juveniles involved in gang activity are, at some point, truant from school.

School officials have begun working with police departments and local government, finding ways to keep the juveniles in school and at the same time demand more accountability from the parents. In Huntington, West Virginia, a woman was sentenced to 100 days in jail after her child missed 59 days of school. The child was placed in a foster home while the mother was in jail. In Honolulu, if a student misses even four hours of school, the student and parent may be summoned by the police to a special class. If they fail to appear, the case may go to court. In many states, welfare checks can be docked if children are truant.

Anti-Cruising Ordinances

Automobile cruising of city streets has become a major problem and potential danger in some metropolitan areas. It is also a symptom of a lack of more conventional recreational and social opportunities for youth in the community. Cities have adopted anti-cruising ordinances to avoid traffic congestion, maintain access to businesses, and prevent the cruising youth from intimidating customers away from businesses. Cruising also calls for an increase in the number of police on duty in an area, pulling them from other patrol areas or adding to budget problems.

The innocent days of cruising, as portrayed in the film *American Graffiti,* have given way to shootings, fights, and drug dealing. The intent of the anti-cruising ordinances is not to curtail fun for participants but to avoid the more serious problems. Even the original cruising capital, Modesto, California, allows cruising only once a year, and may eliminate it altogether. Violation of the anti-cruising ordinances is cause for police citation. More effective policing results when checkpoints are set up and cruisers are required to provide driver's licenses, proof of insurance, and current vehicle registration. Cruisers, once aware of this tactic, often disperse rather than take the risk having their vehicles impounded and receiving citations for more serious violations of the motor vehicle code.

Loitering is similar to the cruising problem. Many young people "hang out" around certain businesses, making nuisances of themselves, littering, and driving away potential customers. Loitering laws often become a civil rights issue and can result in retaliation to the business. Simple solutions are sometimes the easiest. A midwestern convenience store that played popular music on its outside speakers found that it had a problem with loitering. When the manager changed to classical music, the loitering ceased, and sales went up. If an area that attracts loitering becomes less desirable to those causing a nuisance, the problem will probably go away.

School Uniforms/Dress Codes

The current push for school uniforms has been the result of popular clothing styles becoming associated with certain street gangs. Schools and parents first attempted to adopt dress codes to protect innocent students form the dangers of wearing gang-style clothing. Too often young people are hurt or even killed for wearing the wrong colors or not giving clothing items up to gang members on demand. The rapidly changing fashion trends of street gangs sometimes make dress codes obsolete before they become effective.

The solution in some areas, and even entire states such as California, is to establish school uniforms and laws to support them. The benefits of uniforms includes elimination of clothing competition, reduced budgets for school clothes, and a sense of equality among students from different economic levels.

The elimination of desirable clothing that gang members see as potential trophies to be taken from innocents is also a safety measure. Establishing school uniforms may be the only way to stop these senseless crimes.

Long Beach, California's school district, with over 58,000 students, found that during the 1994–1995 school year, the first year that it adopted a school uniform policy, crime statistics declined significantly in all reported crime categories. Other large school districts across the country, in such places as Chicago and Miami, are considering a similar policy.

Corporal Punishment

The great amount of publicity that Michael Fay received when he was sentenced to a public caning in Singapore for a vandalism spree caused many opportunistic politicians to recommend similar policies in the United States. In 1993 the public debate reached President Clinton, when he personally appealed for leniency for Fay. Many people thought that this incident showcased what was wrong with American justice today, and that we need to reevaluate our sentencing and penalties.

Many people think that swift and severe penalties are the answer to the problems of delinquent youth. Several proposals have been made across the country to introduce paddling as an appropriate punishment for such crimes as graffiti. In 1996 the California state legislature debated introducing corporal punishment back into its schools. At the same time, New Hampshire legislators proposed a bill to publicly paddle graffiti vandals as a means of shaming them.

This solution does not, however, address the causes of juvenile crime. Public humiliation really has a minimal impact on youth who have little or no self-esteem in the first place. Restitution is a more effective solution: it not only punishes but raises awareness of crime and its consequences.

Laws aren't the only way city governments can crack down on gang crime. Local government needs to support financially and publicly community groups that focus on gang alternatives. Funds can be raised to support gang alternative programs and athletics in those neighborhoods where gangs have taken a foothold. In January of 1995 a Minnesota state task force recommended spending more money on crime prevention programs rather than incarceration. The report noted that prevention costs less than prisons.

Federal Government

The federal government has taken steps to combat gang activity on a national level. As gangs become more sophisticated and violent, the federal government has introduced programs such as Operation Triggerlock and the career criminal statutes. On November 4, 1993, the U.S. Senate voted to pump $22.2 billion into the fight against violent crime, including putting 100,000 new police officers on the streets. The bill included

$3 billion to build and operate regional prisons;

$1 billion to build jails, correctional boot camps, and other minimum security facilities;

$500 million to build and operate secure institutions to house violent juveniles;

$1.8 billion to prevent violence against women.

Law Enforcement Prevention Strategies

1. Establish and train a special gang unit. This can be a full-time "special assignment," or a number of officers can take the assignment as a collateral duty.
2. Document gang members and associates through police reports as well as field interviews. If you are unsure of criteria for documentation, contact your district attorney or state department of justice for guidelines.
3. Relay obtained information to local school administrators as needed. Communicate openly with neighboring law enforcement agencies.
4. Participate in or formulate county/multicounty law enforcement gang task forces.
5. Identify and maintain close contact with gang members, especially leaders.
6. Establish a local task force in conjunction with the school district, parks and recreation, chamber of commerce, and concerned parents and citizens.
7. Support the schools' anti-gang curriculum. Give extra patrols to schools at the beginning and end of each school day.
8. Develop "officer friendly" programs such as Here's Looking at You 2000, or DARE. Implement these programs in elementary schools.
9. Develop and implement a crime prevention program including a neighborhood watch component.
10. Be a visible presence at all youth-oriented events.
11. Support local "Friday Night Live" programs in the community.
12. Establish abatement programs with the community to eliminate drug houses and gang hangouts.
13. Obtain agreements by the district attorney's office to refrain from plea-bargaining cases originating in drug-free zones.

14. Educate the community by offering gang seminars through the school district or local service organizations.
15. Invite assistance through programs that encourage neighborhood policing.

Rick's Report
CHECK IT OUT FOR YOURSELF

I received a call from an angry woman who said that her street had been vandalized last night and that there was graffiti written everywhere. She asked if I could come to her street and decipher the meaning, if any, of this malicious act. I agreed and told her that I would be there within 30 minutes. Graffiti is my newspaper, and I find it necessary to read the graffiti in order to keep up on gang activity in the city. The etched scribblings and the spray-painted walls hold a wealth of information if you know what you're looking at.

I met the woman as planned and found her street covered with gang graffiti. I explained to her what the symbols and letters represented. A few minutes after my arrival, a city employee arrived in a pick-up truck. His job is to paint over any graffiti that may have appeared overnight.

I walked the street and spoke with some children who were approximately 8 years old. They immediately told me that the boys who did the "funny writing" lived in the blue apartments around the corner and said they would show me which apartment they lived in. We walked to the middle of the block, and they pointed out an upstairs apartment that faced the alley.

I knocked on the door of the apartment and a lady in her mid-thirties answered. I told her that I was a gang detective and asked if I could speak to her for a few minutes. I entered the apartment and explained that there was a rash of graffiti and asked if she had any sons. She said that she had two boys, one was 16 years old and the other was 13. She emphatically denied any possibility that her sons were involved in gangs. I asked her if there was anything in the boys' bedroom that might indicate that they were in a gang. She said that she didn't think so but wasn't sure because the boys didn't allow her in the bedroom.

Her last comment immediately piqued my interest and I asked her if her boys were home. She said that they were at school and that they should be home in the afternoon. I told her that if she didn't mind, I would like to take a brief look at her sons' room to see if there was anything there that we should be concerned with. She said that there was nothing in the room and that I could check it out for myself if I wanted. She led me to the bedroom and opened the door.

Much to her surprise, there was a 17-year-old boy asleep in her son's bed. The boy wasn't hers and she had never seen him before this morning. There were two beds in the room, and each bed was etched with gang symbols from one end to the other. Included was the name of the gang and her sons' monikers. These were the same names that had mysteriously appeared up and down the street during the previous night. There were numerous pictures covering the walls. The pictures were of juveniles who were all dressed in blue and "throwing gang signs." Scattered about the room were packages of bandannas that had yet to be opened. Lying in a corner of the room were a mound of car stereos. Needless to say, the woman was surprised and shocked to find out that her sons were involved in gangs.

I advised the woman to have a chat with her sons and to eliminate all the gang-related paraphernalia from their room, including the extra body under the blankets. I told her to have the boys sand down the beds and remove the graffiti. In addition, I asked if she could find the time to occasionally be a parent and check the boys' room. It is important for parents to know their children's friends and the friends' families. Most important, children should not run the house. Make it your business to "check it out."

Since my visit, the only contact with the family has been when her youngest boy was punched in the face for wearing blue clothes. The boys stay home at night, and overnight guests are screened at the door.

finding Help and Information: A Resource Guide

FINDING INFORMATION

No single book can be a complete resource on juvenile street gangs; this section is provided to help readers gather more detailed information on areas of interest. In your search for information about juvenile street gangs in your area, the first step is to contact local officials, such as the state attorney general, the superintendent of schools, the police department, and the mayor's office. These officials should be able to tell you about local anti-gang efforts and programs.

Your local library is also an excellent source of information, especially if it is equipped with computerized databases to assist in your search for current lists of books and articles. Try topics such as youth gangs, street gangs, juvenile crime, crime, gangs, and juvenile violence when searching these databases. Many libraries participate in the interlibrary loan program so that you can obtain from other libraries books that are not available in your local branch.

The Internet now has several excellent Web sites with detailed information on street gangs in localities nationally and internationally. We hesitate to cite any specific one due to the ever-changing availability of sites on the Internet. Search for information under the same categories as listed above for library research and current sites will begin appearing as you surf through the Net.

A final source that is becoming increasingly useful as its resources grow is the Justice Information Center, which provides several categories of gang information. Their address and phone number are listed under "People, Organizations, and Programs."

BIBLIOGRAPHY

General Information

BOOKS

Albanese, Jay S. *Crime in America: Some Existing and Emerging Issues.* Englewood Cliffs, N.J.: Regents/Prentice Hall, 1993.

Almonte, Paul. *Street Gangs.* Toronto, Calif.: Crestwood House, 1994.

Anderson, Elijah. *A Place on the Corner.* Chicago: University of Chicago Press, 1976.

Barden, Renardo. *Gangs.* Vero Beach, Fla.: Roarke Corporation, 1989.

Biskup, Michael D. *Youth Violence.* San Diego, Calif.: Greenhaven Press Incorporated, 1992.

Block, Carolyn Rebecca, and Block, Richard. *Street Gang Crime in Chicago.* Washington, D.C.: U.S. National Institute of Justice, 1993.

Butler, Robert Olen. *The Deuce.* New York: Simon and Schuster, 1989.

Cartwright, D.; Tomson, D.S.; and Schwartz, H. *Gang Delinquency.* Monterey, Calif.: Brooks Cole, 1975.

Cashmere, E. Ells. *No Future: Youth and Society.* London: Heinemann Educational Books, Ltd., 1984.

Cervantes, Richard C. *Substance Abuse and Gang Violence.* Newbury Park, Calif.: Sage Publications Inc., 1992.

Cloward, Richard A., and Ohlin, Lloyd E. *Delinquency and Opportunity: A Theory of Delinquent Gangs.* New York: The Free Press, 1960.

Cohen, Albert Kircidel. *Delinquent Boys: The Culture of the Gang.* New York: The Free Press, 1971.

Conley, Catherine H. *Street Gangs: Current Knowledge & Strategies.* Lancaster, Pa.: Diane Publishing Company, 1994.

Covey, Herbert C.; Menard, Scott; and Franzase, Robert J. *Juvenile Gangs.* Springfield, Ill.: Charles C. Thomas, 1992.

Cruz, Nicky, and Buckingham, Jamie. *Run Baby Run.* South Plainfield, N.J.: Bridge Publishing, Inc., 1987.

DeCanio, Margaret. *Encyclopedia of Violence: Origins, Attitudes, Consequences.* New York: Facts On File, 1993.

Devore, Cynthia DiLaura. *Kids & Gangs.* Edina, Minn.: Abdo & Daughters, 1994.

Dolan, Edward F. *19 Youth Gangs.* New York: Julian Messner, 1984.

Dryfoos, Joy G. *Adolescents at Risk: Prevalence and Prevention.* New York: Oxford University Press, 1990.

Dunston, Mark S. *Street Signs: An Identification Guide of Symbols of Crime and Violence.* Sacramento: Performance Dimensions Publishing, 1992.

Friedman, Lawrence H. *Crime and Punishment in American History.* New York: Basic Books, 1993.

Gardner, Sandra. *Street Gangs in America.* New York: Franklin Watts, 1992.

Goldentyer, Debra. *Gangs.* Austin, Tex.: Raintree Steck Vaughn. 1994.

Goldstein, Arnold P. *Delinquent Gangs: A Psychological Perspective.* Champaign, Ill.: Research Press, 1991.

Greenberg, Keith E. *Out of the Gang.* Minneapolis, Minn.: Lerner Publications Co., 1992.

Hinojosa, Maria. *Crews: Gang Members Talk to Maria Hinojosa.* Orlando, Fla.: Harcourt Brace Jovanovich, 1995.

Hoenig, Gary. *Reaper: The Story of a Gang Leader.* Indianapolis, Ind.: Bobbs-Merrill, 1975.

Huff, C. Ronald. *Gangs in America*. Newbury Park, Calif.: Sage Publications Inc., 1990.

Jackson, Robert K. *Understanding Street Gangs*. Placerville, Calif.: Custom Publishing. 1985.

Klein, Malcolm. *The American Street Gang: Its Nature, Prevalence & Control*. New York: Oxford University Press, Inc., 1995.

Klein, Malcolm W., and Maxson, Cheryl L. *Street Gang Violence: Twice as Great or Half as Great*. Newbury Park, Calif.: Sage Publications, 1991.

Knox, George W. *An Introduction to Gangs*. Berrien Springs, Mich.: Vande Vere Publishing, Ltd., 1991.

――――. *National Gangs Resource Handbook: An Encyclopedic Reference*. Bristol, Ind.: Wyndham Hall Press, 1994.

Knox, Mike. *Gangsta in the House*. Troy, Mich.: Momentum Books, 1995.

Lyman, Michael D. *Gangland: Drug Trafficking by Organized Criminals*. Springfield, Ill.: Charles C. Thomas, 1989.

Maxon, Cheryl L. *Street Gangs and Drug Sales: A Report to the National Institute of Justice*. Los Angeles: Center for Research on Crime and Social Control, University of Southern California, 1993.

McKinney, Kay C. *Juvenile Gangs: Crime and Drug Trafficking*. Washington, D.C.: Office of Juvenile Justice and Delinquency Prevention, 1988.

Needle, Jerome A. and Stapleton, William V. *Police Handling of Youth Gangs*. Washington, D.C.: U.S. Dept. of Justice, American Justice Institute, 1983.

Oliver, Marilyn Tower. *Gangs: Trouble in the Streets*. Springfield, N.J.: Enslow Publishers, 1995.

Osman, Karen. *Gangs*. San Diego, Calif.: Lucent Books, 1992.

Padilla, Felix M. *The Gang as an American Enterprise*. New Brunswick, N.J.: Rutgers University Press, 1992.

Prothrow-Stith, Deborah, and Weissman, Michaele. *Deadly Consequences*. New York: HarperCollins Publishers, 1991.

Rolfe, Peter Lars, and Greeson, Zelma. *Gangs USA*. Boulder, Colo.: Paladin Press, 1994.

Rosen, Roger, and McSharry, Patra. *Street Gangs: Gaining Turf, Losing Ground*. New York: Rosen Publishing Group, 1991.

Rosenbaum, Dennis P., and Grant, Jane D. *Gang and Youth Problems in Evanston: Research Findings and Policy Options*. Evanston, Ill.: Illinois Center for Urban Affairs and Policy Research, Northwestern University, 1983.

Sandars, William B. *Gangbangs and Drive-Bys*. Hawthorn, N.Y.: Aldijne De Gruyter, 1994.

Sanders, Wiley B. *Juvenile Offenders of 1000 Years*. Chapel Hill: University of North Carolina Press, 1970.

Schwartz, Gary. *Beyond Conformity or Rebellion: Youth and Authority in America*. Chicago, Ill.: University of Chicago Press, 1987.

Schwendiger, Herman and Julia. *Adolescent Subcultures and Delinquency*. New York: Praeger, 1985.

Short, James F. *Group Process and Gang Delinquency*. Chicago: University of Chicago Press, 1974.

Skolnick, Jerome H.. *Drugs, Gangs, and Law Enforcement*. Sacramento: California Department of Justice, 1990.

――――. *Gang Organization and Migration*. Sacramento: California Department of Justice, Office of the Attorney General, 1989.

――――. *The Social Structure of Street Drug Dealing*. Sacramento: California Department of Justice, 1988.

Stark, Evan. *Everything You Wanted to Know About Street Gangs.* New York: Rosen Publishing, 1992.

Sterling, Claire. *Thieves' World.* New York: Simon and Schuster, 1994.

Thrasher, Frederic. *The Gang: The Study of 1313 Chicago Street Gangs.* Chicago: University of Chicago Press, 1936.

Valentine, Bill. *Gang Intelligence Manual: Identifying and Understanding Modern Day Violent Gangs in the United States.* Boulder, Colo.: Paladin Press, 1995.

Van Camp, Lisa, and Wright, Ed. *Gangs: The Epidemic Sweeping America.* Northville, Mich.: Midwest Publishing, Inc., 1994.

Webb, Margot. *Coping with Street Gangs.* New York: Rosen Publishing Group, 1995.

———. *Gangs: A Statewide Directory of Programs, Prevention.* Sacramento, Calif.: The Center, 1994.

Weiner, Neil A., and Wolfgang, Marvin E., eds. *Violent Crime, Violent Criminals.* Newbury Park, Calif.: Sage Publications, Inc., 1989.

Wright, Richard. *Rite of Passage.* New York: HarperCollins, 1994.

Yablonsky, Lewis. *The Violent Gang.* New York: Penguin Books, 1970.

Annual Report to the Legislature. Sacramento: California Office of Criminal Justice Planning, California Gang Violence Suppression Program, 1990.

Crack Down on Gangs. Sacramento: California Office of the State Attorney General, Crime Prevention Center, 1992.

Gang Resource Guide. Sacramento: California District Attorneys Association, 1994.

Gangs 2000: A Call to Action (The Attorney General's Report on the Impact of Criminal Street Gangs on Crime and Violence in California by the Year 2000). Sacramento: California State Department of Justice, Division of Law Enforcement, Bureau of Investigations, 1993.

National Conference on Youth Gangs and Violent Juvenile Crime: A Summary of the Proceedings. Reno, Nev.: National Criminal Justice Association, 1992.

Organized Crime in California. Annual Report to California Legislature. Sacramento: California Deptartment of Justice, Bureau of Investigations, 1988.

State Task Force on Gangs and Drugs: Final Report. Sacramento: California Council on Criminal Justice, 1989.

Street Gangs and Youth Unrest. Chicago: Chicago Tribune Educational Service Department, 1971.

ARTICLES

Abramowitz, Michael. "Street Gang's 'Language' Becomes its Albatross." *Washington Post,* August 25, 1991, A3.

Barich, Bill. "The Crazy Life." *New Yorker,* November 3, 1986, 97–98.

Bergman, Brian, "Wild in the Streets: Teenage Gangs Wreak Havoc in Winnipeg." *Maclean's,* August 14, 1995, 18.

Boyle, Gregory J. "Self-Esteem: A Matter of Life, Death." *Los Angeles Times,* January 28, 1990, M7.

Breen, Lawrence, and Allen, Martin M. "Gang Behavior: Psychological and Law Enforcement." *FBI Law Enforcement Bulletin,* February 1983, 19–24.

Came, Berry, and Burke, Dan. "Gang Terror." *Maclean's,* May 22, 1989, 36.

Castro, Janice. "Gang Members Take to the Sea," *Time,* November 18, 1991, 21.

Gates, F. Daryl, and Jackson, Detective Robert. *The Police Chief* 57, no. 11 (November 1990): 20–25.

Gwynne, S.C. "Up from the Streets." *Time*, April 1990, 34.

Holmstrom, David. "Gangs That 'Secede' From Society." *Christian Science Monitor*, January 18, 1991, 10.

Hull, Jon D. "No Way Out." *Time*, August 17, 1992, 38–40.

Hutson, H. Range; Anglin, Deirdre; Kyriawa, Demetrios; Hart, Joel; Spears, Kelvin. "The Epidemic of Gang-Related Homicides in Los Angeles County from 1979 through 1994." *Journal of the American Medical Association*, October 4, 1995, 1031.

Johnson, Dirk. "Teen-agers Who Won't Join When Drug Dealers Recruit." *New York Times*, January 4, 1990, A1.

Katz, Jesse. "Religious Coalition Plans Major Anti-Gang Effort." *Los Angeles Times*, February 26, 1992, B4.

Leland, John. "Rap as Public Forum on Matters of Life and Death." *New York Times*, March 12, 1989, H29.

Maugh, Thomas H. "Study Finds Rapid Growth of Gangs." *Los Angeles Times*, February 17, 1992, B3.

McGarvey, Robert. "Gangland: L.A. Super Gangs Target America." *American Legion Magazine*, February 1991, 25.

McKinley, James C. "Gangs That Dance to a Violent Beat." *New York Times*, September 6, 1990, B4.

Miller, Annetta. "Do Gang Ads Deserve a Bad Rap?" *Newsweek*, October 21, 1991, 55.

Mydans, Seth. "Not Just the Inner City: Well-To-Do Join Gangs." *New York Times*, April 10, 1990, A7.

———. "Trophies from the Gang Wars: Wheelchairs." *New York Times*, December 6, 1990, A1.

Peoples, Tamecus. "Resisting the Gang." *Los Angeles Times*, June 18, 1990, B7.

Popkin, James. "Bombs Over America: You Name It, They Use It." *U.S. News & World Report*, July 29, 1991, 18.

Roberts, Paul Craig. "So You Say You're Not a Gang Member? Read On." *Business Week*, February 21, 1994, 22.

Ross, Yazmin. "Central America's Latest War." *World Press Review*, May 1993, 20.

Sands, Shannon, and Woodyard, Chris. "Hard-Core Gangs Attract Middle-Class Imitators." *Los Angeles Times*, December 25, 1989, A3.

Seamonds, Jack; Minerbrook, Scott; Moore, Marilyn; Haukins, Steve; Ostrolf, Roberta. "Ethnic Gangs and Organized Crime." *U.S. News & World Report*, January 18, 1988, 229.

Smolich, Thomas H. "When a Homeboy Dies, No One Rests in Peace." *Los Angeles Times*, July 21, 1990, B7.

Stanley, Alessandro. "Los Angeles, All Ganged Up" (Child Warriors). *Time*, June 18, 1990, 50.

Starr, Mark. "Chicago's Gang Warfare." *Newsweek*, January 28, 1985, 32.

Sullivan, Randall. "Leader of the Pack" *Rolling Stone*, August 28, 1986, 50–52.

Takata, Sasan, and Zeritz, Richard. "Youth Gangs in Racine: An Examination of Community Perceptions." *Wisconsin Sociologist*, 1987, 132–139.

Telander, Rick, and Ilic, Mirko. "Senseless: In America's Cities, Kids are Killing Kids Over Sneakers and Other Sports Apparel Favored by Drug Dealers." *Sports Illustrated,* May 14, 1990, 36.

Walker, Jill. "Los Angeles Isn't Alone in Problems with Gangs." *Washington Post*, July 3, 1990, A10.

Wilkinson, Tracy, and Chavez, Stephanie. "Elaborate Death Rites of Gangs." *Los Angeles Times,* March 2, 1992, A1.

Williams, Alex. "Is Peace Breaking Out Among New York Gangs?" *New Yorker,* April 18, 1994, 40.

Witkin, Gordon. "Enlisting the Feds in the War on Gangs." *U.S. News & World Report,* March 6, 1995, 38.

"Ethnic Gangs & Organized Crime." *U.S. News & World Report,* January 18, 1989, 29–31.

"Family Values: The Gangster Version." *Harper's Magazine,* April 1985, 18.

"Gangs That Rival the Mob." *U.S. News & World Report,* February 3, 1986, 29.

"Raiders' Silver and Black Popular with Denver Gangs." *Jet,* November 26, 1990, 49.

"Scorecard." *Newsweek,* August 10, 1992, 6.

"Slain Over a Baseball Cap." *New York Times,* May 18, 1989, A19.

"Today's Gangs Cross Cultural and Geographic Bounds from School Safety Update." *Education Digest,* May 1992.

"Urban Peace and Justice Summit." *Progressive,* July 1993, 12.

"You See a Red Rag, Shoot." *Sports Illustrated,* May 14, 1990, 46.

REPORTS

California Council on Criminal Justice. "State Task Force on Gangs and Drugs, Final Report." Sacramento, Calif., 1989.

California Department of Justice. "Gangs 2000: A Call to Action," The Attorney General's Report on the Impact of Criminal Street Gangs on Crime and Violence in California by the Year 2000. March 1993.

Office of the Attorney General. "Report on Youth Gang Violence in California." Sacramento, Calif., 1988.

Sacramento County Sheriff's Department. "Guide to Bad Boys." Sacramento, Calif., 1992.

Walker, Judith. "Chicago Works Together," Summary Report for the Chicago Intervention Network. Chicago, 1986.

Youth Initiatives Task Force. "Investing in Youth: Final Report." Milwaukee, Wis., 1985.

MAGAZINES

Barrio Warriors Magazine, P.O. Box 6669, East Los Angeles, CA 90022

Community

BOOKS

Adler, P.A.*Wheeling and Dealing: An Ethnography of an Upper-Level Drug Dealing and Smuggling Community.* New York: Columbia University Press, 1985.

Anderson, Elijah. *Street Wise: Race, Class, and Change in an Urban Community.* Chicago: University of Chicago Press, 1990.

Banales, Eddie. *From Gangs to Grace: The Story of Pomona's Eddie Banales.* Pomona, Calif.: FACES (Family and Community Educational Services), 1990.

Bryant, D. *Community Responses Crucial for Dealing with Youth Gangs.* Washington, D.C.: U.S. Deptartment of Justice, Office of Juvenile Justice and Delinquency Prevention, 1989.

Canada, Geoffrey. *Fist Stick Knife Gun.* Boston, Mass.: Beacon Publishing Co., 1995.

Fagan, Jeffery. *Social Processes of Delinquency and Drug Use Among Urban Gangs.* Newbury Park, Calif.: Sage Publications, 1990.

Fremon, Celeste. *Father Greg & The Homeboys.* New York: Hyperion, 1995.

Goldstein, Arnold P., and Huff, Ronald C. *Gang Intervention Handbook.* Champaign, Ill.: Research Press, 1992.

Inciardi, James A.; Horowitz, Ruth; and Pottieger, Anne E. *Street Kids, Street Drugs, Street Crime: An Examination of Drug Use and Serious Delinquency in Miami.* Beaumont, Calif.: Wadsworth Publishing Co., 1993.

Korem, Dan. *Streetwise Parents, Foolproof Kids.* Richardson, Tex.: International Focus Press, 1995.

Kornblum, William. *Blue Collar Community.* Chicago: University of Chicago Press, 1974.

Kretzmann, John P., and McKnight, John L. *Building Communities from the Inside Out: A Path Toward Finding and Mobilizing a Community's Assets.* Evanston, Ill.: Northwestern University, 1993.

MacCloud, Jay. *Ain't No Making It: Leveled Aspirations in a Low Income Community.* Boulder, Colo.: Westview Press, 1987.

Mann, Stephanie, and Blakeman, M.C. *Safe Homes, Safe Neighborhoods.* Berkeley: Nolo Press, 1993.

McKibbin, Marie Paula. *The Citizens' Handbook of California Street Gangs.* Sacramento: McGeorge School of Law, University of the Pacific Center for Research, 1992.

Muehlbauer, Gene, and Dodder, Laura. *The Losers: Gang Delinquency in an American Suburb.* New York: Praeger, 1983.

Sliwa, Curtis, and Schwartz, Murray. *Street Smart.* Reading, Mass.: Addison-Wesley Publishing Company, 1982.

Spergel, Irving. *The Youth Gang Problem: A Community Approach.* Oxford University Press, 1995.

Webb, Margot. *Gangs: A Community Response.* Sacramento: The Center, 1994.

Westerman, Ted D., and Burfeind, James W. *Crime and Justice in Two Societies: Japan and the United States.* Pacific Grove, Calif.: Brooks/Cole Publishing Company, 1991.

Wheeler, Lonnie, and Marshall, Joseph Jr. *Street Soldier.* New York: Delacorte Press, 1996.

Criminal Street Gangs. Trenton, N.J.: New Jersey Commission of Investigations, 1993.

Gangs: A Community Response. Sacramento, Calif.: California Office of the Attorney General, Crime and Violence Prevention Center, 1994.

Gangs, Crime and Violence in Los Angeles: Findings and Proposals. Los Angeles: Los Angeles County, Office of the District Attorney, 1992.

Information Access Guide—A Comprehensive List of Community Policing Resources. Washington, D.C., 1996.

Los Angeles County Gang Task Force Report on the State of Los Angeles Gangs. Los Angeles: Los Angeles County, 1992.

Partnerships Against Violence: Promising Programs. Washington, D.C.: U.S. National Criminal Justice Reference Service, 1994.

The Prevention of Youth Violence: A Framework for Community Action. Atlanta: Centers for Disease Control and Prevention, 1993.

What You Need to Know About Gangs and Drugs: A Handbook for Poverty Owners of Los Angeles. Los Angeles: Los Angeles City Attorney's Office, 1993.

Youth Gangs and Drugs: Communities at Risk. Davis, Calif.: University of California at Davis, 1988.

Youth Violence Prevention and Intervention: The Community Response. Sacramento, Calif.: California Senate Office of Research, 1995.

ARTICLES

Armstrong, Scott. "Antigang Law Targets Parents." *Christian Science Monitor*, May 9, 1989, 8.

———. "Latest Answer to Gangs Draws Fire." *Christian Science Monitor*, December 31, 1991, 6.

———. "Western Cities Battle Gang Violence." *Christian Science Monitor*, January 4, 1989, 8.

Baker, Bob. "L.A. Outrage Makes Little Impact on Gang Epidemic." *Los Angeles Times*, January 30, 1989, sec. I, p. 1.

Bird, Brian. "Reclaiming the Urban War Zones." *Christianity Today*, January 15, 1990, 16–20.

Bosc, Michael. "Street Gangs No Longer Just a Big-City Problem." *U.S. News & World Report*, July 16, 1984, 108–109.

Bremner, Brian. "Murder on Main Street." *Business Week*, January 14, 1991, 42.

Brower, Montgomery. "Gang Violence: Color It Real." *People Weekly*, May 2, 1988, 42–47.

Broyles, William Jr. "Letter From L.A." *Esquire*, July 1992, 37.

Bryant, Danny. "Action, Not Words." *Los Angeles Times*, April 6, 1992, B5.

Calderon, Julio. "Curbing Gang Violence" (letter to the editor). *Los Angeles Times*, October 2, 1989, sec II, p. 4.

Carney, Jay. "Sunbelt Import." *Time*, August 18, 1986, 17.

Cole, Lewis. "Hyper Violence." *Rolling Stone*, December 1, 1994, 106.

Davis, Patricia. "Violent Groups of Middle-Class Teens Disturb Peace of Suburbia." *Washington Post*, October 22, 1991, B1.

del Olmo, Frank. "Orange County Can Step in to Diminish Gang Violence." *Los Angeles Times*, September 25, 1989, sec II, p. 5.

DeMont, John. "A Town in Terror: Hoodlums Harass a Small Nova Scotia Community." *Maclean's*, November 8, 1981, 50–51.

DeMott, John S. "Have Gang, Will Travel." *Time*, December 9, 1985, 34.

Doyle, Brian. "The Streets According to Chief Crazy Lady." *U.S. Catholic*, October 1984, 25–31.

Editorial. "A Dress Code for Success: How to Squelch Gangs but not Kids." *Los Angeles Times*, July 17, 1991, B6.

Editorial. "How to Gang Up on Trouble." *Los Angeles Times*, May 5, 1990, B6.

Eng, Lily, and Smith, Lynn. "San Clemente Sees its First Gang Slaying." *Los Angeles Times*, November 19, 1990, A23.

Fennell, Tom. "In the Cross Fire: Gang Related Violence Claims Innocent Lives." *Maclean's*, May 9, 1994, 19.

Fisher, Luke, "The Brutal Truth: Violent Gangs Instill Fear in Once-Staid Ottawa." *Maclean's*, November 13, 1995, 66.

Fisher, Marc. "The Word on the Street Is Death." *Washington Post*, February 12, 1989, C1.

Grau, Julie. "There Are No Children Here." *Time*, September 12, 1994, 44.

Gregor, Anne. "Death Among the Innocent." *Maclean's*, May 22, 1989, 38.

Haslanger, Phil. "A Rival to the Gangs." *The Progressive*, October 1986, 15.

Hatt, Doug. "Marks of Cain: An Illinois Doctor Helps Ex-Gang Members Lose Their Telltale Tattoos." *People Weekly*, November 20, 1995, 177.

Hedges, Stephen J. "When Drug Gangs Move to Nice Places." *U.S. News & World Report*, June 5, 1989, 42.

Horovitz, Bruce. "Agency Uses Ads to Fight L.A. Gangs and Their Graffiti." *Los Angeles Times*, January 17, 1990, D5.

Hudson, Berkeley. "Children Increasingly Fall Victim to Gang Violence." *Los Angeles Times*, October 27, 1991, A1.

Katz, Jack, and Marks, Daniel. "Much of What We Do to Fight Gangs Turns Out to Be Their Best Recruiter." *Los Angeles Times*, January 25, 1989, sec. II, p. 7.

Katz, Jesse. "Jim Brown Taps Potential of 'Baddest Cats' in City." *Los Angeles Times*, September 24, 1991, A1.

Klein, Malcolm W.; Cunningham, Lea C.; and Maxon, Cheryl L. "Crack, Street Gang and Violence." *Criminology* 29:4 (April 1979).

Kramer, Jeff. "Council Rejects Curfew After Anguished Debate." *Los Angeles Times*, March 26, 1992, J3.

Lacey, Marc. "No Sporting Chance: Danger Lurks for Fans as Gangs Adopt Pro Attire." *Los Angeles Times*, March 20, 1991, B1.

Lasley, James. "LAPD Proves That Muscle Works." *Los Angeles Times*, May 13, 1990, M7.

Lewis, Gregg A. "The Insane Dragons Meet the Unknown Vice Lords." *Christianity Today*, November 20, 1987, 10.

Lingwall, Jill. "Gangs in Des Moines: Getting Them to SCAT (Strategic Complement Against Thugs)." *Public Management*, November 1990, 15.

Mayer, Jane. "Street Dealers." *Wall Street Journal*, September 8, 1989, A1.

McEvoy, Alan. "Combating Activities in Schools: What Does and Doesn't Work." *Education Digest*, October 1990, 31.

Molina, Gloria. "Law on Parental Responsibility" (letter to the editor). *Los Angeles Times*, July 11, 1989, sec. II, p. 6.

Monroe, Sylvester. "Complaints About a Crackdown." *Time*, July 16, 1990, 20.

Murr, Andrew. "When Gangs Meet the Handicapped." *Newsweek*, May 7, 1990, 70.

Mydans, Seth. "Street Gangs That Duel with Paint, Not Guns." *New York Times*, November 6, 1989, B1.

Pillsbury, Samuel H. "How Many Parents Can We Prosecute?" *Los Angeles Times*, May 10, 1989, sec. II, p. 7.

Pope, Victoria, and Level, Sandy. "Crack Invades a Small Town." *U.S. News & World Report*, April 22, 1996, 34–44.

Presser, Arlynn Leiber. "On the Other Side of the Tracks." *National Review*, November 29, 1993, 46.

Reinhold, Robert. "Fearing Gang Violence, School Forfeits a Game." *New York Times*, November 3, 1991, sec. 1, p. 12.

Robinson, Pamela J. "Recreation's Role in Gang Intervention." *Parks & Recreation*, March 1992, 54.

Ross, Elizabeth. "Fighting Crime by Getting the Community Involved." *Christian Science Monitor*, December 30, 1991, 9.

Sager, Mike. "Death in Venice." *Rolling Stone*, September 22, 1988, 64–68.

Salgado, Mike. "Whose Rights First?" *Los Angeles Times*, January 9, 1992, B7.

Shryer, Tracy. "Chicago Officials Hope Nights on the Court Can Keep Young Men Out of Jail." *Los Angeles Times*, February 12, 1990, A4.

Spergel, Irving A., and Curry, G. David. "Gang Homicide, Delinquency, and Community." *Criminology* 26:3 (March 1989).

Stolberg, Sheryl. "Engulfed in a Sea of Spray Paint." *Los Angeles Times*, January 8, 1992, A1.

Tabor, Mary B. W. "Police Try Beantown Comics." *New York Times*, August 4, 1991, A4.

Thompson, Ginger. "Mother Arrested Under Gang Law Denies Blame." *Los Angeles Times*, May 31, 1989, sec. I, p. 1.

———. "Mother Seized, Charged Over Son's Street Gang Ties." *Los Angeles Times*, May 2, 1989, sec I, p. 1.

Timnick, Lois. "Holding Ground." *Los Angeles Times*, October 24, 1991, J1.

Tuohy, Lynn, and Sudo, Phil. "Dealing Death: At a Housing Project in Hartford, CT, Teens Trade Drugs with the Nonchalance of Seasoned Businessmen." *Scholastic Update*, November 17, 1989, 4.

Will, George F. "A 'West Coast Story.' " *Newsweek*, March 28, 1988, 76.

Willwerth, James. "Fighting the Code of Silence." *Time*, February 19, 1990, 59.

Winkel, Vince. "An Open Door for Youth." *Christian Science Monitor*, July 28, 1989, 14.

Wood, Tracy. "1 Killed, 8 Hurt as Fresno Gang Members Go on Rampage in City." *Los Angeles Times*, September 4, 1990, A3.

"Charge is dismissed in Test of Law Linking Parents to Gang Activity." *New York Times*, June 11, 1989, 13.

"Chicago Plans Sports Action for the Gangs." *New York Times*, December 2, 1989, 10.

"Dadz in the 'Hood: Gang Warfare." *The Economist*, November 4, 1995, 33.

"The Drug Gangs." *Newsweek*, March 28, 1988, 20–25.

"Gangs Put $5,000 Bounty on Drug Activist's Life." *Jet*, January 15, 1990, 38.

"Gang Violence and Control in the Los Angeles and San Francisco Areas with a View to What Might Be Done by the Federal Government." Hearing before the Subcommittee on Juvenile Justice of the Committee on the Judiciary U.S. Congress. Westwood, Calif.: San Francisco, Calif. Washington, D.C., 1983.

"Poor Parent Charge Dropped for Mother of Gang Member." *New York Times*, June 10, 1989, 12.

"Priest Threatens to Expel Pupils Involved in Gangs." *Jet*, April 9, 1984, 30.

"Taking on the Gangs." *Los Angeles Times*, February 4, 1989, sec. II, p. 8.

"You Can Only Take So Much." *Time*, October 24, 1983, 32.

Education

BOOKS

Ackley, N. *Gangs in School: Breaking Up Is Hard to Do*. Washington, D.C.: U.S. Deptartment of Justice, Office of Juvenile Justice and Delinquency Prevention, 1984.

Arthur, Richard, and Erickson, Edsel. *Gangs and Schools*. Holmes Beach, Fla.: Learning Publications, Inc., 1992.

Axelson, Roland G. *The Psychological Influence of Street Gangs on School Aged Youth: A Case Study in Hartford, CT*. Hartford, Conn.: ThutWorld Education Center, 1984.

Barry, Rosemary J. *Gang War Workbook* (supplement to *Gang War* below, Paul Kropp). Saint Paul, Minn.: EMSC Publishing, 1984.

Bibson, James W. *Warrior Dreams*. New York: Hill & Wang Incorporated, 1994.

Brown, Sandra A. *Counseling Victims of Violence*. Alexandria, Va.: American Association for Counseling and Development, 1991.

Capuzzi, Dave, and Gross, Douglas R. *Youth at Risk: A Resource for Counselors, Teachers, and Parents*. American Association for Counseling and Development, 1989.

Johnson, Louanne. *My Posse Don't Do Homework*. New York: St. Martin's Press, 1992.

Kropp, Paul. *Gang War (Gang War Workbook* above, Rosemary J. Barry). Saint Paul, Minn.: EMC Publishing, 1982.

Mathews, Jay. *Escalante, the Best Teacher in America.* New York: Henry Holt and Company, 1988.

Riley, Kevin W. *Street Gangs and the Schools: A Blueprint for Intervention.* Bloomington, Ind.: Phi Delta Kappa Educational Foundation, 1991.

Spergel, Irving A., and Curry, G. David. *Gangs, Schools, and Communities.* Chicago: University of Chicago, School of Social Science Administration, 1987.

Spergel, Irving, and Alexander, Alba. *A School Based Model.* Chicago: National Gang Suppression and Intervention Program, School of Social Science Administration, University of Chicago in Cooperation with the Office of Juvenile Justice and Delinquency Prevention, 1991.

Webb, Margot. *Our Alert: Gang Prevention: School In-Service.* Sacramento: California Department of Education, 1994.

Williams, Stanley (Tookie), and Becnel, Barbara Cottman. *Tookie Speaks Out Against Gang Violence.* New York: Rosen Publishing Group, 1996.

Gang Prevention Through Targeted Outreach. Atlanta: Boys & Girls Clubs of America, 1993.

Preventing Violence: A Framework for Schools and Communities. Seattle: Comprehensive Health Education Foundation, 1994.

Safe Schools: A Planning Guide for Action. Sacramento: California Department of Education and Office of the State Attorney General, Crime Prevention Center, 1989.

Toward Better and Safer Schools: A School Leader's Guide to Delinquency Prevention. Washington, D.C.: National School Boards Association, 1994.

Violence in the Schools: How America's School Boards Are Safeguarding Our Children. Alexandria, Va.: National School Board Association, 1993.

ARTICLES

Clay, Douglas A., and Aquila, Frank D. "'Spitting the Lit'—Fact or Fad?" *Phi Delta Kappan,* September 1994, 65–68.

Lee, Felicia, R. "Violence Outside New York Schools." *New York Times,* November 14, 1989, A20.

McEvoy, Alan W. "Combating Gang Activities in Schools." *Education Digest,* October 1990, 31–34.

Miller, Bobbi. "Gone Too Far." *Los Angeles Times,* July 21, 1991, M5.

Mydans, Seth. "On Guard Against Gangs at a Los Angeles School." *New York Times,* November 19, 1989, sec. 1, p. 1.

Pasternak, Judy. "At School, Survival Comes First (In the Crossfire: L.A.'s Gang Crisis: Part 1)." *Los Angeles Times,* February 5, 1989, sec. I, p. 1.

Putka, Gary. "Combating Gangs." *Wall Street Journal,* April 23, 1991, A1.

Sanchez, Flora, and Anderson, Mary Lou. "Gang Mediation: A Process That Works." *Principal Magazine,* May 1990.

Stephens, Ronald D. "Gangs, Guns, and School Violence." *USA Today,* January 29, 1994.

Stover, Del. "Dealing with Youth Gangs in the Schools." *Education Digest,* February 1987, 30–33.

Sudo, Philip. "Turf Wars." *Scholastic Update* (Teachers' edition), November 17, 1989, 6.

Walker, Jill. "New Schools for Gangs Pose Unique Segregation Concern." *Washington Post,* April 11, 1990, A3.

"Today's Gangs Cross Cultural and Geographic Bounds." *Education Digest,* May 1992, 8–10.

Corrections

BOOKS

Allen, Bud, and Bosta, Diana. *Games Criminals Play*. Sacramento: Rae John Publishers, 1989.

Bensinger, Gad J., and Larigio, Arthur J. *Gangs and Community Corrections*. Chicago: Loyola University, 1992.

Bromley, Max L.; Halsted, James B.; and Territo, Leonard. *Crime & Justice in America*. St. Paul, Minn.: West Publishing Co., 1995.

Camp, George, and Camp, Camille Graham. *Prison Gangs: Their Extent, Nature and Impact on Prisons*. Washington, D.C.: U.S. Deptartment of Justice, 1985.

Davis, James R. *Street Gangs: Youth, Biker, and Prison Groups*. Dubuque, Iowa: Kendall/Hunt Publishing Co., 1982.

Drowns, Robert W., and Hess, Kären M. *Juvenile Justice*. St. Paul, Minn.: West Publishing Co., 1995.

Henslin, James M., ed. *Deviance in American Life*. New Brunswick, N.J.: Transaction Publishers, 1989.

Jackson, Robert K., and McBride, Wesley D. *Understanding Street Crimes*. Placerville, Calif.: Custom Publishing Co., 1986.

Jacobs, James B. *Stateville: The Penitentiary in Mass Society*. Chicago: University of Chicago Press, 1997.

Kenney, John P.; Pursuit, Dan G.; and Fuller, Donald E. *Police Work with Juveniles and the Administration of Juvenile Justice*. Springfield, Ill.: Charles C. Thomas, 1989.

Klein, Malcolm W., and Maxson, Cheryl L. *Gangs and Cocaine Trafficking*. Newbury Park, Calif.: Sage Publications, 1991.

Morgan, Lanier. *The Understanding and Modification of Delinquent Behavior*. Rev. Ed. San Diego: Libra Publishers, Inc., 1992.

Short, James F., Jr., ed. *Delinquency, Crime and Society*. Chicago: University of Chicago Press, 1976.

Siegel, Larry, and Senna, Joseph J. *Juvenile Delinquency: Theory, Practice and Law*. St. Paul, Minn.: West Publishing Co., 1991.

Sutton, J. *Stubborn Children: Controlling Delinquency in the United States*. Berkeley, Calif.: University of California Press, 1988.

Weisheit, Ralph A., and Culbertson, Robert G. *Juvenile Delinquency: A Justice Perspective*. Prospect Heights, Ill.: Waveland Press, Inc., 1990.

Dictionary of Desperation. Washington, D.C.: National Alliance of Businessmen, 1976.

Gangs in Correctional Facilities: A National Assessment. Laurel, Md.: American Correctional Association, 1993.

Prison Gangs in the Community. Sacramento, Calif.: California Board of Corrections, 1978.

Research Report—Conditions of Confinement: Juvenile. Washington, D.C.: Detention and Corrections Facilities. U.S. Deptartment of Justice, August 1994.

Security Threat Groups, Symbols and Terminology. Washington, D.C.: U.S. Department of Justice, Federal Bureau of Prisons, 1994.

What Works: Promising Interventions in Juvenile Justice. Washington, D.C.: U.S. Office of Juvenile Justice and Delinquency Prevention, 1994.

ARTICLES

Baird, L.H. "Prison Gangs: Texas." *Corrections Today*, July 18, 1986, 12–22.

Foote, Donna. "California's Teen Gulags." *Newsweek*, July 4, 1994, 4.

Kornblum, William. "Ganging Together: Helping Gangs Go Straight." *Social Issues and Health Review #2*, 1987, 99–104.

Mendoza, Ramon. "My Journey Through the CYA." *California Youth Authority Quarterly*, Winter 1980, 4.

Sahagun, Louis. "Ex-Cons, Young Recruits Reviving East L.A. Gangs." *Los Angeles Times*, December 9, 1989, A1.

PERIODICALS

Prison Life, Prison Life, Inc., 111 S. Ninth Street, Ste. 3, Columbia, MO 65201

Asian Gangs

BOOKS

Beach, W.G. *Oriental Crime in California*. Stanford: Stanford University Press, 1932.

Bresler, Fenton. *The Chinese Mafia*. New York: Stein and Day, 1980.

Cher, Ming. *Spider Boys*. Fairfield, N.J.: Morrow Publishing, 1995.

Chin, Ko-lin. *Chinese Subculture and Criminality: Non-Traditional Crime Groups in America*. Westport, Conn.: Greenwood Press, 1990.

English, T.J. *Born To Kill: America's Most Notorious Vietnamese Gang and the Changing Face of Organized Crime*. Fairfield, N.J.: Morrow Publishing, 1995.

Garland, Sherry. *Shadow of the Dragon*. Orlando, Fla.: Harcourt Brace, 1993.

Huston, Peter. *Tongs, Gangs, and Triads—Chinese Crime Groups in North America*. Boulder, Colo.: Paladin Press, 1995.

Kaono, Jerry. *Pacific Island Gangs: An Emerging Phenomenon*. Carson, Calif.: privately printed, (213) 830–1123, 1992.

Kaplan, David E., and Dubro, Alec. *YaKuza: The Explosive Account of Japan's Criminal Underworld*. Reading, Mass.: Addison-Wesley, 1986.

Posner, Gerald L. *Warlords of Crime—Chinese Secret Societies: The New Mafia*. Blacklick, Oh.: McGraw-Hill, 1988.

Vigil, James, and Yun, Steve Chong. 1990. *Vietnam Youth Gangs in Southern California*. Newbury Park, Calif.: Sage Publications, 1990.

Nightmare: Vietnamese Home Invasion Robberies. Falls Church, Va.: Association of Asian Crime Investigators, 1992.

ARTICLES

Burke, Dan. "Inside the Gangs: An Underworld Reign of Terror." *Maclean's*, March 25, 1991, 22.

Goad, Jim. "Big Trouble in Little Saigon." *Playboy*, May 1991, 82.

Goldberg, Jeffrey. "My Life as a Chinese Gangster." *New York*, July 17, 1995, 34.

Hamilton, Kendall; Glick, David; and Rice, Jeff. "The Bloods and Crips of the Promised Land." *Newsweek*, May 13, 1996, 72–73.

Kaihla, Paul. "Terror in the Streets: Ruthless Asian Gangs Bring a New Wave of Violence to Canadian Cities." *Maclean's*, March 25, 1991, 18.

Leo, John. "Parasites on Their Own People." *Time*, July 8, 1985, 76.

Lorch, Donatella. "Hong Kong Boy." *New York Times*, January 6, 1991, sec. 1, p. 13.

Quinn, Hal. "Empire of the Triads: An Asian 'Mafia' Flexes its Muscle." *Maclean's*, March 25, 1991, 25.

Stone, Michael. "Killer Cowboys: The Violent Saga of the City's Deadliest Drug Game." *New York*, December 13, 1993, 58–66.

Willwerth, James. "From Killing Fields to Mean Streets." *Time*, November 18, 1991, 103.

"To be a Flying Dragon." *Harper's Magazine*, July 1990, 32.

Black Gangs

BOOKS

Baker, Phillip. *Blood Posse*. New York: St. Martin's Press, 1995.

Barrett, Leonard E. *The Rastafarians*. Boston: Beacon Press, 1988.

Bing, Leon. *Do or Die*. New York: HarperCollins, 1991.

Burbridge, Edward K. *Chicago Boy: The Life and Crimes of a Southside Street Fighter*. West Covina, Calif.: LA and Chicago River Underground Press, 1991.

Dawley, David. *A Nation of Lords: The Autobiography of the Vice Lords*. Prospect Heights, Ill.: Waveland Press, Inc., 1992.

Gunst, Laurie. *Born Fi' Dead: A Journey Through the Jamaican Posse Underworld*. New York: Henry Holt & Co., 1995.

Hagedorn, John. *People and Folks*. Chicago: Lake View Press, 1988.

Keiser, Lincoln R. *The Vice Lords: Warriors of the Street*. New York: Holt, Rinehart, and Winston, 1979.

McCarthy, Terrance. *The Vice Lords: Portrait of a Gang* (document). Chicago: Chicago Police Department, 1983.

Mowry, Jess. *Way Past Cool*. New York: Farrar Straus Giroux, 1992.

Perkins, Useni E. *Explosion of Chicago's Black Street Gangs*. Chicago: Third World Press, 1987.

Sale, Richard T. *The Blackstone Rangers: A Reporter's Account of Time Spent with the Street Gang on Chicago's South Side*. New York: Random House, 1971.

ShaKur, SaniyKa, a.k.a. Scott, Kody. *Monster: The Autobiography of an L.A. Member*. New York: Penguin Books, 1993.

Sipchen, Bob. *Baby Insane and the Buddha*. New York: Doubleday, 1993.

Taylor, Carl S. *Dangerous Society*. East Lansing, Mich.: Michigan State University Press, 1990.

ARTICLES

Bing, Leon. "A Gangbanger Squints at Life and Death Through 'Graveyard Eyes.' " *Los Angeles Times*, August 11, 1991, M3.

———. "When You're a Crip (or a Blood)." *Harper's Magazine*, March 1989, 51.

Bonfante, Jordan. "Entrepreneurs of Crack: An L.A. Street Gang Transforms Itself into a Cross-country Cocaine Empire—Until the FBI Busts It All Over." *Time*, February 27, 1995, 22.

Conlon, Edward. "The Pols, the Police and the Gerry Curls." *American Spectator*, November 1994, 36.

English, T.J. "Rude Boys." *Playboy*, October 1991, 86.

Gunst, Laurie. "Jamaican Drug Gangs—Johnny-Too-Bad and the Sufferers." *Nation*, November 13, 1989, 549–569.

Ice-T. "To Live & Die in L.A." *Playboy*, February 1994, 62.

James, George. "Youth's Death is Called Act of Vengeance By Mistake." *New York Times*, October 24, 1995, 82.

Nossiter, Adam. "Zulu Nation, Cultural Group (or Youth Gang?) Is Banned in Its Bronx Home." *New York Times*, October 4, 1995, 12.

ShaKur, Sanyika. "Can't Stop, Won't Stop: The Education of a Crip Warlord." *Esquire*, April 1993, 87.

"Gang Leaders Begin New Agenda: Unity." *Jet*, May 24, 1993, 5.

"Ghaddafi's Goons: A Chicago Gang's Terrorist Plot." *Time*, December 7, 1987, 27.

"Federal Judge Grants New Trial for 3 El Rukins." *Jet*, June 28, 1993, 38.

Hispanic Gangs

BOOKS

Frias, Gus. *Barrio Warriors: Homeboys or Peace*. Los Angeles: Diaz Publications, 1982.

Glick, Ronald, and Moore, Joan. *Drugs in Hispanic Communities*. New Brunswick, N.J.: Rutgers University Press, 1990.

Gonzalez, Alfredo Guerra. *Mexicano/Chicano Gangs in Los Angeles: A Social Historical Case Study* (unpublished dissertation). Berkeley: University of California, 1981.

Horowitz, Ruth. *Honor and the American Dream: Culture and Identity in a Chicano Community*. New Brunswick, N.J.: Rutgers University Press, 1983.

Mierer, Matt S., and Rivera, Reliciano. *The Chicanos: A History of Mexican Americans*. New York: Hill and Wang, 1972.

Mirande, Alfredo. *The Chicano Experience: An Alternative Perspective*. South Bend, In.: Notre Dame Press, 1985.

Moore, J. W. *Going Down to the Barrio: Homeboys and Homegirls in Charge*. Philadelphia: Temple University Press, 1991.

———. *Homeboys: Gangs, Drugs and Prison in the Barrio of L.A.* Philadelphia: Temple University Press, 1978.

Rodriguez, Luis J. *Always Running—La Vida Loca, Gang Days in L.A.* New York: Simon & Schuster, 1994.

Romo, Richard. *East Los Angeles: History of fhe Barrio*. Austin, Tex.: University of Texas, 1983.

Vigil, James Diego. *Barrio Gangs: Street Life and Identity in Southern California*. Austin, Tex.: University of Texas Press, 1988.

Latin Gang Member Recognition Guide. Phoenix, Ariz.: Phoenix Police Department, 1981.

ARTICLES

Arias, Anna Maria. "Texas Gets a Taste of Blood." *Hispanic*, December 1991, 46.

James, George. "Gang Tried to Kill Officer as a Rite, Prosecutors Say." *New York Times,* November 4, 1995, 27.

LeBlanc, Adrian Nicole. "White Manny's Locked Up." *New York Times Magazine*, August 14, 1994, 26.

Rodriguez, Luis J. "Rekindling the Warrior: Gangs Are Part of the Solution Not of the Problem." *Utne Reader*, July–August 1994, 58.

Rodriguez, Richard. "Gangstas." *Mother Jones*, January–February 1994, 46.

Stone, Michael. "Killer Cowboys: The Violent Saga of the City's Deadliest Drug Game." *New York*, December 13, 1993, 58.

"Family Values: The Gangster Version." *Harper's Magazine*, April 1995, 18.

White Gangs

BOOKS

Bennett, Jay. *Skinhead*. New York: Ballantine Books, 1991.

Bing, Leon. *Smoked*. New York: HarperCollins, 1993.

Christensen, Loren. *Skinhead Street Gangs*. Boulder, Colo.: Paladin Press, 1994.

English, T. J. *The Westies*. New York: William Morrow & Co., Inc., 1994.

Gaines, Donna. *Teenage Wasteland—Suburbia's Dead End Kids*. New York: Harper Perennial, 1992.

Hamm, Mark S. *American Skinheads: The Criminology & Control of Hate Crime*. New York: Praeger Publishers, 1994.

Knight, Nick. *Skinhead*. London: Omnibus Press, 1982.

Korem, Danny. *Suburban Gangs: The Affluent Rebels*. Richardson, Tex.: International Focus Press, 1994.

Lavigne, Yves. *Hell's Angels*. New York: Carol Publishing Group, 1990.

Monti, Daniel J. *Wannabe: Gangs in Suburbs and School*. Cambridge, Mass.: Basil Blackwell, 1994.

Muehlbauer, Gene, and Dodder, Laura. *The Losers: Gang Delinquency in an American Suburb*. New York: Praeger Publishers, 1983.

Peck Richard. *Bel-Air Bambi and the Mall Rats*. New York: Laureleaf, 1993.

Ridgeway, James. *Blood in the Face*. New York: Thunders Mouth Press, 1995.

Rosen, Fred. *Blood Crimes*. New York: Pinnacle Books, 1996.

Thompson, Hunter S. *Hell's Angels: A Strange and Terrible Saga*. New York: Random House, 1966.

ARTICLES

Applebome, Peter. "New Report Warns of an Alliance Between Gangs and Racist Groups." *New York Times*, February 6, 1989, A7.

Came, Barry. "A Growing Menace: Violent Skinheads Are Raising Urban Fears." *Maclean's*, January 23, 1989, 43–44.

Chua-Eoan, Howard. "Enlisted Killers." *Time*, December 18, 1995, 44.

Galvin, Regina. "Admitted 'Skinhead' Found Guilty of Shooting." *Army Times*, July 15, 1996, 16.

——. "Admitted 'Skinhead' Found Guilty of Shooting." *Esquire*, April 1996, 102–112.

——. "Pride and Prejudice: Inside the Minds of Army Skinheads." *Army Times*, January 8, 1996.

Kaihla, Paul. "Violence Is Nice. Honestly." *Maclean's*, May 22, 1989, 40.

King Wayne. "Violent Racism Attracts New Breed: Skinheads." *New York Times*, January 1, 1989, sec. 1, p. 35.

MacNamara, Mark. "The Lost Kids of the Palisades." *Los Angeles Magazine*, December 1990, 142.

Van Biema, David. "When White Makes Right." *Time*, August 9, 1993, 40–42.

Vistica, Gregory L. "Extremism in the Ranks." *Newsweek*. March 25, 1996, 34–36.

Girl Gangs

BOOKS

Adler, F. *Sisters in Crime: The Rise of the New Female Criminal.* Blacklick, Ohio: McGraw-Hill, 1975.

Brooks, William Allen. *Girl Gangs: A Survey of Teen-Age Drug Addicts, Sex Crimes, Rape, Kleptomania, Prostitution, Truancy, and Other Deviations.* New York: Padell Book Company, 1952.

Cain, Maureen, ed. *Growing Up Good: Policing the Behavior of Girls in Europe.* London: Sage Publications, 1989.

Campbell, Anne. *The Girls in the Gang: A Report from New York City.* Cambridge, Mass.: Basil Blackwell, 1991.

Chesney-Lind, Meda, and Sheldon, Randall G. *Girls, Delinquency, and Juvenile Justice.* Belmont, Calif.: Wadsworth Publishing Co., 1996.

Hanson, K. *Rebels in the Streets: The Story of New York's Girl Gangs.* Old Tappan, N.J.: Prentice-Hall, 1964.

Oates, Joyce. *Foxfire: Confessions of a Girl Gang.* New York: E.P. Dutton, 1993.

Quicker, John. *Homegirls: Characterizing Chicano Gangs.* San Piedro, Calif.: International Universities Press, 1983.

Sikes, Gini. *8 Ball Chicks.* New York: Doubleday, 1996.

ARTICLES

Abner, Allison. "Gangsta Girls: Gang Membership Among Young Black Girls Is Rising." *Essence*, July 1994, 64.

Dunham, Elizabeth. "Bad Girls." *Teen Magazine*, August 1995, 52.

Efron, Sonni. "Violent, Defiant Vietnamese Form Girl Gangs." *Los Angeles Times*, December 12, 1989, A3.

Kantrowitz, Barbara, and Leslie, Connie. "Wild in the Streets." *Newsweek*, August 2, 1993, 40–46.

Mydans, Seth. "Life in Girls' Gang: Colors and Bloody Noses." *New York Times*, January 29, 1990, A1.

O'Maley, Suzanne. "Girls N the Hood." *Harper's Bazaar*, October 1993, 238.

Sikes, Gini. "Girls in the 'hood." *Scholastic Update*, February 11, 1994, 20.

Taylor, Carl S. "Can Buy Me Love." *Harper's Magazine*, July 1990, 32.

Waller, Sheila. "Girls in the Gang: A Nineties Nightmare." *Cosmopolitan*, August 1994, 166.

"My Boyfriend Was in a Gang." *Teen Magazine*, February 1995, 38.

Gang History

BOOKS

Bloch, Herbert A., and Niederhoffer, Arthur. *The Gang*. Westport, Conn.: Greenwood Press, 1958.

Gilbert, J. A. *Cycle of Outrage: America's Reaction to the Juvenile Delinquent in the 1950's.* New York: Oxford University Press, 1986.

Haskins, James. *Street Gangs: Yesterday and Today*. New York: Hastings House, 1974.

Jankowski, Martin Sanchez. *Islands in the Street—Gangs and American Urban Society*. Berkeley, Calif.: University of California Press, 1991.

Liebow, Elliot. *Tally's Corner: A Study of Negro Streetcorner Men*. Boston: Little, Brown and Company, Inc., 1967.

Miller, Walter B. *Violence by Youth Gangs and Youth Groups as a Crime Problem in Major American Cities*. Washington, D.C.: U.S. Government Printing Office, 1975.

Olivero, M. J. *Honor, Violence, and Upward Mobility: A Case Study of Chicago Gangs During the 1970's and 1980's*. Edinburg, Tex.: University of Texas–Pan American Press, 1991.

Perkins, Useni E. *Explosion of Chicago's Black Street Gangs: 1900 to Present*. Chicago: Third World Press, 1987.

Reisner, Robert. *Two Thousand Years of Wall Writing*. Chicago: Cowles Book Company, 1971.

Ro, Ronin. *Gangsta Merchandising the Rhymes of Violence*. New York: St. Martin's Press, 1996.

Rolfe, P., and Greeson, Z. *Gangs USA*. Boulder, Colo.: Paladin Press, 1992.

Sifakis, Carl. 1982. *The Encyclopedia of American Crime*. New York: Facts On File, 1982.

Spergel, Irving. *Youth Gangs: Continuity and Change*. Chicago: University of Chicago Press, 1990.

Suttles, Gerald D. *The Social Order of the Slum: Ethnicity and Territory in the Inner City*. Chicago: University of Chicago Press, 1968.

Thrasher, Frederick. *The Gang*. Chicago: University of Chicago Press, 1927, 1963.

Vigil, James Diego. *The Established Gang, Gangs: The Origins and Impact on Contemporary Youth in the United States*. Albany, N.Y.: State University of New York Press, 1993.

Whyte, William F. *Street Corner Society: The Social Structure of an Italian Slum*. 3rd ed. Chicago: University of Chicago Press, 1981.

ARTICLES

Clark, Charles A. "Background." *CQ Researcher*, October 11, 1991, 762.

Harrison, Eric. "8-State Raid Aims 'Death Blow' at Notorious Chicago Gang." *Los Angeles Times*, October 28, 1989, A2.

Satanic

BOOKS

Drury, Nevill. *Dictionary of Mysticism and the Occult*. San Francisco: Harper & Row Publishers, 1985.

Kahaner, Larry. *Cults That Kill: Probing the Underworld of Occult Crime*. New York: Warner Books, 1988.

Larson, Bob. *Satanism: The Seduction of America's Youth*. Nashville, Tenn.: ThomasNelson Publishers, 1989.

Pulling, Pat. *The Devil's Web*. Lafayette, La.: Vital Issues Press, 1989.

Robbins, Rossell Hope. *The Encyclopedia of Witchcraft & Demonology*. New York: Crown Publishers, Inc., 1981.

Sparks, Beatrice, ed. *Jay's Journal*. New York: Pocket Books, 1979.

Stratford, Lauren. *Satan's Underground*. Eugene, Oreg.: Harvest House, 1988.

Victor, Jeffrey S. *Satanic Panic—The Creation of a Contemporary Legend*. Chicago: Open Court, 1994.

Warnke, Mike; Balsiger, Dave; and Jones, Les. *The Satan Seller*. South Plainfield, N.J.: Bridge Publishing Inc., 1972.

ARTICLES

Fine, Gary Alan, and Victor, Jeffrey. "Satanic Tourism: Adolescent Dabblers and Identity Work." *Phi Delta Kappan*, September 1994, 70.

REPORT

Wooden, Wayne S. "Profiles of Teenage Skinheads and Satanists in Southern California." Pomona, Calif.: Cal Poly Pomona Press, 1991.

People, Organizations & Programs

BOOKS

Callison, William, and Colocino Richards, Nancy. *Substance Abuse, Dropout and Gang Prevention Strategies*. Fullerton, Calif.: Students at Risk, Inc., 1991.

Smith, Peggy. *The Gang Incident Tracking System Report*. Santa Ana, Calif.: Orange County Chief's and Sheriff's Association, 1994.

Spergel, Irving A., and Curry, G. David. *Strategies and Perceived Agency Effectiveness in Dealing with Youth Gang Problems*. Newbury Park, Calif.: Sage Publications, 1990.

———. *Survey of Youth Gang Problems and Programs in 45 Cities and Sites*. Chicago, Ill.: University of Chicago, School of Social Science Administration, 1990.

———. *Youth Gangs: Problem and Response*. Chicago, Ill.: University of Chicago, School of Social Science Administration, 1990.

Street Gangs. Rockville, Md.: U.S. Department of Justice, Office of Justice Programs, National Institute of Justice, 1993.

State and Local Programs: Youth, Drugs and Violence. Rockville, Md.: U.S. Department of Justice, Bureau of Justice Assistance, 1995.

ORGANIZATIONS

American Correctional Association
8025 Laurel Lakes Court
Laurel, MD 20707
(301) 206-5100
Publishes a yearbook with statistical information and names and addresses of facilities and personnel in corrections across the United States.

Boys and Girls Clubs of America
Gang Intervention Services
1230 W. Peachtree Street NW
Atlanta, GA 30309-3494
(404) 815-5764
Programs to help youth at risk and involved in gang activities.

California Office of the Attorney General
Crime and Violence Prevention Center
1515 K Street
Sacramento, CA 95814
Gangs: A Statewide Directory of Programs.

California Office of Criminal Justice Planning
Gang Violence Suppression Program
1130 K Street, Suite 300
Sacramento, CA 95814
California Statewide Directory of Anti-Gang Efforts.

Center to Prevent Handgun Violence, The
1225 I Street NW, Suite 1100
Washington, D.C. 20005
(202) 289-7319
Information on handgun violence.

Children's Defense Fund
25 East Street NW
Washington, D.C. 20001
(800) CDF-1200
Publications promoting children's causes.

Citizenship and Law-Related Education
(CLRE) Center, The
9738 Lincoln Village Drive
Sacramento, CA 95827
(916) 228-2322

Community Policing Consortium
1726 M Street NW, Suite 801
Washington, D.C. 20036
(202) 833-3305
www.communitypolicing.org
Publishes newsletter on community policing programs.

FACES (Family and Community Education Services)
P.O. Box 1781
Pomona, CA 91769
(714) 623-4995
Community gang intervention program.

Gang Crime Section
Chicago Police Deptartment
1121 S. State Street
Chicago, IL 60605
(312) 744-6328
Gang intelligence on Midwest gangs.

Institute for Intergovernmental Research
P.O. Box 12729
Tallahassee, FL 32317
(904) 385-0600, ext. 259 or 285
Information from the National Youth Gang Center.

Juveniles Out of Gangs (JOG)
San Diego City Schools
San Diego, CA 92101-5729
Community gang intervention program.

Miami Police Deptartment Gang Detail
Community Relations Section
400 NW Second Avenue
Miami, FL 33128
(305) 579-6620
Gang information for the southeast United States.

Midnight Basketball League
Walker, Gil
534 E. 37th Street
Deptartment P
Chicago, IL 60653
Information about midnight basketball programs.

Mothers Against Violence
154 Christopher Street, 2nd Floor
New York, NY 10014
(212) 255-8484
Community mobilization about violence.

National Association for Mediation in Education (NAME)
205 Hampshire House, Box 33635
University of Massachusetts
Amherst, MA 01003
(413) 545-2462
Promotes school conflict resolution programs.

National Clearinghouse for Alcohol Information
P.O. Box 2345
Rockville, MD 20852
Information on alcohol abuse.

National Clearinghouse for Drug Abuse Information
P.O. Box 416
Kensington, MD 20795
Information on drug abuse.

National Crime Prevention Council
1700 K Street NW, 2nd Floor
Washington D.C. 20006-3817
(202) 466-6272
Information on crime prevention.

National Criminal Justice Reference Service
Justice Information Center
Box 6000
Rockville, MD 20849-6000
(301) 251-5500
www.ncjrs.org
The starting point for any search of government information and resources about street gangs. The Web site leads to many additional national and international sites.

National Federation of Parents for Drug-Free Youth
8730 Georgia Avenue, Suite 200
Silver Springs, MD 20910
Hotline: (800) 554-KIDS, 9 A.M.–5 P.M. EST M–F
Information on drug abuse.

National School Safety Center (NSSC)
4165 Thousand Oaks Boulevard., Suite 290
Westlake Village, CA 91362
(805) 373-9977
Information and publications about school safety.

National Victims Resource Center
Box 6000–AIQ
Rockville, MD 20850
Information on crime prevention.

Paramount Plan: The Alternatives to Gang Membership
City of Paramount
16400 Colorado Avenue
Paramount, CA 90723-5091
(213) 220-2140
Community gang intervention program.

Police Executive Research Forum
2300 M Street NW, Suite 910
Washington, D.C. 20037
(202) 466-7820

Project Yes
Orange County Department. of Education
200 Kalmus Drive
P.O. Box 9050
Costa Mesa, CA 92628-9050
(714) 966-4320
Anti-gang and antidrug curriculum.

Regional Educational Alliance for Gang Activities (REAGA)
Puget Sound Educational Service Agency
12310 80th Avenue S.
Seattle, WA 98178
(206) 772-6944
Gang information in northwest United States.

SANE/Gang Curriculum
Substance Abuse and Narcotics Education Program
Los Angeles County Sheriff's Department
211 W. Temple Street
Los Angeles, CA 90012
School drug and alcohol education program.

Save Our Streets
Weller Grossman Productions
14144 Ventura Boulevard, Suite 200
Sherman Oaks, CA 91423
(213) 634-7777
e-mail: sosusa@aol.com
Syndicated television show that presents information about anti-gang efforts in communities and current programs throughout the country.

S.T.A.R. Decision-Making Process
Jefferson Center for Character Education
202 South Lake Avenue, Suite 240
Pasadena, CA 91101
(818) 729-8130
School program for self-esteem.

Youth Development, Inc.
1710 Centro Familia SW
Albuquerque, NM 87105
(505) 873-1604
Community gang intervention programs.

Index

Numbers in **boldface** indicate major treatment of a topic.